CONTENTS

Editor	Sandra Tooze
Assistant Editor	Jean Dale
Graphic Technician	Patrick Glassford

ACKNOWLEDGEMENTS

Many thanks to Derek Dawe and Ivan MacGee for their help in fact-checking parts of the manuscript, Ralph Brough for his background information on Wade, Joy Damsell for her assistance in answering my enquiries, Bill Walker for his help regarding backstamps, Cynthia and Jenny for answering questions and to J.A. Stringer for his assistance with Wade Ireland products.

Companies

My thanks to the following companies for supplying information and photographs concerning the Wade products they commissioned:

Bell's Whisky (United Distillers), C&C International, Granada Television, Guiness PLC, Harrods Knightsbridge, The Highland Distilleries Co. PLC, Imperial Tobacco Limited, The International Association of Jim Beam Bottles and Specialties Club, The Irish Mist Liqueur Company Ltd., Keenan Antiques, Lang Brothers Limited, Lofthouse of Fleetwood Ltd., Lyon's Tetley, National Westminster Bank PLC, Phillips Auctioneers and Valuers, Ringtons Ltd., Robyn Hood Distilleries Ltd., Silver State Specialties, Smiths Crisps, Taunton Cider PLC, Thorntons Chocolates and Vaux Breweries Ltd.

Institutions

I am grateful to the following institutions for their research assistance:

The Barrie Reference Library, The British Newspaper Library, British Telecom, the Metro Toronto Reference Library and Stroud Public Library.

Contributors

Thanks also to the following collectors for their photographs and data:

Sheila and Brian Chappell, Jenny Chinnery, S.A. Cockerill, Tom Fish, Ann Glatzel, Marion and Gareth Hunt, Peg Johnson, Vera and Ian MacKay, P.M. McNicholl, Joanne and Don Mandryk, Pam and John Marshall, David Maund, Margaret Neate, Robin Pennington, Stuart Pickford, Ginny Plunkett, B. and P. Powell, Janet Robinson, Fiona Shoop, Val Turner, Kim and Derek Watson, Carol and John Woolner, Joanne Yadro and those who wish to remain anonymous.

HOW TO USE THIS CATALOGUE

The Listings

On the pages that follow Wade models are listed, illustrated, described and priced.

The measurements of the models are given in millimetres. Items such as figurines, most animals and birds, tankards, decanters and water jugs are measured according to their **height**. For relatively flat objects—ashtrays, dishes, trays and the like—the measurement listed is the **diameter** of a round item, the **side** of a square or the **longest length** of a rectangle or oval. For a few items, both height and width are provided.

Although the publisher has made every attempt to obtain and photograph all models listed, several pieces, naturally, have not come into the publisher's possession.

A Word on Pricing

The purpose of this catalogue is to give readers the most accurate, up-to-date retail prices for Wade models in the United States, Canada and the United Kingdom.

To accomplish this The Charlton Press continues to access an international pricing panel of Wade experts who submit prices based on both dealer and collector retail price activity, as well as current auction results in U.S., Canadian, and U.K. markets. These market figures are carefully averaged to reflect accurate valuations for the Wade models listed herein in each of these three markets.

Please be aware that prices given in a particular currency are for models in that country only. The prices published herein have not been calculated using exchange rates — they have been determined solely by the supply and demand within the country in question.

A necessary word of caution. No pricing catalogue can be, or should be, a fixed price list. This catalogue should be considered as a guide only, one that shows the most current retail prices based on market demand within a particular region.

Current models, however, are priced differently. They are priced according to the manufacturer's suggested retail price in each of the three market regions. It should be noted, however, that it is likely that dealer discounting from these prices will occur.

The prices published herein are for items in mint condition.

The only exception is the prices for the cellulose figures, which are listed for models with a moderate degree of glaze flaking. Collectors are cautioned that a repaired or restored piece may be worth as little as 50 percent of the value of the same model in mint condition. Those collectors interested strictly in investment potential must avoid damaged items.

All relevant information must be known about an item in order to make a proper valuation. When comparing auction prices to catalogue prices, collectors and dealers should remember two important points. First, to compare "apples and apples", be sure that auction prices include a buyer's premium, if one is due. Prices realized for models in auction catalogues may not include this additional cost. Secondly, if an item is restored or repaired, it may not be noted in the listing, and as a result, the price will not be relective of that same piece in mint condition.

The Numbering System

All models are numbered consecutively in the section in which they appear. Each section has the following letter prefixes:

AC:	Advertising and Commissioned Products
A:	Animals
B:	Birds
C:	Commemorative Ware
F:	Figures
J:	Jugs, Steins and Tankards
L:	Liquor Products
MB:	Money Boxes
SM:	Shaving Mugs

One mould may produce more than one variation of model. The difference may be in colouring or lettering on the item, as long as it does not affect the mould. When more than one variation of a model occurs, one style number is assigned to the mould and the varieties produced from that mould are indicated by a lower-case letter. For example, model F-61 was produced in five variations, resulting in F-61a to F-61e.

When a derivative of an item is produced, it is indicated by the number 1 following the model number from which it was made. Thus the number of the derivative F-25dl indicates it was produced from model F-25d.

INTRODUCTION

History

In the early 1930s, Wade consisted of three potteries—A.J. Wade Ltd., George Wade & Son Ltd. and Wade Heath and Co. Ltd.— with Wade Ulster (Ireland) being acquired in the mid 1940s. At first the company mainly produced gas burners for domestic lighting, although a small amount of gift ware was made as well. Later, Wade's chief output was insulating products, bobbins, thread guides and tiles. The company even made cone heads for guided missles in the early 1960s.

At the onset of World War II, the government permitted the production of essential ceramics only. All gift ware production came to an end, with parts of the potteries being used as emergency food stores for the duration of the war. Afterwards the potteries were engaged in replacing the essential ceramics that had been destroyed by bombing. By the early 1950s, the George Wade Pottery began producing small collectable figures and animals.

Between 1955 and 1969 Wade Heath and Company Limited worked with Reginald Corfield (Sales) Ltd., of Redhill, Surrey (under the trademark of Regicor London), to produce a range of promotional and point-of-sale advertising ware. These earthenware products were produced by Wade Heath at its Royal Victoria Pottery in Burslem.

The Reginald Corfield sales force worked closely with the distilling, brewing and tobacco industries. Many original water jugs and ashtrays were created for specific clients and were retained as exclusive shapes for particular brands.

In 1958 the three English Wade potteries were restructured under the name Wade Potteries Ltd., later renamed Wade PLC. Wade (Ulster) Ltd. was renamed Wade Ireland in 1966.

The association with Reginald Corfield was discontinued in October 1969, and Wade Heath formed its own product, design and marketing company, called Wade PDM (PDM also stood for point of sale, design and marketing). This company specializes in advertising products for the distilling, brewing and tobacco industries, although it is not limited to those areas. It has become one of the leading suppliers of advertising products in the U.K.

In 1989 Wade PLC was taken over by Beauford PLC and renamed Wade Ceramics Ltd., which is still in operation today. Wade Ireland was renamed Seagoe Ceramics and continued to manufacture domestic tableware until 1993, when it reverted back to the production of industrial ceramics.

The Production Process

The Wade potteries manufacture a particularly hard porcelain body which has been used in many different products. It consists of a mixture of ball clays, china clay, flint, felspar, talc, etc., some ingredients imported from Sweden, Norway and Egypt. These materials are mixed in large vats of water, producing a thick sludge or "slip." The slip is passed into a filter to extract most of the water, leaving large flat "bats" of porcelain clay, approximately two feet square and three inches thick. The clay bats are dried and then ground into dust ready for the forming process. Paraffin is added to the dust to assist in bonding and as a lubricant to remove the formed pieces from the steel moulds. Once pressed into the required shape, the clay articles are allowed to dry, then all the press marks are removed by sponging and "fettling," the scraping off of surplus clay with a sharp blade.

One or more ceramic colours is applied to the model, which is then sprayed with a clear glaze that, when fired, allows the colours underneath to show through. This process is known as underglaze decoration. On-glaze decoration—which includes enamelling, gilding and transfer printing—can also be done after the article has been glazed and fired.

Modellers

HARPER, WILLIAM K., 1954-1962
Bard of Armagh
Irish Emigrant
Little Crooked Paddy
Little Mickey Mulligan
Molly Malone
Phil the Fluter
Star of County Down
Widda Cafferty

HOLMES, KEN, 1975–present
Dunbar Cake Decorators, wedding cake topper
The Great Priory of England and Wales, Knight Templar
Imperial Tobacco, St. Bruno Key Ring
J.W. Thornton delivery van money boxes
Lyons Tetley Tea Brew Gaffer items
Lyons Tetley Tea delivery van money boxes
My Fair Ladies
Sophisticated Ladies

LANG, FAUST, 1939
Brown Bear
Budgerigar on Branch
Budgerigars
Chamois Kid
Cockatoo
Ermine
Grebe
Highland Stag
Horse
Monkey on Tree
Panther
Parrot
Weasel

MASLANKOWSKI, ALAN, 1975
The Cheetah and Gazelle
The Connoisseur's Collection
University Treasures, Razorback Pigs
The World of Survival series

MELLOR, FREDERICK, 1979
Peter Thompson, The Thistle and the Rose Historical Chess Set

STABLER, PHOEBE, 1962-1963
Dan Murphy
Eileen Oge
Mother MacCree

SZEILOR, JOHN, LATE 1940s-EARLY 1950s
Siamese Kittens
Begging Puppy

VAN HALLEN, JESSIE, 1930-1939
Lady figures
Large dog models

THE CHARLTON STANDARD CATALOG(

WADE

Volume One: General Is(
Second Edition

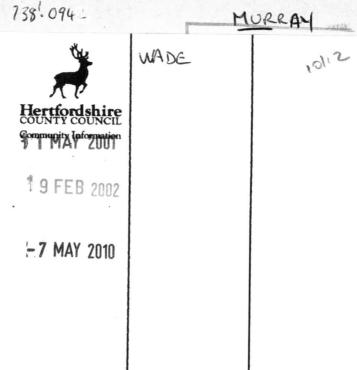

The Charlton Press
TORONTO, ONTARIO ❖ BIRMINGHAM, MICHIGAN

Canadian Cataloguing in Publication Data

Murray, Pat.
The Charlton standard catalogue of Wade
2nd ed.
Previously published under title: Pre-war and more Wades.
Contents: v. 1. General issues — v. 2. Decorative ware —
v. 3 Tableware.
Includes index.
ISBN 0-88968-139-2 (v. 1). - ISBN 088968-181-3 (v. 2)
ISBN 0-88968-183-X (V. 3)
1. George Wade and Son - Catalogs. 2. Figurines - England -
Catalogs. 3. Miniature pottery - England - Catalogs.
I. Title. II. Title: Pre-war and more Wades.

NK8473.5.W33M8 1996   738.8'2   C95-932732-0

Printed in Canada
in the Province of Ontario

The Charlton Press

Editorial Office
2010 Yonge Street
Toronto, Ontario M4S 1Z9
Telephone: (416) 488-4653   Fax: (416) 488-4656
Telephone: (800) 442-6042   Fax: (800) 442-1542

Insuring Your Models

As with any other of your valuables, making certain your models are protected is very important. It is paramount that you display or store any porcelain items in a secure place, preferably one safely away from traffic in the home.

Your models are most likely covered under your basic homeowner's policy. There are generally three kinds of such policies — standard, broad and comprehensive. Each has its own specific deductible and terms.

Under a general policy your models are considered part of the contents and are covered for all of the perils covered under the contractual terms of your policy (fire, theft, water damage and so on). However, since some models are extremely delicate, breakage is treated differently by most insurance companies.

There is usually an extra premium attached to insure models against accidental breakage by or carelessness of the owner. This is sometimes referred to as a "fine arts" rider. You are advised to contact your insurance professional to get all the answers.

In order to help protect yourself, it is critical that you take inventory of your models and have colour photographs taken of all your pieces. This is the surest method of clearly establishing, for the police and your insurance company, any items lost or destroyed. It is also the easiest way to establish their replacement value.

Backstamps

A large variety of different ink stamps were used by both the Wade Heath and George Wade potteries from the late 1920s to 1953, most of them in black ink. Large ink stamps were used on large-based models and small stamps on small models. Because the two potteries shared moulds and backstamps, it is extremely difficult to say which pottery produced which models. As a broad guideline, however, it can be assumed that models of animals, birds and human figures marked with a green or brown ink stamp were made in the Wade Heath Pottery.

Green ink stamp, early 1930s-1953

Brown ink stamp, early 1930s-1953

Green ink stamp, c.1948-1953

Some of the hollow figures, produced from the 1930s to the early 1950s, were not marked because, due to the hole in the bottom or a sloping bottom rim, there was no room for a stamp. These models are marked with a variety of Wade England and Wadeheath backstamps handwritten in black ink.

Handwritten, 1930s-1939

Handwritten, 1930s-1939

Handwritten, 1930-1939

From the early 1950s, the George Wade Pottery has also used several types of impressed and embossed Wade England backstamps, which are incorporated into the mould. Transfer printed backstamps were first used in the George Wade and Wadeheath potteries in 1953, and they are still in use today.

Impressed, early 1960s

Impressed, 1994

Embossed, 1954-1993

Wade Regicor and later Wade PDM produced commissioned ware from 1955 to the present. Several styles and colours of transfer-printed backstamps can be found with Wade Regicor and Wade PDM on them.

Transfer print, 1955-1968

Transfer print, 1969-1984

Transfer print, 1990 to the present

Wade Ireland used a wide variety of impressed and embossed marks in the 1950s, and reissued models from the original moulds still carried the 1950s backstamps. Because the colours remained the same, it is difficult to determine the age of some Wade Ireland models. Also in the 1950s, some figures had various types of ink-stamped Wade Ireland backstamps, which were used until 1991. Beginning in 1962 Wade Ireland began using transfer printed backstamps.

Impressed, early 1950c-1980s

Transfer print, 1977-1986

ADVERTISING AND
COMMISSIONED PRODUCTS
1953 to the present

From 1953 to the present, Wade Ceramics has produced - through Wade Regicor then Wade PDM — a huge range of earthenware jugs, ashtrays and ancillary items for use as commissioned and advertising products, making it one of the leading suppliers of these items in the United Kingdom. The Royal Victoria, George Wade and Wade Ireland potteries all produced these models.

The items in this section were used to advertise various companies and products, with the exception of liquor advertising. All liquor-related advertising items can be found in the section entitled Liquor Products.

Advertising and commissioned products can be found under the headings of the sponsoring companies or brand names, which are listed alphabetically.

Please note that some dates in this section are approximate only, when no information on production start or end dates is available. They indicate the earliest and latest dates of the backstamps used; they do not imply that the product was made continuously during the range of dates.

BACKSTAMPS

Wade Regicor and Wade PDM Backstamps

Wade Regicor and Wade PDM transfer-printed backstamps are found in black, blue, yellow, white, green, red and gold. The colour of the backstamps varied in order to contrast with the base colour of the models. The dating of a product is not determined by the colour of the backstamp, but by its style.

1984–1990: "Wade p d m England," with spaces between the letters *pdm*

1955–1962: "Wade Regicor, London England" in between two upright rows of nine laurel-type leaves, large size (18 mm x 20 mm)

1962–1968: "Wade Regicor, London England" in between two upright rows of nine laurel-type leaves, small size (13 mm x 13 mm)

1990–1996: "Wade P D M England" or "Wade P D M Made in England" within two red lines, one thick, the other thin

Private Backstamps

As well as the Wade Regicor and Wade PDM backstamps, many advertising and commissioned items produced from 1953 to the present are marked with some type of Wade England transfer print. Others are more elaborate and can be embossed or impressed. They can include details of the commissioning company and/or the occasion for which the product was created. Some companies have omitted a backstamp, believing that their name decorating the top of the item was sufficient, and a few companies do not have their name on the product at all.

1968–1969: "Reginald Corfield Limited Redhill Surrey" printed in a circle, with "Wade Regicor England" printed through the circle

1969–1984: "Wade pdm England" printed in a circle (this was the first Wade PDM backstamp)

ACCESS BANKING

ASHTRAY, 1955-1962

This ashtray is decorated with a transfer print of a bank card.

Photograph not available at press time

Backstamp: "Wade Regicor, London England," laurel leaves, large size

No.	Description	Colourways	Shape/Size	U.S.$	Can.$	U.K.£
AC-1	Ashtray	Green; white/green print, lettering "Access Your Flexible Friend"	Oval/153	20.00	25.00	8.00

ADDIS LTD.

SHAVING MUGS, c.1965–c.1980

These shaving mugs were produced intermittently for Addis Ltd. of England in white and beige. These mugs have four drainage holes as apposed to the of Culmark shaving mugs which have only one drainage hole.

Steam Coach by Gurney, 1827 (AC-2c)

Bi-Plane, R.A.F. (AC-2n)

Backstamp: **A.** Red transfer print "Wade England"
 B. Green transfer print "Wade England"
 C. Brown transfer print "Wade England"

No.	Description	Colourways	Size	U.S.$	Can.$	U.K.£
AC-2a	La Mancelle by Bollee, 1878	White; multi -coloured print	90	25.00	30.00	12.00
AC-2b	Steam Car	White; multi-coloured print	90	25.00	35.00	12.00
AC-2c	Steam Coach by Gurney, 1827	White; multi-coloured print	90	25.00	30.00	12.00
AC-2d	Steam Engine	White; multi-coloured print	90	25.00	30.00	12.00
AC-2e	Steam Roller by Aveling, 1893	White; multi-coloured print	90	25.00	30.00	12.00
AC-2f	Rotary Cultivator by Rickett, 1858	White; multi-coloured print	90	25.00	30.00	12.00
AC-2g	Her Majesty by Burrell, 1897	White; multi-coloured print	90	25.00	30.00	12.00
AC-2h	Steam Omnibus by Thornycroft, 1902	White; multi-coloured print	90	25.00	30.00	12.00
AC-2i	Vintage Ford Car	Beige; brown print	90	15.00	20.00	8.00
AC-2j	Convertible Car, 1920	Beige; brown print	90	15.00	20.00	8.00
AC-2k	Bentley Car	Beige; brown print	90	15.00	20.00	8.00
AC-2l	Spitfire Plane, RAF	Beige; brown print	90	15.00	20.00	8.00
AC-2m	Bi-Plane, RAF	Beige; brown print	90	15.00	20.00	8.00

BARRATT HOMES

ASHTRAY, 1984-1990

The print on this ashtray is of a helicopter flying over trees.

Photograph not available at press time

Backstamp: "Wade p d m England"

No.	Description	Colourways	Shape/Size	U.S.$	Can.$	U.K.£
AC-3	Ashtray	Green; black print, lettering "Barratt"	Square/110	10.00	15.00	5.00

BENSON AND HEDGES CIGARETTES

ASHTRAY AND CIGARETTE LIGHTER, 1969-1984

Wade produced the hollow cube into which a lighter was fitted. The lettering is on the front of the cube.

Photograph not available at press time

Backstamp: "Wade pdm England"

No.	Description	Colourways	Shape/Size	U.S.$	Can.$	U.K.£
AC-4	Ashtray	Black/gold; gold lettering "Benson & Hedges Special Filter"	Rectangular/242	15.00	20.00	8.00
AC-5	Lighter	Light brown; black lettering "Benson & Hedges"	Rectangular/114	25.00	30.00	12.00

BOOTS THE CHEMIST

TEDDY BEAR BOOKENDS AND UTENSIL POT, 1988–1989

Bookends

Utensil Pot

Backstamp: Unmarked

No.	Description	Colourways	Size	U.S.$	Can.$	U.K.£
AC-6a	Bookend - Bear Reading	White; black eyes; brown nose; blue jumper	150	40.00	45.00	20.00
AC-6b	Bookend - Bear Waving	White; black eyes; brown nose; blue dungarees	150	40.00	45.00	20.00
	Bookends (Pair)			80.00	100.00	40.00
AC-7	Utensil Pot	White; black eyes; brown nose; blue jumper	133	40.00	45.00	20.00

BOULDRAY BRASS AND METAL FOUNDRIES

TRAYS, 1958-1965

Bouldray trays were adapted from the base of Wade *Whimtrays,* with the backstamp changed to "Bouldray." Models made of brass, black metal or a combination of black metal and brass, produced by Bouldray Brass, were attached to the trays with a screw through a hole in the base of the tray.

Card Trumps (AC-8), Swallow Ring (AC-16)

Cockerel (AC-9a), Stag (AC-15)

Backstamp: Raised "Bouldray Wade Porcelain 2 Made in England"

No.	Description	Colourways	Size	U.S.$	Can.$	U.K.£
AC-8	Card Trumps	Brass frame; white plastic cards; yellow tray	90	15.00	20.00	8.00
AC-9a	Cockerel	Black metal/brass cockerel; yellow tray	75	15.00	20.00	8.00
AC-9b	Cockerel	Brass cockerel; yellow tray	75	15.00	20.00	8.00
AC-10	Cornish Pixie on Mushroom	Brass pixie/mushroom; pink tray	60	15.00	20.00	8.00
AC-11a	Crinoline Lady/Rose Bush	Brass figure; black tray	70	15.00	20.00	8.00
AC-11b	Crinoline Lady/Rose Bush	Brass figure; blue tray	70	15.00	20.00	8.00
AC-11c	Crinoline Lady/Rose Bush	Brass figure; pink tray	70	15.00	20.00	8.00
AC-12a	Duck	Black metal duck; blue tray	55	15.00	20.00	8.00
AC-12b	Duck	Brass metal duck; black tray	55	15.00	20.00	8.00
AC-13	Jenny Lind	Brass figure; yellow tray	75	15.00	20.00	8.00
AC-14	Rearing Horse	Black horse; yellow tray	65	15.00	20.00	8.00
AC-15	Stag	Brass stag; yellow tray	75	15.00	20.00	8.00
AC-16	Swallow Ring	Brass ring; blue/white swallow (from "Swallow Posy Bowl"); yellow tray	72	15.00	20.00	8.00

CANDLE HOLDERS, 1963-1965

As with the Bouldray trays, the candle holders, which were formerly used as Wade's 1959–1960 *First Whimsies Zoo Lights*, had a hole drilled in the base and a miniature metal model was attached with a screw through the bottom. The models are brass, black metal and black metal with some brass. Wade supplied the base only; the metal figure was supplied and attached by Bouldray Brass.

Black Cat (AC-17)

Duck (AC-20b)

Backstamp: Raised "Wade Porcelain made in England"

No.	Description	Colourways	Size	U.S.$	Can.$	U.K.£
AC-17	Black Cat	Black metal/brass cat; yellow holder	50	15.00	20.00	8.00
AC-18a	Cockerel	Black metal/brass cockerel; blue holder	45	15.00	20.00	8.00
AC-18b	Cockerel	Black metal/brass cockerel; pink holder	45	15.00	20.00	8.00
AC-18c	Cockerel	Black metal/brass cockerel; yellow holder	45	15.00	20.00	8.00
AC-18d	Cockerel	Brass cockerel; blue holder	45	15.00	20.00	8.00
AC-19	Cornish Pixie	Brass pixie; blue holder	50	15.00	20.00	8.00
AC-20a	Duck	Black metal/brass duck; blue holder	45	15.00	20.00	8.00
AC-20b	Duck	Brass duck; blue holder	45	15.00	20.00	8.00
AC-21a	Rearing Horse	Black metal/brass horse; yellow holder	45	15.00	20.00	8.00
AC-21b	Rearing Horse	Brass horse; yellow holder	45	15.00	20.00	8.00

BOURNE OF HARLESDON

NURSERY AND OTHER DOOR PLAQUES, c.1965

These door plaques, which were produced by Wade for Bourne of Harlesdon, were sold by Bourne under its own name.

Backstamp: Raised "Bourne of Harlesdon"

No.	Description	Colourways	Size	U.S.$	Can.$	U.K.£
AC-22a	Bedroom	White; multi-coloured print	105 x 57	50.00	70.00	25.00
AC-22b	Girl's Room	White; multi-coloured print	105 x 57	50.00	70.00	25.00
AC-22c	Kitchen	White; multi-coloured print	105 x 57	50.00	70.00	25.00
AC-22d	Lounge	White; multi-coloured print	105 x 57	50.00	70.00	25.00
AC-22e	Nursery	White; multi-coloured print	105 x 57	50.00	70.00	25.00
AC-22f	Linen Cupboard	White; multi-coloured print	105 x 57	50.00	70.00	25.00

BRITISH OVERSEAS AIRWAYS CORPORATION

ASHTRAYS, JUGS AND TANKARDS, 1950-c.1970

B.O.A.C. (now known as British Airways) commissioned these products from Wade Heath through its association with Regicor. Seven items advertised B.O.A.C. and one advertised British Airways.

The round water jug has a recessed handle and an ice-check spout. The transfer print on style AC-28a is missing the periods after each initial of B.O.A.C. When the mistake was noticed, the prints were changed with the periods inserted.

Ashtray (AC-23)   **Water Jug (AC-28a)**

Backstamp: A. "Wade Regicor London England," laurel leaves, large size
B. "Wade Regicor London England," laurel leaves, small size
C. Transfer print "Wade PDM England"

No.	Description	Colourways	Shape/Size	U.S.$	Can.$	U.K.£
AC-23	Ashtray	Grey-blue; white print	Circular/142	30.00	35.00	15.00
AC-24	Ashtray	Blue/white; multiple red/blue "British Airways"	Circular/216	25.00	30.00	12.00
AC-25	Ashtray	Grey-blue; white B.O.A.C. print	Square/120	20.00	30.00	10.00
AC-26	Ashtray	Dark blue; white B.O.A.C. print	Square/140	20.00	30.00	10.00
AC-27	Ashtray	Grey-blue; white B.O.A.C. print	Square/140 clipped corners	20.00	30.00	10.00
AC-28a	Water Jug	Grey-blue; white BOAC; black/white crest	133	40.00	45.00	20.00
AC-28b	Water Jug	Grey-blue; white B.O.A.C.; black/white crest	133	40.00	45.00	20.00
AC-29	Tankard	Grey-blue tankard; white B.O.A.C. crest	1/2 pint/100	40.00	45.00	20.00
AC-30	Tankard	Grey-blue tankard; white B.O.A.C. crest	Pint/120	50.00	70.00	25.00

BRITVIC SOFT DRINKS

ASHTRAY, 1990-1995

Photograph not available at press time

Backstamp: "Wade P D M Made in England" within two red lines

No.	Description	Colourways	Shape/Size	U.S.$	Can.$	U.K.£
AC-31	Ashtray	Black/orange; white lettering "Britvic"	Round/120	10.00	15.00	5.00

CAMPBELL MOTOR EXPORTS LTD.
AUCKLAND, NEW ZEALAND

TIRE DISHES, 1966

Wade produced two tire dishes for the Campbell Motor Group of Auckland, New Zealand. The dishes depict the Peugeot and Rambler cars sold by Campbell Motors and were given as gifts to the purchasers of those cars. Only 500 of each dish were produced. Campbell Motors was sold to the Challenge Corporation in 1975 and ceased business in the early 1980s.

Rambler, 1902

Backstamp: A. Black transfer print "1902 Rambler, Model D. In the first year 1,500 were sold, establishing Rambler as the world's second massed produced automobile. N.Z. Rambler Distributors, Campbell Motor Exports Ltd Auckland"
B. Unknown

No.	Description	Colourways	Size	U.S.$	Can.$	U.K.£
AC-32a	Peugeot	White; grey rim; black print	125	20.00	30.00	10.00
AC-32b	Rambler, 1902	White; grey rim; black print	125	20.00	30.00	10.00

CANADA DRY

ASHTRAY, 1955-1962

Photograph not available at press time

Backstamp: "Wade Regicor, London England," laurel leaves, large size

No.	Description	Colourways	Shape/Size	U.S.$	Can.$	U.K.£
AC-33	Ashtray	Pale blue; red lettering "Canada Dry Sparkling Drinks"	Shield/127	30.00	35.00	15.00

CANADIAN COLLEGES AND UNIVERSITIES

TANKARDS, 1960-c.1980

Commissioned for various Canadian colleges and universities, these traditional pint tankards are found in black, white or blue glazes with a gold or multi-coloured name and crest of the institution on the front. The "Queen's University Tankard" was made from a different mould than the others; it resembles a stein and has a square handle and two raised bands round the top and bottom halves.

University of Guelph (AC-34f)

Backstamp: A. Red or green transfer print "Wade England"
B. Red transfer print "Wade England"

No.	Description	Colourways	Size	U.S.$	Can.$	U.K.£
AC-34a	Dalhousie University	Black; gold print	118	15.00	20.00	12.00
AC-34b	Humber College	Black; gold print	118	15.00	20.00	12.00
AC-34c	Niagara College	Royal blue; gold print	118	15.00	20.00	12.00
AC-34d	Ryerson Polytechnical Inst.	Black; gold print	118	15.00	20.00	12.00
AC-34e	Ryerson Polytechnical Inst.	White; gold print	118	15.00	20.00	12.00
AC-34f	University of Guelph	Royal blue; gold print	118	15.00	20.00	12.00
AC-34g	University of Waterloo	Royal blue; gold print	118	15.00	20.00	12.00
AC-34h	Waterloo Lutheran Univ.	Royal blue; gold print	118	15.00	20.00	12.00
AC-35	Queen's University	White; gold bands; red/yellow/blue crest	146	15.00	20.00	12.00

CARROLLS CIGARETTES

ASHTRAY, 1955-1962

Photograph not available at press time

Backstamp: "Wade Regicor, London England," laurel leaves, large size

No.	Description	Colourways	Shape/Size	U.S.$	Can.$	U.K.£
AC-36	Ashtray	White; red/black lettering "Carrolls Virginia Cigarettes Number 1"	Oval/224	15.00	20.00	8.00

CAVALIER PANATELLAS

ASHTRAY, 1955-1962

Photograph not available at press time

Backstamp: "Wade Regicor, London England," laurel leaves, large size

No.	Description	Colourways	Shape/Size	U.S.$	Can.$	U.K.£
AC-37	Ashtray	Light grey; red/black lettering "Cavalier Panatellas"	Oval/228	15.00	20.00	8.00

CREST HOTELS

ASHTRAYS, 1969-1990

Ashtray (AC-38)

Ashtray (AC-39)

Backstamp: A. "Wade pdm England"
B. "Wade p d m England"

No.	Description	Colourways	Shape/Size	U.S.$	Can.$	U.K.£
AC-38	Ashtray	Pale blue; black print, lettering "Crest Hotels"	Rectangular/210	15.00	20.00	8.00
AC-39	Ashtray	Maroon; gold print, lettering "Crest Hotels"	Rectangular/170	15.00	20.00	8.00

CROSSE AND BLACKWELL

PLOUGHMAN'S PLATE, LATE 1980s

Wade produced this heavily embossed "Ploughman's Plate" as a promotional line for the British pickle company, Crosse and Blackwell. The plate has "Crosse and Blackwell" embossed on the top rim and "Branston, the Perfect Pickle for a Ploughman" around the rim.

Backstamp: Black transfer print "Rockingham by Wade England"

No.	Description	Colourways	Size	U.S.$	Can.$	U.K.£
AC-40	Plate	Dark honey brown	225	30.00	35.00	15.00

CULMAK LTD.

BARBERS SHOP SHAVING MUG, c.1965

The "Barbers Shop Shaving Mug," with a rolled rim on the top and on the base, is the same style originally used by Victorian barbers.

Backstamp: Red transfer print "Wade England"

No.	Description	Colourways	Size	U.S.$	Can.$	U.K.£
AC-41	Shaving Mug	Beige; gold rim; brown print	88	25.00	30.00	12.00

SHAVING MUGS, c.1980

These shaving mugs have only one drainage hole in the soap bowl.

Wolseley (AC-42g)

Backstamp: **A.** Black transfer print "Wade Made in England"
B. Green transfer print "Wade England"
C. Red transfer print "Wade England"

No.	Description	Colourways	Size	U.S.$	Can.$	U.K.£
AC-42a	Ford	White; multi-coloured print	80	25.00	30.00	12.00
AC-42b	H.M.S Victory	White; black print	80	20.00	30.00	10.00
AC-42c	Nelson	White; black print	80	20.00	30.00	10.00
AC-42d	Nelson's Column	White; black print	80	20.00	30.00	10.00
AC-42e	Rolls-Royce, 1909	White; multi-coloured print	80	25.00	30.00	12.00
AC-42f	Steam Engine Train	White; green/black print	80	25.00	30.00	12.00
AC-42g	Wolseley	White; multi-coloured print	80	25.00	30.00	12.00

DEBENHAMS

REX THE RETRIEVER, 1993

This model was commissioned by Debenhams to commemorate the installation of its new computerized retrieval system, which was christened "Rex" by the installers of the system. Only 250 models were produced.

Backstamp: Raised "Wade England"

No.	Description	Colourways	Size	U.S.$	Can.$	U.K.£
AC-43	Retriever	Fawn	153	125.00	155.00	65.00

DUNBAR CAKE DECORATORS, SCOTLAND

WEDDING CAKE TOPPER, 1992

This model was produced in all white; however, the staff of Dunbar Cakes decorated some with lace and other materials. Less than three thousand of these figures have been made.

Backstamp: Black print "Wade England"

No.	Description	Colourways	Size	U.S.$	Can.$	U.K.£
AC-44	Bride and Groom	White	100	70.00	90.00	35.00

DUNHILL CIGARETTES

ASHTRAYS AND WATER JUGS, 1968-1984

The water jugs are rectangular with ice-check spouts.

Ashtray (A-46)

Backstamp: A. "Reginald Corfield Limited Redhill Surrey," "Wade Regicor England"
B. Transfer printed "Wade pdm England"

No.	Description	Colourways	Shape/Size	U.S.$	Can.$	U.K.£
AC-45	Ashtray	Black; red label with gold lettering "Dunhill"	Square/177	15.00	20.00	8.00
AC-46	Water Jug	Black; gold lettering "Dunhill International Cigarettes"	140	25.00	30.00	12.00
AC-47	Water Jug	Maroon; black lettering "Dunhill International Cigarettes"	146	25.00	30.00	12.00
AC-48	Water Jug	Black; red label; gold lettering "Dunhill"	171	25.00	30.00	12.00

EMBASSY CIGARETTES

WATER JUG, 1969-1984

This water jug is square with an ice-check spout.

Photograph not available
at press time

Backstamp: "Wade pdm England"

No.	Description	Colourways	Size	U.S.$	Can.$	U.K.£
AC-50	Water Jug	Royal blue; white lettering "Embassy Regal"	146	30.00	35.00	15.00

EMBASSY HOTELS

ASHTRAY, 1984-1990

Photograph not available at press time

Backstamp: "Wade p d m England"

No.	Description	Colourways	Shape/Size	U.S.$	Can.$	U.K.£
AC-51	Ashtray	White; blue lettering "Embassy Hotels"	Round/120	8.00	10.00	3.00

555 CIGARETTES

ASHTRAY AND WATER JUG, 1955-1984

The ashtray has a large "555" in the centre. The water jug is round with an ice-check spout and "555" is the only decoration.

Photograph not available at press time

Backstamp: **A.** "Wade Regicor, London England," laurel leaves, large size
B. "Wade pdm England"

No.	Description	Colourways	Shape/Size	U.S.$	Can.$	U.K.£
AC-52	Ashtray	White; blue "555"	Round/140	15.00	20.00	8.00
AC-53	Water Jug	Dull blue; gold "555"	Round/165	25.00	30.00	12.00

GARDNER MERCHANT CATERING SERVICES

TRINKET BOX, 1986

The trinket box was commissioned by the British firm of Gardner Merchant Catering Services to commemorate 100 years in business. It was presented to Gardner's employees.

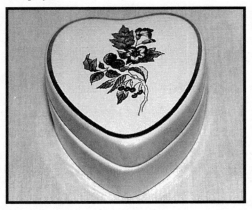

Backstamp: Purple transfer print "Royal Victoria Pottery Wade Staffordshire England," with "Gardner Merchant a century of catering service, 1886–1986" in gold letters

No.	Description	Colourways	Size	U.S.$	Can.$	U.K.£
AC-54	Trinket Box	White/gold band; purple/green flower, berries	42 x 80	25.00	30.00	12.00

GLOW WORM GAS FIRES

GLOW WORM PENCIL HOLDER, DATE UNKNOWN

This comical pencil holder was produced as a promotional item for Glow Worm Gas Fires and used in company offices and showrooms.

Backstamp: Unknown

No.	Description	Colourways	Size	U.S.$	Can.$	U.K.£
AC-55	Pencil holder	Pink worm; black gloves, golf bag; orange golf ball	101	70.00	90.00	35.00

GRANADA TELEVISION

ROVERS RETURN TEA CADDY AND TEAPOT

The tea caddy and teapot were produced for Granada Television studio tours as promotional items for its long-running British television series, "Coronation Street." The round jar, which could be used as a tea caddy or a biscuit barrel, has a transfer print of the Rovers Return Inn on the front. It could be purchased at the studio gift shop or by mail order. The original price was £14.95. The teapot has the same print on the front, and its original price, in the gift shop or by mail order, was £15.95.

Photograph not available
at press time

Backstamp: Unknown

No.	Description	Colourways	Size	U.S.$	Can.$	U.K.£
AC-56	Tea Caddy	White; green/brown/yellow print	185	40.00	45.00	20.00
AC-57	Teapot	Unknown	Unknown	40.00	45.00	20.00

GRAY FINE ARTS

PLAQUES, c.1988–c.1990

Irish Artists Plaques

Wade Ireland produced a number of plaques for Gray Fine Arts of Belfast, which had prints of works by Irish artists on the fronts. Some plaques have holes in the rim for hanging, others have a small string loop glued to the backs and some have a foot on the back (with and without a slotted stand). All the plaques were produced in the typical Irish grey/green glaze and had multi-coloured prints.

Spaniel and Pheasant (AC-62)

Cobbler (AC-58a)

Backstamp: **A.** Leaflet in box "This ornament is Irish Porcelain especially made by Wade of Portadown for the Manufacturers Gray Fine Arts of Belfast"
B. Label on plaque "One in a series of Paintings by Irish Artist James Gray All Copyrights reserved" and "Manufactured by Gray Fine Arts—Belfast—Ireland"
C. Label "Manufactured by Wade of Portadown"

No.	Description	Colourways	Shape/Size	U.S.$	Can.$	U.K.£
AC-58a	Cobbler	Grey-green; multi-coloured print	Oblong/110 hanging	70.00	90.00	35.00
AC-58b	Reaper	Grey-green; multi-coloured print	Oblong/110 hanging	70.00	90.00	35.00
AC-58c	Spaniel and Pheasant	Grey-green; multi-coloured print	Oblong/110 hanging	70.00	90.00	35.00
AC-59	Couple in Cart	Grey-green; multi-coloured print	Oblong/110 footed	70.00	90.00	35.00
AC-60	Couple in Cart	Grey-green; multi-coloured print	Oblong/110 hanging	70.00	90.00	35.00
AC-61	Couple Sitting in Field	Grey-green; multi-coloured print	Oblong/110 slotted stand	70.00	90.00	35.00
AC-62	Spaniel and Pheasant	Grey-green; multi-coloured print	Oval/100 hanging	70.00	90.00	35.00

Wild Flowers Plaques

Red Clover (AC-66)

Rock Rose (AC-67)

Backstamp: Paper label "One of a series of paintings by Irish Artist Elizabeth McEwen, all copyrights reserved. Manufactured by Gray Fine Arts-Belfast-Ireland"

No.	Description	Colourways	Shape/Size	U.S.$	Can.$	U.K.£
AC-63a	Primrose	Blue-grey; yellow flowers	Oval/100 hanging	30.00	35.00	15.00
AC-63b	Primula	Blue-grey; yellow flowers	Oval/100 hanging	30.00	35.00	15.00
AC-63c	Red Clover	Blue-grey; pink flowers	Oval/100 hanging	30.00	35.00	15.00
AC-63d	Rose	Blue-grey; white flowers	Oval/100 hanging	30.00	35.00	15.00
AC-64	Flower Unknown	Blue-grey; white flowers	Oval/100 Footed stand	30.00	35.00	15.00
AC-65	Flower Unknown	Blue-grey; white flowers	Oval/100 Slotted stand	30.00	35.00	15.00
AC-66	Red Clover	Blue-grey; pink flowers	Rectangular/100	30.00	35.00	15.00
AC-67	Rock Rose	Blue-grey; yellow flowers	Square/100	30.00	35.00	15.00

THE GREAT PRIORY OF ENGLAND AND WALES

KNIGHT TEMPLAR, 1991
Style One

The "Knight Templar" was commissioned in 1991 by the Great Priory Of England and Wales to commemorate its bicentenary. For the second style of this model, see The Potteries Centre, listed in this section.

Backstamp: Transfer print "Made Exclusively for The Great Priory of England and Wales and its Provinces by Wade Ceramics to Commemorate 1791—The Bicentenary—1991"

No.	Description	Colourways	Size	U.S.$	Can.$	U.K.£
AC-68	Knight Templar	Silver shield; red hat; white cross; black/brown sword, belt	240	325.00	400.00	190.00

GUINNESS PLC

NOVELTY MODELS, 1968

Wade produced 5,000 each of these four models in December 1968 for Guinness PLC. The four models were given to licensees and were not offered to the general public.

Backstamp: Raised "Guinness" on the front rim

No.	Description	Colourways	Size	U.S.$	Can.$	U.K.£
AC-69	Duke of Wellington	Brown/honey brown	90	150.00	225.00	75.00
AC-70	Mad Hatter	Brown/honey brown/greenish grey	85	150.00	225.00	75.00
AC-71	Sam Weller	Brown/honey brown	80	150.00	225.00	75.00
AC-72	Tweedle Dum and Tweedle Dee	Brown/honey brown	75	150.00	225.00	75.00

HARRODS OF KNIGHTSBRIDGE

TEAPOT, 1993

Backstamp: Black transfer print "Harrods Knightsbridge"

No.	Item	Description	Size	U.S.$	Can.$	U.K.£
AC-73	Teapot	White; multi-coloured print of store	135	100.00	145.00	55.00

HAYWOODS TOBACCONISTS

WATER JUG, 1955–1962

This round jug resembles the shape known as a "Dutch jug" and has been used by the Wade Heath Pottery in its range of tablewares since the early 1930s. It has an open spout.

Photographs not available
at press time

Backstamp: "Wade Regicor, London England," laurel leaves, large size

No.	Description	Colourways	Size	U.S.$	Can.$	U.K.£
A-74	Water Jug	White; black lettering "Haywoods Wholesale Tobacconists Brighton"	140	50.00	70.00	25.00

IMPERIAL CHEMICAL INDUSTRIES (I.C.I.)

ATROMID-S MAN, 1967

The British pharmaceutical manufacturer Imperial Chemical Industries produced a drug called Atromid-S, which was used for weight reduction for patients at risk from heart disease. The "Atromid-S Man" depicts a person likely to suffer from heart disease, an overweight man sitting on a beer crate with a pint of beer in his hand. It was given by salesmen to general practitioners as a sales promotion. This model has been found in Germany named "Regelan."

Backstamp: A. Raised "Wade England I.C.I." and "Atromid S"
               B. Raised "Atromidin Wade England I.C.I."

No.	Description	Colourways	Size	U.S.$	Can.$	U.K.£
AC-75a	Atromid-S Man	Dark blue all over	Small/80	90.00	130.00	45.00
AC-75b	Atromid-S Man	Honey brown all over	Small/80	90.00	130.00	45.00
AC-76a	Atromid-S Man	Black all over	Large/205		Rare	
AC-76b	Atromid-S Man	Brown shirt, box; red trousers	Large/205		Rare	

IMPERIAL TOBACCO COMPANY LIMITED

ASHTRAY, CIGARETTE LIGHTER AND WATER JUG, 1969-1984

Water Jug, Ashtray, Lighter

Backstamp: "Wade pdm England"

No.	Description	Colourways	Size	U.S.$	Can.$	U.K.£
AC-77	Ashtray	Maroon/deep red; gold lettering "Imperial International Filter Virginia"	115	15.00	20.00	8.00
AC-78	Cigarette Lighter	Maroon/red/gold; gold/black lettering "Imperial International Filter Virginia"	108	25.00	30.00	12.00
AC-79	Water Jug/ ice-check spout	Burgundy; red/gold lettering "Imperial International Filter Virginia"	153	25.00	30.00	12.00

ST. BRUNO KEY RING, 1986–1987

Backstamp: Unmarked

No.	Description	Colourways	Size	U.S.$	Can.$	U.K.
AC-80	Key Ring	White; red-brown patches; yellow pouch	30	10.00	15.00	5.00

THE INTERNATIONAL FEDERATION OF ESPERANTUS RAILWAYMEN

BROOCH, 1963

Produced for the 1963 Congress of the International Federation of Esperantus Railwaymen, this urn-shaped brooch is decorated with a lariat wreath, open wings and the inscription "Esperanto XV a Kongreso De I.F.E.F. Stoke on Trent Majo 1963." Only one brooch is known.

Photograph not available
at press time

Backstamp: Black transfer "Wade England"

No.	Description	Colourways	Size	U.S.$	Can.$	U.K.£
AC-81	Brooch	White/green	40		Rare	

KEENAN, PATTY

CHRISTMAS ORNAMENTS, 1994–1995

"Santa's Sleigh," produced for Christmas 1994, was commissioned by Patty Keenan of Pennsylvania, U.S.A., in a limited edition of 2,000. The "Rocking Horse," designed by Robert Oughton of Hellam, Pennsylvania, was produced for Christmas 1995 in a limited edition of 2,500.

Santa's Sleigh

Rocking Horse

Backstamp: Red ink stamp "Wade made in England"

No.	Description	Colourways	Size	U.S.$	Can.$	U.K.£
AC-82	Santa's Sleigh	White; red coat	40	30.00	35.00	15.00
AC-83	Rocking Horse	Grey; dark grey mane, tail, rocker	38	30.00	35.00	15.00

KEITH AND HENDERSON

ASHTRAYS, 1969-1984

Photograph not available
at press time

Backstamp: "Wade pdm England"

No.	Description	Colourways	Shape/Size	U.S.$	Can.$	U.K.£
AC-84	Ashtray	Brown; gold lettering "Keith & Henderson Cloth for a Connoisseur"	Rectangular/205	15.00	20.00	8.00
AC-85	Ashtray	Brown; white lettering "Keith & Henderson Cloth for a Connoisseur"	Square/140	15.00	20.00	8.00

L - B KINGSIZE CIGARETTES

WATER JUG, 1969-1984

This rectangular water jug has an ice-check spout.

Photograph not available
at press time

Backstamp: "Wade pdm England"

No.	Description	Colourways	Size	U.S.$	Can.$	U.K.£
AC-86	Water Jug	White; black/red lettering "L-B Kingsize"	153	25.00	30.00	12.00

LEGAL AND GENERAL ASSURANCE SOCIETY LTD.

ASHTRAYS, 1955-1969

Photograph not available
at press time

Backstamp: **A.** "Wade Regicor, London England," laurel leaves, large size
B. "Reginald Corfield Limited Redhill Surrey," "Wade Regicor England"

No.	Description	Colourways	Shape/Size	U.S.$	Can.$	U.K.£
AC-87	Ashtray	Blue; white lettering "Legal & General Assurance Society Limited"	Square/146	15.00	20.00	8.00
AC-88	Ashtray	Black; white lettering "Legal and General Assurance Society Ltd"	Square/140	15.00	20.00	8.00

LEGAL AND GENERAL PROPERTY LTD.

MILLBANK TOWER VASE, 1993

This oblong vase represents the Millbank Tower Building.

Backstamp: Dark blue print "An original Design for Legal and General Property Ltd by Wade England"

No.	Description	Colourways	Size	U.S.$	Can.$	U.K.£
AC-89	Tower	Grey/dark blue, white lettering	160	25.00	30.00	12.00

LESNEY PRODUCTS AND CO. LTD.

GIFT TRAYS, 1961–c.1975

Only the trays of these models were produced by Wade. The metal and/or plastic models were mounted on the backs of the trays by Lesney Products and Co. Ltd., a British company famous for its Matchbox miniature car models. A large variety of Lesney products are found on the trays, but most have a Matchbox car, bus or train on the back rim.

Titled "Gifts By Lesney, Ceramic Tray" on the packaging, the trays are found in six different shapes—kidney, oval, round, square, semi-oval and triangular shapes—and in four colours. Some trays have been found with a silver label on the front edge that names the model.

The kidney- and oval-shaped trays were previously used by Wade in 1957 and 1958 as the "Doggie Dish" (kidney shape) and the "Swallow Dish" (oval shape).

Buildings and Figures

The Mermaid

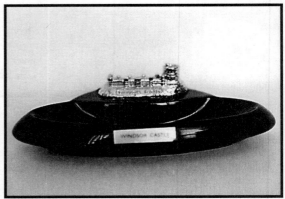

Windsor Castle

Backstamp: **A.** Impressed "Wade Made In England"
B. Raised "R.K. Product by Wade of England"
C. Raised "S42/9"

No.	Description	Colourways	Shape/Size	U.S.$	Can.$	U.K.£
AC-90	Buckingham Palace (plastic)	Silver palace; black tray	Oval/33 x 150	25.00	30.00	12.00
AC-91	Edinburgh Castle (metal)	Gold model; dark brown tray	Round/77 x 110	25.00	30.00	12.00
AC-92	The Mermaid (metal)	Gold mermaid; dark brown tray	Round/77 x 110	25.00	30.00	12.00
AC-93	London Bridge (metal)	Silver bridge; green tray	Kidney/40 x 100	25.00	30.00	12.00
AC-94	Tower Bridge (metal)	Silver bridge; brown tray	Kidney/40 x 100	25.00	30.00	12.00
AC-95a	Windsor Castle (metal)	Silver castle; black tray	Semi-oval/55 x 150	25.00	30.00	12.00
AC-95b	Windsor Castle (plastic)	Silver castle; black tray	Semi-oval/55 x 150	25.00	30.00	12.00

Transportation

Duke of Connaught Locomotive

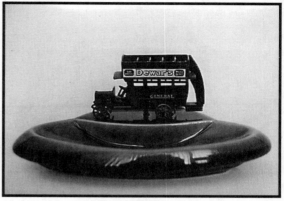

B Type Bus "Dewar's"

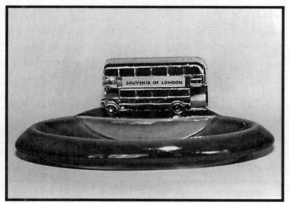

Bus "Souvenir of London"

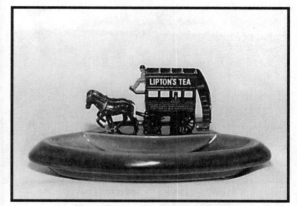

Horse Drawn Bus "Lipton's Tea"

Backstamp: A. Raised "Wade Porcelain Made in England," 1961
B. Raised "R.K. Product by Wade of England"
C. Raised "S42/8"
D. Raised "Made in England Lesney"

No.	Description	Colourways	Shape/Size	U.S.$	Can.$	U.K.£
AC-96a	B Type Bus, "Dewars"	Red metal bus; green tray	Semi-oval/65 x 150	40.00	45.00	20.00
AC-96b	Bus, "Players Please"	Red metal bus; green tray	Semi-oval/55 x 150	40.00	45.00	20.00
AC-96c	Horse Drawn Bus, 1899, Lipton's Teas	Red metal bus; green tray	Semi-oval/65 x 150	40.00	45.00	20.00
AC-97a	Bus, "Cliftonville"	Silver plastic bus; black tray	Semi-oval/55 x 150	25.00	30.00	12.00
AC-97b	Bus, "Souvenir of London"	Silver plastic bus; green tray	Semi-oval/55 x 150	25.00	30.00	12.00
AC-98a	Duke of Connaught Locomotive, 1897	Black metal train; honey-brown tray	Semi-oval/65 x 150	40.00	45.00	20.00
AC-98b	Duke of Connaught Locomotive, 1897	Green metal train; beige tray	Semi-oval/65 x 150	40.00	45.00	20.00
AC-99	Ford	Silver metal car; black tray	Triangular/90 x 150	40.00	45.00	20.00

Maxwell Roadster 1911

Mercer Raceabout Sportscar 1913

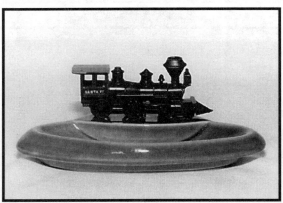

Santa Fe Train

Spitfire Pen Holder

Backstamp: **A.** Raised "Wade Porcelain Made in England"
B. Raised "R.K. Product by Wade of England"
C. Raised "S42/8"
D. Raised "Made in England Lesney"

No.	Description	Colourways	Shape/Size	U.S.$	Can.$	U.K.£
AC-100	Maxwell Roadster, 1911	Gold metal car; black tray	Square/50 x 130	40.00	45.00	20.00
AC-101	Mercer Raceabout Sportscar, 1913	Silver metal car; black tray	Triangular/70 x 135	40.00	45.00	20.00
AC-102a	Rolls Royce, 1907	Silver metal car; black tray	Semi-oval/50 x 130	40.00	45.00	20.00
AC-102b	Rolls Royce, 1907	Gold metal car; green tray	Semi-oval/50 x 130	40.00	45.00	20.00
AC-103	Sailing Ship	White plastic ship; black tray	Semi-oval/90 x 145	25.00	30.00	12.00
AC-104a	Santa Fe 4-4-0 American "General" Locomotive, 1862	Red/silver metal train; honey-brown tray	Semi-oval/65 x 150	40.00	45.00	20.00
AC-104b	Santa Fe 4-4-0 American "General" Locomotive, 1983	Red/green metal train; beige tray	Oval/65 x 150	40.00	45.00	20.00
AC-105a	Spitfire Pen Holder	Silver metal plane; black tray	Triangular/100 x 145	25.00	30.00	12.00
AC-105b	Spitfire Pen Holder	Brass metal plane; royal blue tray	Triangular/100 x 145	25.00	30.00	12.00

Animals and Fish

Pike (plastic)

Roach (plastic)

Backstamp: Raised "R.K. Product by Wade of England"

No.	Description	Colourways	Shape/Size	U.S.$	Can.$	U.K.£
AC-106	Hare (metal)	Beige hare; green tray	Semi-oval/90 x 150	25.00	30.00	12.00
AC-107a	Pike (metal)	White fish; green tray	Semi-oval/65 x 150	25.00	30.00	12.00
AC-107b	Pike (metal)	Green fish; honey-brown tray	Semi-oval/65 x 150	25.00	30.00	12.00
AC-108a	Pike (plastic)	White fish; honey-brown tray	Semi-oval/65 x 150	25.00	30.00	10.00
AC-108b	Pike (plastic)	Grey fish; honey-brown tray	Semi-oval/65 x 150	25.00	30.00	10.00
AC-109	Perch (plastic)	Green fish; honey-brown tray	Semi-oval/65 x 150	25.00	30.00	10.00
AC-110	Roach (plastic)	Green fish; honey-brown tray	Semi-oval/65 x 150	25.00	30.00	10.00
AC-111	Squirrel (metal)	Brown squirrel; green tray	Semi-oval/90 x 150	25.00	30.00	12.00

THE LICENCES AND GENERAL INSURANCE COMPANY LTD

DISH, c.1950-c1960

Photograph not available
at press time

Backstamp: Red transfer print "Wade England"

No.	Description	Colourways	Shape/Size	U.S.$	Can.$	U.K.£
AC-112	Dish	White; black print, lettering "The Licences and General Insurance Company Ltd"	Circular/110	8.00	10.00	3.00

LOFTHOUSE OF FLEETWOOD LTD.

FISHERMAN'S FRIEND TEAPOT

This teapot , commissioned by the manufacturer of Fisherman's Friend Throat Lozenges, is the same shape as that used for Wade's "English Life Conservatory Teapot," which was produced from 1988 to 1994.

Backstamp: Black and red transfer print "Made Exclusively for Lofthouse of Fleetwood Ltd by Wade England" and two red lines

No.	Description	Colourways	Size	U.S.$	Can.$	U.K.£
AC-113	Teapot	White; multi-coloured prints	114	50.00	70.00	25.00

THE LONDON TEA AND PRODUCE CO. LTD.

TEA CADDY, 1984

Backstamp: Unknown

No.	Description	Colourways	Size	U.S.$	Can.$	U.K.£
AC-114	Tea Caddy	Off white; brown print	101	30.00	35.00	15.00

LONDON ZOO

150TH ANNIVERSARY CELEBRATION DISH, 1979

This dish was produced to celebrate the 150th anniversary of the London Zoo.

Backstamp: Raised "No 3"

No.	Description	Colourways	Size	U.S.$	Can.$	U.K.£
AC-115a	Dish	Grey blue	120	25.00	30.00	12.00
AC-115b	Dish	Honey brown	120	25.00	30.00	12.00
AC-115c	Dish	Green	120	25.00	30.00	12.00

LUCKY STRIKE CIGARETTES

ASHTRAYS, 1990-1995

Photograph not available
at press time

Backstamp: "Wade P D M Made in England"

No.	Description	Colourways	Shape/Size	U.S.$	Can.$	U.K.£
AC-116a	Ashtray	White; red/black lettering "Lucky Strike"	Round/177	10.00	15.00	5.00
AC-116b	Ashtray	Deep blue; red/black/white lettering "Lucky Strike"	Round/177	10.00	15.00	5.00
AC-117	Ashtray	Deep blue; red/black/white lettering "Lucky Strike"	Round/205	10.00	15.00	5.00

LYONS TETLEY LTD.

COFFEE MUG AND COOKIE JAR, 1990-1994

The coffee mug was issued in 1990 and the cookie jar from 1993 to 1994.

Coffee Mug   Cookie Jar

Backstamp: **A.** Gold transfer "Made exclusively for Lyons Tetley by Wade"
             B. White print "An original design for Lyons Tetley by Wade England"

No.	Description	Colourways	Size	U.S.$	Can.$	U.K.£
AC-118	Coffee mug	Black mug; multi-coloured print; gold lettering "Lyons Fresh Ground Coffee"	90	25.00	30.00	12.00
AC-119	Cookie Jar/Gaffer	Dark blue; brown hat; white lettering "Cookies"	215	40.00	45.00	20.00

CRUET SET, 1990–1992

Sydney Pepper Pot, Brew Gaffer Salt Cellar

Backstamp: Black transfer print "Wade England"

No.	Description	Colourways	Size	U.S.$	Can.$	U.K.£
AC-120	Brew Gaffer Salt Cellar	Light brown hat, slippers; white coat; red tie; blue trousers	90	70.00	90.00	35.00
AC-121	Sidney Pepper Pot Sydney/Gaffer (Pair)	Light brown hat, slippers; white coat; blue dungarees	100	70.00 125.00	90.00 155.00	35.00 65.00

MONEY BOXES, 1989–1990

The "Brew Gaffer Money Box" was produced in a limited edition of 10,000 and came with a numbered certificate of authenticity. The delivery vans were produced in 1990.

Brew Gaffer

Lyons' Coffee Delivery Van

Tetley's Teas Delivery Van

Backstamp: **A.** Black transfer print "Made exclusively for Lyons Tetley by Wade"
B. White transfer print "Manufactured Exclusively for Lyons Tetley Wade Made in England," impressed "Wade"

No.	Description	Colourways	Size	U.S.$	Can.$	U.K.£
AC-122	Brew Gaffer	Brown cap, slippers; white coat, shirt; red tie; blue trousers	140	80.00	100.00	40.00
AC-123	Lyons' Coffee Delivery Van	Dark green; gold/white lettering "Lyons' Coffee Est 1904"	140	70.00	90.00	35.00
AC-124	Tetley's Teas Delivery Van	Dark blue; gold/white lettering "Tetley's Teas Est 1837	140	70.00	90.00	35.00

TEAPOTS AND TOAST RACK, 1989-1994

The two-cup teapot was issued in 1989 and the "Sydney Teapot" in 1990. The "Brew Gaffer and Sydney Teapot" and toast rack were offered as mail-in premiums from "The Tetley Tea Folk Catalogue."

Two-Cup Teapot

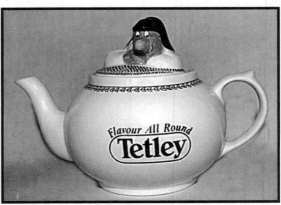
Sydney Teapot

Toast Rack; Brew Gaffer and Sydney Teapot

Backstamp: **A.** Black print "Two cup Teapot specially made by Wade Potteries for Lyons Tetley Ltd"
B. Black transfer "Made exclusively for Lyons Tetley by Wade"
C. White print "An original design for Lyons Tetley by Wade England"

No.	Description	Colourways	Size	U.S.$	Can.$	U.K.£
AC-125	Two-Cup Teapot	Dark blue teapot; white lettering "Tetley"	120	30.00	35.00	15.00
AC-126	Sydney Teapot	White teapot; brown hat, shoes; white overall; brown/black rope ladder; blue lettering "Flavour All Round Tetley"	135	50.00	70.00	25.00
AC-127	Brew Gaffer and Sydney Teapot	Dark blue; brown/blue/white print	127	50.00	70.00	25.00
AC-128	Toast Rack	Dark blue; brown/blue/white print	70	30.00	35.00	15.00

LYONS TEA IRELAND LTD.

WORLD CUP FOOTBALL TEAPOT, 1990

This football-shaped teapot, with the knob on the lid depicting a football boot, was produced as a promotional item for Lyons Tea Ireland when Ireland qualified for the 1990 World Cup football competitions.

Backstamp: Unknown

No.	Description	Colourways	Size	U.S.$	Can.$	U.K.£
AC-129	Football	White; black boot, patches on ball	155	70.00	90.00	35.00

LYONS TETLEY LTD. AND ESSO PETROLEUM

GAFFER AND NEPHEW VAN TEA CADDY, 1994–1995

Lyons Tetley and Esso Petrol stations in Britain joined forces in a promotion that lasted from September 1994 to February 1995. Purchasers of £6 worth of Esso petrol were given a Tiger Token, and 200 of these tokens were needed to obtain the "Gaffer and Nephew Van Tea Caddy." The caddy has moulded figures of the Tetley Tea Gaffer as the driver and his nephew sitting beside him.

Backstamp: White print "An Original Design For Lyons Tetley By Wade England"

No.	Description	Colourways	Size	U.S.$	Can.$	U.K.£
AC-130	Tea Caddy	Blue; brown/white/blue figures	127	150.00	225.00	75.00

R.H. MACY & CO. INC.

TEAPOT, 1989

The world famous Macy's department store of New York commissioned the Wade pottery to produce a teapot representing its building. Wade used the mould from the *English Life* series "Queen Victoria Pub Teapot" and decorated the teapot with a transfer print of the Macy's store front.

Photograph not available at press time

Backstamp: Black transfer "Made in England Expressly for R.H. Macy & Co. Inc., New York N.Y. 10001 ⇑Μαχψ.∀

No.	Description	Colourways	Size	U.S.$	Can.$	U.K.£
AC-131	Teapot	White; red/white/yellow print	145	30.00	35.00	15.00

MARLBORO CIGARETTES

ASHTRAYS, 1984-1995

Photograph not available at press time

Backstamp: **A.** "Wade p d m England"
B. "Wade P D M Made in England"

No.	Description	Colourways	Shape/Size	U.S.$	Can.$	U.K.£
AC-132a	Ashtray	White; yellow/red lettering "Marlboro"	Hexagonal/190	15.00	20.00	8.00
AC-132b	Ashtray	Black; red/white lettering "Marlboro"	Hexagonal/190	15.00	20.00	8.00
AC-132c	Ashtray	White; red/black lettering "Marlboro"	Hexagonal/190	15.00	20.00	8.00

MARSTON'S

CRUETS, c.1950-c.1960

Photograph not available at press time

Backstamp: Red printed "Wade England"

No.	Description	Colourways	Size	U.S.$	Can.$	U.K.£
AC-133a	Pepper Pot	Beige; brown/black lettering "Marston's Good Food Quality and Value"	114	8.00	10.00	3.00
AC-133b	Salt Cellar	Beige; brown/black lettering "Marston's Good Food Quality and Value"	114	8.00	10.00	3.00

MINSTER GINGER ALE

WATER JUG, 1962-1968

This water jug has a recessed handle and an open spout.

Photograph not available at press time

Backstamp: "Wade Regicor, London England," laurel leaves, small size

No.	Description	Colourways	Shape/Size	U.S.$	Can.$	U.K.£
AC-134	Water Jug	Black, white/gold lettering "Minster Ginger Ale"	Round/120	25.00	30.00	12.00

PENCIL AND PEN-AND-INK HOLDERS

The pencil holders, made in the shape of a 1950s television set, were produced as a private commission in 1987 for someone with the initials *SM*, but whose name was not recorded. The TVs with the bear cub have gold knobs and a coloured transfer print of the bear in different poses.

The pen-and-ink holder has four holes with the letters *MB* and a star in a circle on the front. It was produced circa 1980.

TV/Bear Cub Sleeping

Pen-and-ink Holder

Backstamp: Embossed "Wade (SM) England"
Pen-and-Ink holder — Unmarked

No.	Description	Colourways	Size	U.S.$	Can.$	U.K.£
AC-136c	TV/Bear Cub Eating	Pearlised; gold knobs, brown/green print	90	25.00	30.00	12.00
AC-136d	TV/Bear Cub Sleeping	Pearlised; gold knobs, brown/green print	90	25.00	30.00	12.00
AC-136b	TV/Bear Cub Walking	Pearlised; gold knobs, brown/green print	90	25.00	30.00	12.00
AC-136a	TV/Blank Screen	Off white	90	15.00	20.00	8.00
AC-137	Pen-and-Ink Holder	Off white; blue print	35 x 85	25.00	30.00	12.00

MULBERRY GALLERY OF GREAT BRITAIN

MUSTANG P-5 AIRPLANE WALL PLATE, c.1965

A limited edition of 2,500 wall plates was produced for the Mulberry Gallery circa 1965. So far only one plate has been reported.

Photograph not available at press time

Backstamp: Black transfer print "Wade North American P-5 Mustang by Robert Taylor, one of a Limited Edition of 2,500 Fine English Bone China Plates Created exclusively for the Mulberry Gallery of Great Britain by Wade Potteries PLC"

No.	Description	Colourways	Size	U.S.$	Can.$	U.K.£
AC-138	Plate	White; multi-coloured print	165	70.00	90.00	35.00

NATIONAL TRUST

TEAPOTS, 1989

Only two teapots are known to have been produced for the British National Trust. Two moulds from the *English Life* teapots were used. With the addition of new multi-coloured transfer prints, the "Flories Flowers Teapot " became the "Alfreston Lodge Teapot" and "The Conservatory Teapot" became the "Blaise Hamlet Cottage Teapot."

Photograph not available at press time

Backstamp: Unknown

No.	Description	Colourways	Size	U.S.$	Can.$	U.K.£
AC-139	Alfreston Lodge	White; multi-coloured print	140	30.00	35.00	15.00
AC-140	Blaise Hamlet Cottage	White; multi-coloured print	135	30.00	35.00	15.00

NATIONAL WESTMINSTER BANK

MONEY BOXES

Mother Panda and Baby, 1989

Backstamp: Raised "Wade England"

No.	Description	Colourways	Size	U.S.$	Can.$	U.K.£
AC-141	Panda and Baby	Black/white	112	30.00	35.00	15.00

Pig Family, 1984–1989

A limited number of "Woody Money Boxes," glazed with 22-karat gold leaf were made exclusively for the board of directors of the National Westminster Bank.

Backstamp: **A.** Raised "Wade"
B. Raised "Wade England"

No.	Description	Colourways	Size	U.S.$	Can.$	U.K.£
AC-142a	Woody (baby)	Pink; white nappy; silver/grey safety pin	135	25.00	30.00	12.00
AC-142b	Woody (baby)	Gold	135	95.00	135.00	50.00
AC-143	Annabel (girl)	Pink; white blouse; green gym slip; blue bag	175	30.00	35.00	15.00
AC-144	Maxwell (boy)	Pink; red/white tie; blue trousers	180	30.00	35.00	15.00
AC-145	Lady Hilary (mother)	Pink; light blue blouse; navy skirt	185	40.00	45.00	20.00
AC-146	Sir Nathaniel Westminster (father)	Pink; black suit; red bow tie, rose	190	50.00	70.00	25.00

MUG, 1987–1989

Backstamp: Red transfer print "Royal Victoria Pottery Wade Staffordshire England"

No.	Description	Colourways	Size	U.S.$	Can.$	U.K.£
AC-147	100's Club Piggy	Pale grey; multi-coloured print	90	25.00	35.00	12.00

NELSON CIGARETTES

ASHTRAY, 1955-1962

Photograph not available
at press time

Backstamp: "Wade Regicor, London England," laurel leaves, large size

No.	Description	Colourways	Shape/Size	U.S.$	Can.$	U.K.£
AC-148	Ashtray	Pale blue; black lettering "Nelson Filter Tipped"	Oval/171	15.00	20.00	8.00

NOTIONS AND NOVELTIES LIMITED OF LONDON

FAMOUS AIRCRAFT TRAYS, 1958-1960

The original price was 3/9d each.

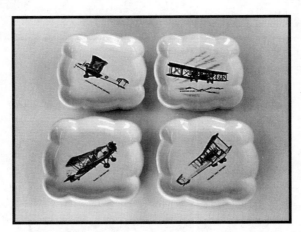

Backstamp: Black print "A Moko line by Wade of England Authenticated by 'Janes all the Worlds Aircraft,'" with the set and dish number

No.	Description	Colourways	Size	U.S.$	Can.$	U.K.£
AC-149a	Bleriots Mono Plane 1909	White dish; black/blue print (Set 1)	103	40.00	45.00	20.00
AC-149b	Fairey "Swordfish"	White dish; yellow/black print (Set 2)	103	50.00	70.00	25.00
AC-149c	Handley Page 0/400 Bomber	White dish; yellow/black print (Set 2)	103	50.00	70.00	25.00
AC-149d	Vickers Vimy Bomber	White dish; yellow/black print (Set 2)	103	50.00	70.00	25.00
AC-149e	Vickers Vimy 1919	White dish; black/blue print (Set 1)	103	40.00	45.00	20.00
AC-149f	Wrights Bi-Plane	White dish; black/blue print (Set 1)	103	40.00	45.00	20.00

PARKINSONS DONCASTER OLD FASHIONED HUMBUGS

ASHTRAY, 1955-1962

Photograph not available
at press time

Backstamp: "Wade Regicor, London England," laurel leaves, large size

No.	Description	Colourways	Shape/Size	U.S.$	Can.$	U.K.£
AC-150	Ashtray	White; red/black lettering "Parkinsons Doncaster Old Fashioned Humbugs"	Round/140	15.00	20.00	8.00

PEARS SOAP

SOAP DISH, 1987

This dish has a gold banner along two sides which proclaims "30 yrs of Miss Pears 1958–1987."

Photograph not available
at press time

Backstamp: Red transfer print "Royal Victoria Pottery—Staffordshire Wade England"

No.	Description	Colourways	Size	U.S.$	Can.$	U.K.£
AC-151	Soap Dish	White; pink flowers; gold banners	20 x 145	15.00	20.00	8.00

PEERAGE BRASS

TRAYS, 1958–1965

Peerage Trays are the same trays used for the Irish Wade *Whimtrays*. With the addition of a hole drilled in the back of the tray, a miniature brass animal or figure, produced by Peerage Brass, was then fixed onto the rim with a screw through the bottom. The client's name was added to the bottom of the tray. They are listed in alphabetical order.

Wired-Haired Terrier; Bear and Staff Warwick

Squirrel with Acorn; Guy De Warwick

Backstamp: Raised "Peerage Wade Porcelain Made in England"

No.	Name	Description	Size	U.S.$	Can.$	U.K.£
AC-152	Bear and Staff Warwick	Brass bear; blue tray	70 x 75	15.00	20.00	8.00
AC-153	Cornish Pixie	Brass pixie; yellow tray	50 x 75	15.00	20.00	8.00
AC-154	Crinoline Lady with Basket	Brass lady; blue tray	60 x 75	15.00	20.00	8.00
AC-155	Esmeralda	Brass girl; blue tray	70 x 75	15.00	20.00	8.00
AC-156	Galleon Victory	Brass galleon; yellow tray	70 x 75	15.00	20.00	8.00
AC-157	Galleon *The Revenge*, 1588	Brass galleon; yellow tray	70 x 75	15.00	20.00	8.00
AC-158	Guy De Warwick	Brass knight; yellow tray	65 x 75	15.00	20.00	8.00
AC-159a	Pekinese	Brass dog; black tray	55 x 75	15.00	20.00	8.00
AC-159b	Pekinese	Brass dog ; yellow tray	55 x 75	15.00	20.00	8.00
AC-160	Rearing Horse	Brass horse; yellow tray	65 x 75	15.00	20.00	8.00
AC-161	Squirrel with Acorn	Brass squirrel; yellow tray	60 x 75	15.00	20.00	8.00
AC-162	Stag	Brass stag; black tray	70 x 75	15.00	20.00	8.00
AC-163	Wire-Haired Terrier	Brass dog; black tray	60 x 75	15.00	20.00	8.00

PETER ENGLAND SHIRT MANUFACTURERS, ENGLAND

ASHTRAY, 1969-1984

This ashtray was modelled in the shape of a sitting cartoon-type lion, with the detailing in black. It was produced in a limited edition of 1,000.

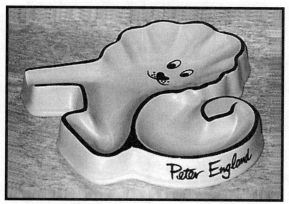

Backstamp: "Wade pdm England" printed in a circle

No.	Description	Colourways	Size	U.S.$	Can.$	U.K.£
AC-164	Ashtray	Bright yellow; black lettering "Peter England"	184	40.00	45.00	20.00

JOHN PLAYER CIGARETTES

ASHTRAY AND WATER JUGS, 1969-1984

This ashtray has a print of cigarettes on it. The water jugs have ice-check spouts and are decorated with a print of the cigarette label.

Photograph not available
at press time

Backstamp: "Wade pdm England" printed in a circle

No.	Description	Colourways	Shape/Size	U.S.$	Can.$	U.K.£
AC-165	Ashtray	Black; white print; gold lettering "John Player Special"	Square/195	15.00	20.00	8.00
AC-166	Water Jug	Black; yellow/black print; gold lettering "John Player"	Rectangular/146	25.00	30.00	12.00
AC-167	Water Jug	Black; gold/yellow lettering "John Player Special Cigarettes"	Rectangular/153	25.00	30.00	12.00

THE POTTERIES CENTRE, WADE COLLECTORS CLUB

BOTTLE OVEN CRUET, 1991

The "Bottle Oven Cruet" was available to members of the Wade Collectors Club.

Backstamp: Black transfer print "Wade England"

No.	Description	Colourways	Size	U.S.$	Can.$	U.K.£
AC-168	Cruet	Dark brown	50	25.00	30.00	12.00

KNIGHT TEMPLAR , 1991
Style Two

The second version of the "Knight Templar" was issued in a limited edition of 100 and made available to members of the Wade Collectors Club. The original issue price was £85.

Backstamp: Red transfer print "Genuine Wade Porcelain" and gold handwritten "Limited Edition — of 100 December 1991"

No.	Description	Colourways	Size	U.S.$	Can.$	U.K.£
AC-169	Knight Templar	White/red robes, shield; red hat	235	250.00	300.00	125.00

PRICE'S PATENT CANDLE COMPANY LTD.

CANDLE HOLDERS, 1963–1982

Between the middle of 1963 and 1982, Wade was commissioned by Price's Patent Candle Company Ltd. to produce a series of candle holders to sell in gift packages with Price's candles. Only the cube candle holder bears the Wade backstamp, other models listed below are marked with their shape numbers and can be easily recognized by their typical Wade glaze and weight.

Backstamp: A. Embossed "Made in England"
B. Embossed "S68/1 Wade England"

No.	Description	Colourways	Size	U.S.$	Can.$	U.K.£
AC-170	Bridge	Off white (S2/6)	37 x 137	8.00	10.00	3.00
AC-171a	Cube	Royal blue (S68/1)	49 x 49	8.00	10.00	3.00
AC-171b	Cube	Honey-brown (S68/1)	49 x 49	8.00	10.00	3.00
AC-172	Daffodil, Small	Brown/grey/blue	19 x 41	6.00	8.00	2.00
AC-173	Daffodil, Large	Brown/grey/blue	35 x 78	8.00	10.00	3.00
AC-174	Hat, Small	Pale green	20 x 42	6.00	8.00	2.00
AC-175	Hat, Large	Black (S2/7)	35 x 70	6.00	8.00	2.00
AC-176a	Ink Bottle	Olive green (S2/16)	43 x 73	8.00	10.00	3.00
AC-176b	Ink Bottle	Pale blue (S2/16)	43 x 73	8.00	10.00	3.00
AC-176c	Ink Bottle	White (S2/16)	43 x 73	8.00	10.00	3.00
AC-177a	Leaf	Dark green	35 x 155	8.00	10.00	3.00
AC-177b	Leaf	Light green	35 x 155	8.00	10.00	3.00
AC-177c	Leaf	Dark/light brown	35 x 155	8.00	10.00	3.00
AC-178	Soap Cake	Off white	19 x 100	8.00	10.00	3.00
AC-179a	Sunflower	Honey-brown/orange-brown	30 x 78	8.00	10.00	3.00
AC-179b	Sunflower	Red-brown/orange-brown	30 x 78	8.00	10.00	3.00
AC-180	Triangle	Pale blue (S62/2)	Unknown	6.00	8.00	2.00
AC-181a	Tulip, Small	Pale blue (S2/18)	43 x 50	6.00	8.00	2.00
AC-181b	Tulip, Small	Maroon (S2/18)	43 x 50	6.00	8.00	2.00
AC-181c	Tulip, Small	Brown (S2/18)	43 x 50	6.00	8.00	2.00
AC-181d	Tulip, Small	White (S2/18)	43 x 50	6.00	8.00	2.00
AC-182a	Tulip, Large	Pale blue	55 x 71	8.00	10.00	3.00
AC-182b	Tulip, Large	Maroon	55 x 71	8.00	10.00	3.00
AC-183a	Water Lily	Mottled brown/blue	24 x 103	8.00	10.00	3.00
AC-183b	Water Lily	Mottled green/brown	24 x 103	8.00	10.00	3.00

RANK FILM ORGANISATION

FRIED GREEN TOMATOES MONEY BOX, 1992

This tomato-shaped money box was produced for the Rank Film Organisation of England to promote its film, *Fried Green Tomatoes*. They were produced in a limited edition of 1,000.

Backstamp: Red print "Wade England"

No.	Description	Colourways	Size	U.S.$	Can.$	U.K.£
AC-184	Money Box	Pale green; dark green letters "Fried Green Tomatoes at the Whistle Stop Cafe"	135 x 155	70.00	90.00	35.00

READY MIXED CONCRETE UNITED KINGDOM LTD.

CIGARETTE BOX, c.1958

This cigarette box is decorated with a black-and-white transfer print of a Ready Mixed Concrete lorry with a large genie, wearing a bowler hat, floating from the mixer.

Photograph not available
at press time

Backstamp: Black ink stamp "Wade England"

No.	Description	Colourways	Size	U.S.$	Can.$	U.K.£
AC-185	Cigarette Box	Black base, print; white lid	50 x 125	40.00	55.00	20.00

CARTOON DISHES, c.1960–1970

Cartoons by Ray Davis

These two sets of dishes are decorated with cartoons by Ray Davis. Set one has a black and white design on a white, square dish, while set two has cartoons that have multi-coloured prints on a white, triangular dish with a gold-lined rim. Only the first set of dishes is signed by Ray Davis.

Set One

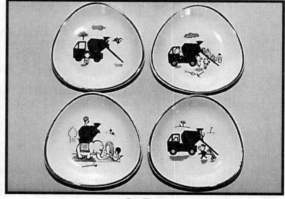

Set Two

Backstamp: **A.** Red transfer print "Wade England," Set one
B. Black transfer print "Wade England," Set two

No.	Description	Colourways	Size	U.S.$	Can.$	U.K.£
AC-186a	Birds and Cement Mixer	Black cement mixer, birds (Set one)	106	10.00	15.00	5.00
AC-187a	Birds and Cement Mixer	Orange cement mixer; black birds (Set two)	106	10.00	15.00	5.00
AC-186b	Dice in Cement Mixer	Black cement mixer, dice (Set one)	106	10.00	15.00	5.00
AC-187b	Dice in Cement Mixer	Orange cement mixer; yellow/white dice (Set two)	106	10.00	15.00	5.00
AC-186c	Elephant Spraying Cement	Black cement mixer, dice (Set one)	106	10.00	15.00	5.00
AC-187c	Elephant Spraying Cement	Orange cement mixer, white elephant (Set two)	106	10.00	15.00	5.00
AC-186d	Golfer and Cement Mixer	Black cement mixer, golfer (Set one)	106	10.00	15.00	5.00
AC-187d	Golfer and Cement Mixer	Orange cement mixer, golfer (Set two)	106	13.00	15.00	5.00

Cartoon by David Langdon

These cartoon dishes were signed by David Langdon. They have a multi-coloured print on a white dish with a gold-lined rim. The cartoons show Ready Mixed Cement being used to repair the Wonders of the World.

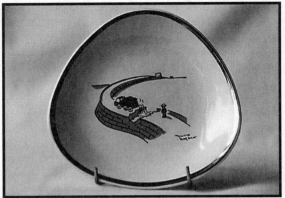

Great Wall of China

Pyramids of Egypt

Backstamp: Green transfer print "Wade PDM England"

No.	Description	Colourways	Size	U.S.$	Can.$	U.K.£
AC-188a	Great Wall of China	Blue wall; red cement mixer	106	10.00	15.00	5.00
AC-188b	Pyramids of Egypt	Blue/white pyramids; red cement mixer	106	10.00	15.00	5.00

REGINALD CORFIELD LTD.

DISH, 1954

This dish advertised Reginald Corfield's colour printing on metal. It is from the same mould as that used for Wade's 1953 "Coronation Dish" with the embossing changed. Inscribed around the rim in embossed letters is "Reginald Corfield Ltd - Colour Printing on Metal - Lombard Road, Merton SW 19." On the inside of the bowl is an inscribed quote from a speech Ralph Waldo Emerson made in 1871: "If a man can write a better book, preach a better sermon, or make a better Mouse trap than his neighbour, though he build his house in the Woods, the world will make a beaten path to his house." The centre of the dish is inscribed with "Regicor - Regd - Trade Mark." In 1955 Wade Heath and Reginald Corfield Ltd. formed a partnership in advertising and promotional wares that lasted 14 years.

Photograph not available
at press time

Backstamp: Embossed "Wade England"

No.	Description	Colourways	Size	U.S.$	Can.$	U.K.£
AC-189	Dish	Light green; green lettering	120	30.00	35.00	15.00

RINGTONS TEA LTD.

BEAKER, 1994

The "Chinese Willow Pattern Beakers" were available from Ringtons for £8.99 per pair.

Backstamp: Black print "Exclusive Willow Pattern Specially Commissioned for Ringtons Ltd, Produced By Wade Ceramics"

No.	Description	Colourways	Size	U.S.$	Can.$	U.K.£
AC-190	Beaker	White; blue print	100	25.00	30.00	12.00

CARRIAGE CLOCK

This rectangular clock is decorated with an all-over floral design against a white background.

Photograph not available
at press time

Backstamp: Black print "Especially Commissioned by Ringtons Ltd, produced By Wade Ceramics"

No.	Description	Colourways	Size	U.S.$	Can.$	U.K.£
AC-191	Carriage Clock	White; multi-coloured flowers	162	50.00	70.00	25.00

TEA CADDIES, 1982–1993

The "Cathedrals and Bridge Tea Caddy" was produced for Ringtons to celebrate its 80th anniversary in 1987. Each panel of the hexagonal jar is ornately decorated with transfer prints of famous Northern landmarks — Durham Cathedral, the Castle and Tyne Bridge in Newcastle-upon-Tyne, Ripon Cathedral, Selby Abbey, York Minister — with Windsor Castle on the lid. The design was based on an original caddy that was produced for Ringtons by the Tyneside pottery of C.T. Maling and Sons in 1929 to commemorate the North East Coast Industries Exhibition of that year. The Wade version is smaller and has slightly different transfers than the original Maling tea caddie. Approximately 36,500 Wade caddies were produced, and when they were originally sold in British stores, they were filled with tea. Ringtons commissioned 120 special editions of the caddy to present to the shareholders, directors and suppliers of Ringtons Tea. These editions can be distinguished by an extra gold line in the ornate decoration and are numbered on the bases.

With the success of the "Cathedrals and Bridge Tea Caddy," Ringtons commissioned a larger version in 1989. It was decorated in a similar way, but the transfer prints were changed to Carlisle Cathedral, Hexham Abbey, Newcastle Cathedral, Ripon Cathedral, Selby Abbey and York Minster, with Durham Cathedral on the lid.

The rectangular "Horse-Drawn Van Tea Caddy" was produced in 1982 to celebrate Ringtons' 75th anniversary. It has a transfer print on it of a 1907 horse-drawn van with the words "Ringtons Tea 1907–1982."

The "Oriental Jar, Willow Pattern Tea Caddy," produced in 1991, has square sloping sides that are wider at the top than at the base and a round lid. It is decorated with the popular Chinese willow pattern. The design is based upon that of an original 1920s Maling tea caddy, produced for Ringtons, that had a round lid, used as a tea measure. Inside the lid is a copy of the original Ringtons trademark, the monogram *RT* on a blue shield.

The "Pagoda, Willow Pattern Tea Caddy," produced in 1993, has square sloping sides that are wider at the base than the top and has a square lid. It is also decorated with the popular Chinese willow pattern. The caddy is the same design as a teapot produced by Maling for Ringtons in 1929.

Cathedrals and Bridge Tea Caddy

Oriental Jar Tea Caddy

Pagoda Tea Caddy

Backstamp: A. Blue transfer print "Made exclusively for Ringtons Ltd. by Wade Potteries to commemorate Ringtons Est. 1907–80th Anniversary based on an original 'Maling' Tea Caddy for Ringtons in the late 1920's"

B. Blue transfer print "Made exclusively for Ringtons Ltd by Wade Potteries based upon an original Maling Cathedral Jar produced for Ringtons in the late 1920s–1989"

C. Black print "Specially Commissioned by Ringtons Ltd, produced By Wade Ceramics—Ringtons—Based upon an Original 'Maling' Tea Caddy Produced for Ringtons in the late 1920's"

No.	Description	Colourways	Size	U.S.$	Can.$	U.K.£
AC-192a	Cathedrals/Bridge	Blue/white	100	70.00	90.00	35.00
AC-192b	Cathedrals/Bridge, Gold	Blue/white/gold trim	100		Rare	
AC-193	Cathedrals and Abbeys	Blue/white	135	60.00	80.00	30.00
AC-194	Horse-Drawn Van, 75th Anniversary	White; black print	160	70.00	90.00	35.00
AC-195	Oriental Jar, Willow Pattern	Blue/white	128	50.00	70.00	25.00
AC-196	Pagoda, Willow Pattern	Blue/white	135	50.00	70.00	25.00

TEAPOTS

Willow Pattern Teapot, 1994

The round four-cup "Willow Pattern Teapot" was available from Ringtons for £13.99.

No.	Description	Colourways	Size	U.S.$	Can.$	U.K.£
AC-197	Teapot	White; blue willow print	138	50.00	70.00	25.00

Street Scenes Collector Teapots, 1993-1994

This set of four teapots was all modelled in the shape of a house. They are decorated with transfer prints of street scenes showing Ringtons delivery vans and their progression from the 1920s horse-drawn van to the modern delivery van of the 1990s. They were available from Ringtons for £16.99 each.

The "Horse-Drawn Van Teapot" was made from the same mould as Wade's "Cricketers Teapot," which was first produced in 1991. The transfer print on this teapot is of a Ringtons Tea horse-drawn van, with a driver delivering a box of Ringtons Tea to a lady outside her house.

The "Motor Delivery Van Teapot, 1940" was taken from the same mould as used for Wade's "Wedding Teapot," which was first produced in 1991. The transfer print on this teapot is of a Ringtons Tea delivery van, with the driver delivering a box of Ringtons Tea to a lady outside her house.

Styles AC-198 and AC-199 were issued in 1993, styles AC-200 and AC-201 in 1994.

Photograph not available
at press time

No.	Description	Colourways	Size	U.S.$	Can.$	U.K.£
AC-198	Horse-Drawn Van, 1920	White; black/grey roof; beige house; white horse; green/yellow cart	177	50.00	70.00	25.00
AC-199	Motor Delivery Van, 1940	White; brown house; grey roof; green/yellow van	177	50.00	70.00	25.00
AC-200	Motor Delivery Van, 1960	White; grey/yellow house; red/white roof; green/yellow van	195	50.00	70.00	25.00
AC-201	Motor Delivery Van, 1990	White; green/yellow house; green/white roof; green/yellow van	177	50.00	70.00	25.00

ROTHMANS CIGARETTES

ASHTRAYS AND TANKARDS, 1969-1995

Tankard AC-205a has a transfer print on it of a Rothmans coach and horses. On the back is a history of the coach: "The Rothmans Coach, travels every day from Pall Mall through the West End of London along the Mall and Carlton Terrace, Rothmans still deliver their famous cigarettes to select Clubs and Embassies by coach and footman. This time honoured custom is a tradition of the House of Rothmans." Tankard AC-205b is decorated with a transfer print of the logo found on a Rothmans King Size Cigarette package.

Backstamp: A. "Wade P D M Made in England"
B. "Wade pdm England"

No.	Description	Colourways	Shape/Size	U.S.$	Can.$	U.K.£
AC-202	Ashtray	Maroon; white lettering "Pall Mall"	Round/177	10.00	15.00	5.00
AC-203	Ashtray	White; blue/red/white lettering "Rothmans King Size"	Round/120	10.00	15.00	5.00
AC-204	Ashtray	White; gold rim; white/blue lettering "Rothmans King Size"	Rectangular/254	15.00	20.00	8.00
AC-205a	Tankard	Amber; black print, lettering "Rothmans of Pall Mall"	Pint/115	25.00	30.00	12.00
AC-205b	Tankard	White; blue/white/red print, lettering "Rothmans King Size"	Pint/115	25.00	30.00	12.00

RUTHERFORD LABORATORIES

TANKARD, 1985

This tankard was commissioned by Rutherford Laboratories to present to its employees. It bears the inscription, "To commemorate the Inauguration of the Pulsed Spallation Neutron Source ISIS at the Rutherford Appleton Laboratory on 1st October 1985."

Photograph not available
at press time

Backstamp: Black print "Manufacturers of Alumina Ceramic Vacuum Vessels for ISIS. Porcelain Wade No 0507"

No.	Description	Colourways	Size	U.S.$	Can.$	U.K.£
AC-206	Tankard	White; multi-coloured print	115	25.00	30.00	12.00

SAFIR CIGARETTES

ASHTRAY, 1955-1962

Photograph not available
at press time

Backstamp: "Wade Regicor, London England," laurel leaves, large size

No.	Description	Colourways	Shape/Size	U.S.$	Can.$	U.K.£
AC-207	Ashtray	White; black lettering "Safir Filter Cigarettes"	Square/146	15.00	20.00	8.00

SALADA TEA CANADA

TEA CADDY, 1984

This tea caddy was first used in Wade's 1982–1983 *Village Stores* series; only the multi-coloured transfer print on the front was changed. Across the front of this caddy is printed "Salon de the Salada Ye olde tearoom." To obtain it the collector had to send in the UPC code from the back of the tea box, plus $13.00 to cover shipping and handling charges.

Backstamp: Transfer print "Village Stores by Wade Staffordshire, England"

No.	Description	Colourways	Size	U.S.$	Can.$	U.K.£
AC-208	Tea Caddy	White; multi-coloured print	191	50.00	70.00	25.00

SCARBOROUGH BUILDING SOCIETY

BASEBALL MONEY BOX

Backstamp: Unknown

No.	Description	Colourways	Size	U.S.$	Can.$	U.K.£
AC-209	Money Box	White ball head; royal blue cap	150	60.00	80.00	30.00

SENIOR SERVICE CIGARETTES

ASHTRAYS, 1962-1968

Photograph not available
at press time

Backstamp: "Wade Regicor, London England," laurel leaves, small size

No.	Description	Colourways	Shape/Size	U.S.$	Can.$	U.K.£
AC-210a	Ashtray	Blue; white lettering "Senior Service"	Round/140	15.00	20.00	8.00
AC-210b	Ashtray	Pale blue; black lettering "Senior Service Satisfy"	Round/140	15.00	20.00	8.00
AC-211	Ashtray	Blue; white lettering "Senior Service"	Triangular/242	15.00	20.00	8.00

7UP SOFT DRINKS

ASHTRAYS, 1955-1968

Backstamp: **A.** "Wade Regicor, London England," laurel leaves, large size
B. "Wade Regicor, London England," laurel leaves, small size

No.	Description	Colourways	Shape/Size	U.S.$	Can.$	U.K.£
AC-212	Ashtray	White; red/black lettering "7UP - Fresh up with Seven-Up The All Family Drink"	Square/146	15.00	20.00	8.00
AC-213	Ashtray	Pale green; multi-coloured lettering "7Up The All Family Drink"	Square/140	15.00	20.00	8.00

SHELL MEX AND BRITISH PETROLEUM

SHELL DISHES, 1953–1956

These shell-shaped dishes were printed with slogans associated with driving. It is believed that they were used as premiums at Shell petrol stations. For 1953 coronation dishes commissioned by Shell Mex and British Petroleum, see the section on commemorative items.

Photograph not available
at press time

Backstamp: Gold transfer print "Wade England A," with raised "BCM/OWL"

No.	Description	Colourways	Size	U.S.$	Can.$	U.K.£
AC-214a	"Keep Right"	Pale blue; gold print	85	20.00	20.00	8.00
AC-214b	"Keep Left"	Pale pink; gold print	85	15.00	20.00	8.00
AC-214c	"Turn Right"	Pale blue; gold print	85	15.00	20.00	8.00
AC-214d	"Shell"	Pale green; gold print	85	15.00	20.00	8.00
AC-214e	"Shell"	Pale green; gold print	85	15.00	20.00	8.00

SILK CUT CIGARETTES

WATER JUG, 1969-1984

This water jug has an ice-catcher spout and is decorated with a transfer print of a label from the cigarette package.

Photograph not available
at press time

Backstamp: "Wade pdm England"

No.	Description	Colourways	Shape/Size	U.S.$	Can.$	U.K.£
AC-215	Water Jug	White; maroon print; gold lettering "Silk Cut"	Rectangular/146	25.00	30.00	12.00

SLIMBRIDGE WILDFOWL TRUST

RUDDY DUCK, 1976

The "Ruddy Duck" is a slip-cast model produced in a bisque porcelain and was commissioned by Sir Peter Scott of the Slimbridge Wildfowl Trust. Only 3,500 models of the "Ruddy Duck" were made. The original price was £1.75.

Backstamp: Unmarked

No.	Description	Colourways	Size	U.S.$	Can.$	U.K.£
AC-216	Ruddy Duck	Red-brown body; black head, wings; blue bill	35	200.00	275.00	100.00

SMITHS CRISPS

MONSTER MUNCHER MONEY BOX, 1987

Backstamp: Impressed "Wade England"

No.	Description	Colourways	Size	U.S.$	Can.$	U.K.£
AC-217	Money Box	Bright blue body; red/white/green/blue/ yellow hat; pink feet	170	95.00	135.00	50.00

SUNDERLAND FOOTBALL CLUB

CENTENARY TANKARD, 1979

This jug was produced in a limited edition to commemorate the centenary of the Sunderland Football Club.

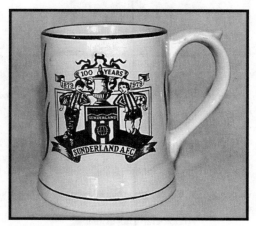

Backstamp: Green transfer print "Wade England"

No.	Description	Colourways	Size	U.S.$	Can.$	U.K.£
AC-218	Tankard	White; purple lustre rim, handle; multi-coloured print	120	95.00	135.00	50.00

SUPERKINGS CIGARETTES

WATER JUG, 1969-1990

These water jugs have ice-check spouts.

Photograph not available at press time

Backstamp: "Wade pdm England"

No.	Description	Colourways	Shape/Size	U.S.$	Can.$	U.K.£
AC-219	Water Jug	Black; gold lettering "Superkings"	Rectangular/146	25.00	30.00	12.00
AC-219	Water Jug	Black; gold lettering "Superkings"	Rectangular/170	30.00	35.00	15.00

TAYLORS MUSTARD

TANKARD, 1963

This half-pint Ulster Ware tankard is shape number I.P.1.

Backstamp: Impressed "Irish Porcelain" curved around shamrock leaf , "Made in Ireland" in straight line under shamrock

No.	Description	Colourways	Shape/Size	U.S.$	Can.$	U.K.£
AC-220	Tankard	Blue/grey; white lettering "1903 1963 Taylors"	1/2 pint/108	10.00	15.00	5.00

TIME LIFE INTERNATIONAL

CIGARETTE BOX, c.1965

The lid of this square cigarette box is decorated with a design of black letters, making up the name *Time Life*.

Photograph not available
at press time

Backstamp: Black print "Expressly Produced For Time Life International" and "Made In England By Wade, Stoke On Trent," with "Design By Alan Fletcher" on the underside of the lid

No.	Description	Colourways	Size	U.S.$	Can.$	U.K.£
AC-221	Cigarette Box	Black box; white/black lid	85 x 135	50.00	70.00	25.00

TOBY INNS

CRUETS, c.1950–c.1960

Backstamp: Red printed "Wade England"

No.	Description	Colourways	Size	U.S.$	Can.$	U.K.£
AC-222a	Pepper Pot	Beige; red/black print, lettering "The Sign of Good Food"	114	8.00	10.00	3.00
AC-222b	Salt Cellar	Beige; red/black print, lettering "The Sign of Good Food"	114	8.00	10.00	3.00
AC-222c	Pepper Pot	Beige; red/black print, lettering "Welcome Food Award"	114	8.00	10.00	3.00
AC-222d	Salt Cellar	Beige; red/black print, lettering "Welcome Food Award"	114	8.00	10.00	3.00

J. W. THORNTON LTD.

MONEY BOXES, 1984–1993

Wade produced five money boxes for J.W. Thornton Ltd. of England, manufacturers of chocolate and toffee: three "Delivery Vans" (1984, 1991 and 1993), a "Letter Box" (1985) and "Peter the Polar Bear" (1989) .The original price for the "Delivery Van" and the "Letter Box" was £3.99 each. The original 1984 "Delivery Van" and the 1993 reissue have solid back doors. A new style of delivery van, with two circular holes in the rear doors, was produced in 1991. The original 1984 "Delivery Van" was reissued for Christmas 1993 in a lighter brown. It was marked "Wade" on the packaging. The original price from Thorntons was £14.95.

1993 Delivery Van, 1991 Delivery Van

Rear 1984 Van (solid); Rear 1991 Van (two holes)

Letter Box

Peter the Polar Bear

Backstamp: **A.** Impressed "Made Exclusively for J. W. Thornton Ltd" on the base and "Thorntons Chocolates 1911" embossed on the side

B. Embossed "Thorntons Estd 1911" on the back

No.	Description	Colourways	Size	U.S.$	Can.$	U.K.£
AC-223	1984 Delivery Van	Chocolate brown	120	70.00	90.00	35.00
AC-224	1991 Delivery Van	Royal blue	120	60.00	80.00	30.00
AC-225	1993 Delivery Van	Light brown	120	50.00	70.00	25.00
AC-226	1985 Letter Box	Chocolate brown	180	70.00	90.00	35.00
AC-227	1989 Peter the Polar Bear	Off white; brown eyes, nose; red/green scarf	160	70.00	90.00	35.00

POTS, 1985 AND 1988

The "Father's Day Plant Pot" was produced in 1985 for Father's Day, and the "Special Toffee Pot" was produced in 1988.

Thornton's Special Toffee

Backstamp: Unmarked

No.	Description	Colourways	Size	U.S.$	Can.$	U.K.£
AC-228	Father's Day Plant Pot	Dark brown; light brown letters	110	70.00	90.00	35.00
AC-229	Special Toffee Pot	Dark brown; light brown letters	110	70.00	90.00	35.00

UNIVERSITY TREASURES

RAZORBACK PIGS, 1981

These hollow models, produced in biscuit porcelain, depict a North American wild pig called a razorback. They were designed by Alan Maslankowski, who modelled Wade's *Survival Animals* series. A limited edition of 500 models was produced for the University of Arkansas, whose football-team mascot is a razorback pig. These models are extremely rare.

Backstamp: Black ink stamp "Wade England"

No.	Description	Colourways	Size	U.S.$	Can.$	U.K.£
AC-230a	Razorback	Dark grey	130	700.00	775.00	350.00
AC-230b	Razorback	Red brown	130	700.00	775.00	350.00

VALOR GAS

TEAPOT, 1990

The British company Valor Gas commissioned this teapot. The mould was taken from the *English Life* series "Antique Shop Teapot." It is decorated with fireplace decals on either side, and the words "Valor Masters of the Living Flame" are printed on the lid. Only 1,000 of these teapots were produced.

Photograph not available
at press time

Backstamp: Black print "Valor a limited edition of 1,000 by Wade"

No.	Description	Colourways	Size	U.S.$	Can.$	U.K.£
AC-231	Teapot	White; red/green prints	153	20.00	30.00	10.00

VAN HEUSEN SHIRTS

TANKARD, c.1970

Tankard (face)

Tankard (back)

Backstamp: "Wade pdm England"

No.	Item	Description	Size	U.S.$	Can.$	U.K.£
AC-232	Tankard	Pale grey; black print, lettering "… continuing the Craftsman's art"	Pint/115	25.00	30.00	12.00

VICEROY CIGARETTES

ASHTRAYS, 1962-1968

Photograph not available
at press time

Backstamp: "Wade Regicor, London England," laurel leaves, small size

No.	Description	Colourways	Shape/Size	U.S.$	Can.$	U.K.£
AC-233	Ashtray	White; black/red lettering "Viceroy Filter Tip"	Oval/171	15.00	20.00	8.00
AC-234	Ashtray	White; green lettering "Viceroy Filter Tip"	Round/140	15.00	20.00	8.00

THE WESTBURY HOTEL, LONDON

DISH, c.1958

Backstamp: Red transfer "Wade England"

No.	Description	Colourways	Size	U.S.$	Can.$	U.K.£
AC-235a	Dish	White; pale blue band; multi-coloured print	110	8.00	10.00	3.00
AC-235b	Dish	White; red band; black print	110	8.00	10.00	3.00

WILLIAMSON AND MAGOR TEA DISTRIBUTORS

ELEPHANT TEA CADDIES, 1990, 1993

The original 1990 "Elephant Tea Caddies" were issued with a matt finish, and the models were decorated with a red and gold design. In 1993 the "Elephant Tea Caddies" were reissued in high-gloss glazes with a gold decoration.

| Elephant Tea Caddy, Earl Grey | Elephant Tea Caddy, English Breakfast |

Backstamp: Black print "Handcrafted and Produced Exclusively for Williamson and Magor by Wade Royal Victoria Pottery" and a silhouette of an elephant

No.	Description	Colourways	Size	U.S.$	Can.$	U.K.£
AC-236a	Earl Grey Tea	Grey matt finish; red/blue/gold decoration	185	70.00	90.00	35.00
AC-236b	Earl Grey Tea	Grey gloss finish; gold decoration	185	70.00	90.00	35.00
AC-236c	English Breakfast Tea	Blue matt finish; red/blue/gold decoration	185	70.00	90.00	35.00
AC-236d	English Breakfast Tea	Blue gloss finish; gold decoration	185	70.00	90.00	35.00

WINSOR AND NEWTON INKS LTD.

BRUSH POT, 1984

These round pots are decorated with a design of a flying griffin and the words "Winsor and Newtons Artists Brushes." They were produced as brush holders for Winsor and Newton inks and used in store displays.

Photograph not available
at press time

Backstamp: Unmarked

No.	Description	Colourways	Size	U.S.$	Can.$	U.K.£
AC-237	Brush Pot	Off white; black print	115	20.00	30.00	10.00

BRUSH AND INK STAND, c.1980

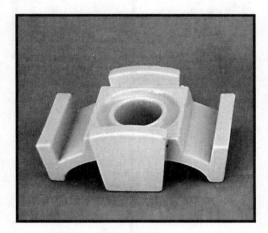

Backstamp: Blue transfer print "Wade Porcelain made in England"

No.	Description	Colourways	Size	U.S.$	Can.$	U.K.£
AC-238	Brush and Ink Stand	Cream	40 x 133	25.00	30.00	12.00

THE YORKSHIRE INSURANCE COMPANY LTD.

DISH, c.1950-c.1960

Backstamp: Red transfer print "Wade England"

No.	Description	Colourways	Shape/Size	U.S.$	Can.$	U.K.£
AC-239	Dish	White; red/gold print "Yorkshire 1824 The Yorkshire Insurance Company Ltd"	Round/110	8.00	10.00	3.00

ANIMALS
c.1930-1991

Wade animal models created from the early 1930s to 1939 and from the late 1940s up to the early 1950s are slip-cast (hollow) and have a circular casting hole in the base. Beginning in the early 1950s, Wade produced some solid models, and afterwards all the models were solid.

The glazes used from the 1930s to the early 1950s are in delicate pastel and natural colours and are very different from the darker colours used from the late 1950s. Many of the models that were first produced in the early 1930s proved to be popular and were reissued in the late 1940s and early 1950s.

BACKSTAMPS

Handwritten Backstamps

Handwritten backstamps were used to mark models from 1930 to 1939.

Black handwritten, 1930-1939

Ink Stamps

Ink stamps were used from 1935 to 1953. The size of the mark has no relevance to the date; large ink stamps were used on models with large bases, small ink stamps on small bases. Many of the smaller models are unmarked.

Green ink stamp, 1940s-1953

Brown ink stamp, early 1940s-1953

Transfer Prints

Beginning in 1953 transfer prints were used

Transfer print, 1953-late 1950s

Transfer print, 1976-1982

CELLULOSE MODELS
c.1935-1939

Alsatian, large size

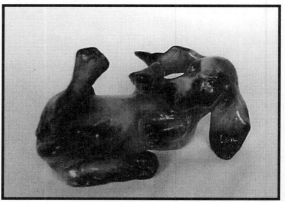

Spaniel Puppy

Panda

Backstamp: A. Black handwritten "Wade Made in England"; black ink stamp of a leaping deer
B. Black handwritten "Wade," stamped "Made in England"; model name

No.	Name	Description	Size	U.S.$	Can.$	U.K.£
A-1	Alsatian	Mottled browns; red tongue	Small/115	125.00	150.00	65.00
A-2a	Alsatian	Mottled yellow/black; pink tongue	Large/255	290.00	325.00	150.00
A-2b	Alsatian	Black/tan; red tongue	Large/255	290.00	325.00	150.00
A-2c	Alsatian	Dark brown all over	Large/255	95.00	135.00	50.00
A-3a	Panda	Black/white	165	95.00	135.00	50.00
A-4	Scottie	Black	120	125.00	150.00	65.00
A-5	Spaniel Puppy	Brown/black	85	125.00	150.00	65.00

Note: The Panda was also produced with a high-gloss, see page 91.

HIGH-GLOSS MODELS
c.1930-c.1979

BEAR CUB, c.1935-c.1939

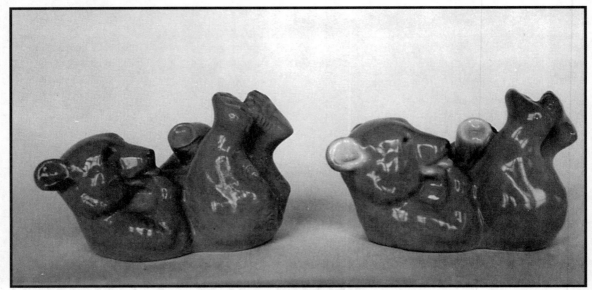

Bear Cub (A-6c, A-6a)

Backstamp: Black handwritten "Wade England"

No.	Name	Colourways	Size	U.S.$	Can.$	U.K.£
A-6a	Bear Cub	Beige; white ears; white honey	50	95.00	135.00	50.00
A-6b	Bear Cub	Brown; white ears; yellow honey	50	95.00	135.00	50.00
A-6c	Bear Cub	Beige all over	50	95.00	135.00	50.00
A-6d	Bear Cub	White; pink ears; brown feet; yellow honey	50	95.00	135.00	50.00

BROWN BEAR, 1939

The "Brown Bear" was modelled by Faust Lang.

Backstamp: Blue handwritten "Wade England 1939 Brown Bear" and the incised signature of Faust Lang

No.	Name	Colourways	Size	U.S.$	Can.$	U.K.£
A-7	Brown Bear	Beige; green/blue/grey rocky base	245	450.00	525.00	250.00

CALVES, c.1930–c.1948

First issued in the early 1930s, these models were reissued in the late 1940s and early 1950s. The reissues can be identified by the backstamp. The original price was 2/6d each.

Calf, eyes closed (A-9); Calf, eyes open (A-10)

Backstamp: A. Handwritten "Wade England"
B. Black ink stamp "Wade England"
C. Black ink stamp "Made in England"

No.	Name	Colourways	Size	U.S.$	Can.$	U.K.£
A-8	Calf, standing	White/brown patches	65	100.00	145.00	55.00
A-9	Calf, mooing, eyes closed	White/brown patches; pink ears; no mouth	45	100.00	145.00	55.00
A-10	Calf, mooing, eyes open	White/brown patches; brown ears; black mouth	45	100.00	145.00	55.00

CAMEL, 1939

Photograph not available
at press time

Backstamp: Unknown

No.	Name	Colourways	Size	U.S.$	Can.$	U.K.£
A-11	Camel	Light/dark brown	200	325.00	400.00	175.00

CATS

ABC Cats, c.1930–c1955

The *ABC Cats* are identified by letters used by Wade in the sales catalogues. Only six cats are illustrated in the publication, but a seventh cat, which is looking at a dish, has been reported.

Originally issued circa 1930, these cats were so popular they were reissued during the late 1940s, and again from 1953 to circa 1955. The price for these models in the 1950s was 1/6d each.

Care must be taken when purchasing an unmarked cat, as many Japanese and German cats have been produced in very similar poses as the *ABC Cats*. Whenever possible, compare such models with marked models first.

Cat A — Sitting cat with paws on ball, bow on left of neck
Cat B — Cat lying on its back, ball held in its front paws
Cat C — Sitting cat looking down at ball
Cat D — Sitting cat with paws on ball, bow on right of neck
Cat E — Drinking from dish of milk
Cat F — Cat on back with ball to mouth

Cat B, Cat A, Cat D, Cat E, Cat C

Backstamp: **A.** Black handwritten "Wade Made in England"
 B. Brown ink stamp "Wade England"
 C. Black transfer "Wade England"

No.	Name	Colourways	Size	U.S.$	Can.$	U.K.£
A-12a	Cat A	White/ginger cat; blue ribbon; yellow ball	38	70.00	90.00	35.00
A-12b	Cat A	White/grey cat; blue ribbon; ball	38	70.00	90.00	35.00
A-12c	Cat A	White/grey cat; blue ribbon; yellow ball	38	70.00	90.00	35.00
A-12d	Cat A	White/grey cat; yellow ribbon; blue ball	25	50.00	70.00	25.00
A-13a	Cat B	White/ginger cat; blue ribbon; yellow ball	27	70.00	95.00	35.00
A-13b	Cat B	White/grey cat; blue ribbon, ball	30	60.00	80.00	30.00
A-13c	Cat B	White/grey cat; yellow ribbon; blue ball	25	50.00	70.00	25.00
A-14a	Cat C	White/ginger cat; blue ribbon; yellow ball	40	70.00	90.00	35.00
A-14b	Cat C	White/grey cat; blue ribbon; ball	40	70.00	90.00	35.00
A-14c	Cat C	White/grey cat; blue ribbon; green ball	35	70.00	90.00	35.00
A-15a	Cat D	White/grey cat; blue ribbon, ball	40	70.00	90.00	35.00
A-15b	Cat D	White/grey cat; blue ribbon; green ball	40	70.00	90.00	35.00
A-15c	Cat D	White/grey cat; blue ribbon; red ball	40	70.00	90.00	35.00
A-16a	Cat E	White/grey cat; blue ribbon, dish	22	70.00	90.00	35.00
A-16b	Cat E	White/grey; cat yellow ribbon; grey dish	25	50.00	70.00	25.00
A-17	Cat F	White/grey cat; blue ribbon, ball	25	70.00	90.00	35.00

Siamese Kittens, c.1948–c1953

Only four models in the *Siamese Kittens* set have been found to date. They were modelled by John Szeilor, who worked at the Wade Heath Royal Victoria Pottery in the late 1940s to the early 1950s, when he left to establish his own pottery, the Szeilor Studio Art Pottery. Some of the early Szeilor Studio figures have a great similarity to his Wade models and are now very collectable.

Kitten, sitting, paw raised   **Kitten, standing**   **Kitten, sleeping**

Backstamp: **A.** Black ink stamp "Wade England"
          B. Black transfer stamp "Wade England"

No.	Name	Colourways	Size	U.S.$	Can.$	U.K.£
A-18	Kitten, sitting, paw down	Off white; grey markings; blue/black eyes	60	60.00	80.00	30.00
A-19	Kitten sitting, paw raised	Off white; grey markings; blue/black eyes	60	60.00	80.00	30.00
A-20	Kitten, standing	Off white; grey markings; blue/black eyes	45	60.00	80.00	30.00
A-21	Kitten, sleeping	Off white; grey markings	35	60.00	80.00	30.00

CHAMOIS KID, 1939

The "Chamois Kid" was modelled by Faust Lang.

Backstamp: Blue handwritten "Wade England 1939 Chamois Kid" and the incised signature of Faust Lang

No.	Name	Colourways	Size	U.S.$	Can.$	U.K.£
A-22	Chamois Kid	Honey/beige; green/blue rocky base	125	250.00	300.00	125.00

DOGS

Airedale, c.1935-1939

Photograph not available
at press time

No.	Name	Colourways	Size	U.S.$	Can.$	U.K.£
A-23	Airedale	Brown/black	180 x 200	200.00	275.00	100.00

Alsatian, c.1935-1939

Backstamp: Blue handwritten "Wade England"; model name

No.	Name	Colourways	Size	U.S.$	Can.$	U.K.£
A-24	Alsatian, small	Dark grey/black; pink tongue	115	200.00	275.00	100.00

Borzoi, c.1935-1939

Photograph not available
at press time

No.	Name	Colourways	Size	U.S.$	Can.$	U.K.£
A-25	Borzoi	White; black patches	300	375.00	475.00	200.00

Bulldog, c.1948

The sitting bulldog wears a sailor cap with "H.M.S. Winnie" on the hat band.

Photograph not available
at press time

Backstamp: Black ink stamp "Wade Made in England"

No.	Name	Colourways	Size	U.S.$	Can.$	U.K.£
A-26	H.M.S. Winnie	Beige; grey muzzle; white/blue sailor cap	100	325.00	400.00	175.00

Dachshunds, c.1930

In these models a dachshund sits begging with its head turned slightly to the front, its tail curled around its front leg. The original price was 2/6d.

Dachshund

Dachshund Mustard Pot Posy Bowl

Backstamp: A. Black handwritten "Wade Made in England"
B. Black handwritten "Wade England"
C. Black handwritten "England"

No.	Name	Colourways	Size	U.S.$	Can.$	U.K.£
A-27a	Dachshund	Red-brown; white chest	80	100.00	145.00	55.00
A-27b	Dachshund	Beige all over	80	100.00	145.00	55.00
A-27c	Dachshund	Dark brown all over	80	100.00	145.00	55.00
A-27d	Dachshund	Beige; white flash on chest	80	100.00	145.00	55.00
A-27e	Dachshund	Dark/light brown	80	100.00	145.00	55.00

Derivatives

Dachshund Posy Bowls, c.1940

Sir George Wade's policy of creating new items by combining unsold stock from the George Wade Pottery and the Wade Heath Pottery produced many unusual and delightful "Stick-em-on-somethings." Unsold models were mounted on a new base with bramble-ware mustard pots or basket-weave egg cups to form posy bowls. The multi-coloured posy bowls usually have a moulded porcelain flower added to the bowl. Posy bowls in one colour with the added flower are rarely seen. All the posy bowls were produced in the Wade Heath Pottery.

Backstamp: Green-brown ink stamp "Wade England"

No.	Description	Colourways	Size	U.S.$	Can.$	U.K.£
A-27c1	Mustard Pot	Dark brown dog; multi-coloured bowl, flower	90	90.00	130.00	45.00
A-27f1	Mustard Pot	Matt green	90	70.00	90.00	35.00
A-27g1	Mustard Pot	Matt cream	90	70.00	90.00	35.00
A-27h1	Egg Cup	Matt green	90	70.00	90.00	35.00

Dalmatian, c.1935-1939

Photograph not available
at press time

Backstamp: Blue handwritten "Wade England"; model name

No.	Name	Colourways	Size	U.S.$	Can.$	U.K.£
A-28	Dalmatian	White/black	220	290.00	325.00	150.00

English Setters, c.1930–c.1955

Backstamp: **A.** Black handwritten "Wade Made in England"
B. Black transfer "Wade England"

No.	Name	Colourways	Size	U.S.$	Can.$	U.K.£
A-29a	English Setter	White; orange patches	50	120.00	150.00	60.00
A-29b	English Setter	White; black patches	50	120.00	150.00	60.00

Puppies, c.1948–c.1953

Produced at the same time as the *Siamese Kittens* and also modelled by John Szeilor, only two puppy models have been found to date.

Puppy Begging

Puppy with Slipper

Backstamp: A. Black hand painted "Wade"
B. Black transfer "Wade England"

No.	Name	Colourways	Size	U.S.$	Can.$	U.K.£
A-30	Puppy Begging	White; beige ears; blue/black eyes; blue collar	60	60.00	80.00	30.00
A-31	Puppy with Slipper	White; beige ears, patch; black/blue eyes; blue slipper	45	60.00	80.00	30.00

Red Setter c.1930-1939

Photograph not available
at press time

No.	Name	Colourways	Size	U.S.$	Can.$	U.K.£
A-32	Red Setter	Red-brown	150	200.00	275.00	100.00

Spaniel, 1935-1939

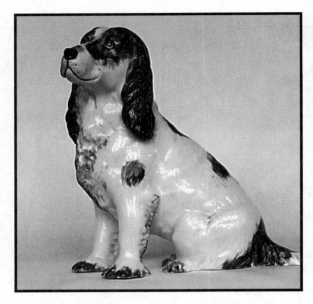

Backstamp: Black handwritten "Wade Made in England," red ink stamp of a leaping deer

No.	Name	Colourways	Size	U.S.$	Can.$	U.K.£
A-33a	Spaniel, seated	White; black markings, nose	135	290.00	325.00	150.00
A-33b	Spaniel, seated	White; brown markings; black nose	135	290.00	325.00	150.00

Spaniel, Seated on Round Base, 1945-1953

Photograph not available
at press time

Backstamp: Unmarked

No.	Name	Colourways	Size	U.S.$	Can.$	U.K.£
A-34	Spaniel, seated on base	Honey/grey body; blue-grey ears; green base	75	50.00	70.00	25.00

Terriers, Begging, c.1935-c.1948

Terrier, begging

Terrier Egg Cup Posy Bowl

Backstamp: A. Black handwritten "Wade Made in England"
B. Black ink stamp "Wade England"

No.	Name	Colourways	Size	U.S.$	Can.$	U.K.£
A-35a	Terrier, begging	White; one black eye, ear	80	120.00	150.00	60.00
A-35b	Terrier, begging	White; light brown ear, eye, collar	80	120.00	150.00	60.00
A-35c	Terrier, begging	White; one black eye, ear	80	120.00	150.00	60.00
A-35d	Terrier, begging	White; two black ears; grey collar	80	120.00	150.00	60.00
A-35e	Terrier, begging	White; two black ears; brown collar	80	120.00	150.00	60.00

Terrier, Standing, 1935-1939

Photograph not available
at press time

No.	Description	Colourways	Size	U.S.$	Can.$	U.K.£
A-36	Terrier, standing	White; brown/black patches	180	200.00	275.00	100.00

Derivatives

Terrier Posy Bowls, c.1948–1953

These derivatives were made from the Style A-35 terriers above.

Backstamp: Green-brown ink stamp "Wade England"

No.	Description	Colourways	Size	U.S.$	Can.$	U.K.£
A-35f1a	Egg Cup	White dog; black ears; multi-coloured bowl	82	90.00	130.00	45.00
A-35g1	Egg Cup	White dog; brown ears; multi-coloured bowl	82	90.00	130.00	45.00
A-35h1	Mustard Pot	Green all over - reglazed	82	70.00	95.00	35.00

West Highland Terrier, c.1948

Photograph not available
at press time

No.	Name	Colourways	Size	U.S.$	Can.$	U.K.£
A-37	West Highland Terrier	White; blue spots	50	70.00	95.00	35.00

DONKEYS

Donkey Foals, c.1938-c.1953

Backstamp: **A.** Black handwritten "Wade England"
B. Black transfer "Wade Ireland"

No.	Name	Colourways	Size	U.S.$	Can.$	U.K.£
A-38a	Donkey Foal	Light grey; black mane	48 x 40	70.00	90.00	35.00
A-38b	Donkey Foal	Beige; black mane, tail tip	50 x 45	70.00	90.00	35.00

Donkeys with Baskets, 1965

The models of a small donkey with large baskets (panniers) on each side was produced by Wade Ireland for a short time in 1965. Some models have been found with the names of Irish towns hand painted on the baskets.

Donkey with Baskets

"Alexford" Donkey with Baskets

Backstamp: Ink stamp "Wade Ireland"

No.	Name	Colourways	Size	U.S.$	Can.$	U.K.£
A-39a	Donkey with Baskets	Grey/blue/green	95	50.00	70.00	25.00
A-39b	"Alexford" Donkey with Baskets	Grey/blue/green	95	50.00	70.00	25.00

ELEPHANT, c.1930, c.1950

The issues of the 1930s and 1950s can be identified by their backstamps. The original price of this model was 2/6d.

Backstamp: **A.** Black handwritten "Wade England," 1930s
B. Black transfer "Wade England," 1950s

No.	Name	Colourways	Size	U.S.$	Can.$	U.K.£
A-40	Elephant	Pale grey; black eyes	50	120.00	150.00	60.00

ERMINE, 1939

The "Ermine," designed by Faust Lang, was made from the same mould as that used for the "Weasel."

Backstamp: Blue handwritten "Wade England 1939 Ermine"

No.	Name	Colourways	Size	U.S.$	Can.$	U.K.£
A-41	Ermine	White; pink ears; black tail tip; blue-grey base	220 x 95	325.00	400.00	175.00

FAWNS, c.1938

These fawn models can be found in a variety of browns and greys. Most of the miniature models have no backstamps.

Fawn, facing right   **Fawn, facing left**

Backstamp: Black handwritten "Wade"

No.	Name	Colourways	Size	U.S.$	Can.$	U.K.£
A-42a	Fawn, facing right	Beige; light brown markings	Miniature/30	80.00	110.00	40.00
A-42b	Fawn, facing right	Beige; dark brown markings	Miniature/30	80.00	110.00	40.00
A-42c	Fawn, facing right	White; grey markings	Miniature/30	80.00	110.00	40.00
A-43a	Fawn, facing left	Off white; light brown markings	Small/61	80.00	110.00	40.00
A-43b	Fawn, facing left	Off white; grey/light brown markings	Small/61	80.00	110.00	40.00

GIRAFFE, 1938

Photograph not available
at press time

No.	Name	Colourways	Size	U.S.$	Can.$	U.K.£
A-44	Giraffe	Cream; beige markings	77	200.00	275.00	100.00

GOATS, c.1930-c.1950

This set was first issued in the 1930s and was so popular that it was reissued in the 1940s and in the 1950s. The issues of the 1930s, 1940s and 1950s can be identified by their backstamps.

Goat

Kid

Backstamp: **A.** Black handwritten "Wade England"
B. Black ink stamp "Made in England"
C. Black transfer "Wade England"

No.	Name	Colourways	Size	U.S.$	Can.$	U.K.£
A-45a	Goat	Beige; creamy brown markings	55	100.00	145.00	55.00
A-45b	Goat	Off white; orange-brown markings	55	100.00	145.00	55.00
A-46a	Kid	Beige; creamy brown markings	45	90.00	130.00	45.00
A-46b	Kid	Off white; fawn markings	40	90.00	130.00	45.00

HORSES

Foals, 1930-1950

Foal, head back

Foal, head down

Backstamp: **A.** Black handwritten "Wade England"
B. Black transfer "Wade England"

No.	Name	Colourways	Size	U.S.$	Can.$	U.K.£
A-47	Foal, head back	Beige; grey mane, tail	Large/65	80.00	110.00	40.00
A-48	Foal, head back	White; grey mane, tail, hooves	Medium/55	70.00	90.00	35.00
A-49	Foal, head back	Beige; grey mane, tail, hooves	Small/40	50.00	70.00	25.00
A-50a	Foal, head down	White; grey mane, tail, hooves	55	80.00	110.00	40.00
A-50b	Foal, head down	Beige; grey mane, tail, hooves	55	80.00	110.00	40.00

Foals, c.1948-1953

Foal, rear leg forward

Backstamp: Black ink stamp "Wade England"

No.	Name	Colourways	Size	U.S.$	Can.$	U.K.£
A-51a	Foal, rear leg forward	Light brown; black mane, tail; brown hooves	120	95.00	135.00	50.00
A-51b	Foal, rear leg forward	White; ginger mane, spots, tail, hooves	120	95.00	135.00	50.00
A-51c	Foal, rear leg forward	White; blue mane, spots, tail, hooves	120	95.00	135.00	50.00
A-52	Foal, rear leg forward	Dark brown; black mane, tail, hooves	108	95.00	135.00	50.00
A-53a	Foal, rear legs parallel	White; pale blue mane, tail, hooves, spots	102	95.00	135.00	50.00
A-53b	Foal, rear legs parallel	Dark brown; black mane, tail, hooves	102	95.00	135.00	50.00

Horse, 1939

This is a Faust Lang model.

Photograph not available
at press time

Backstamp: Blue handwritten "Wade England 1939 Horse" and the incised signature of Faust Lang

No.	Name	Colourways	Size	U.S.$	Can.$	U.K.£
A-54	Horse	Brown; white socks; blue/green base	215	290.00	325.00	150.00

HIPPOPOTAMUS, c.1930

Backstamp: Black handwritten "Wade England"

No.	Name	Colourways	Size	U.S.$	Can.$	U.K.£
A-55	Hippopotamus	Light grey; brown eyes	50 x 90	100.00	145.00	55.00

IBEX RAMS, c.1939–c.1953

Photograph not available
at press time

Backstamp: **A.** Black handwritten "Wade Made in England," c.1939
B. Black ink stamp "Wade Made in England," c.1948-1953

No.	Name	Colourways	Size	U.S.$	Can.$	U.K.£
A-56a	Ibex Ram	White; grey horns; green/beige rock base	80 x 65	95.00	135.00	50.00
A-56b	Ibex Ram	Cream/beige; dark grey horns; blue/grey rock base	80 x 65	95.00	135.00	50.00

LAMBS, 1930-c.1955

This set comprises three running lambs with long tails. The first two styles are very similar, but one lamb has its legs apart and the other has its legs closer together. Due to their delicate legs and tails, these models are easily damaged. Their original price was 2/6d each.

Lamb, Tail out (left) Lamb Tail down (right)

Backstamp: **A.** Black handwritten "Wade Made in England"
B. Black handwritten "Wade England"
C. Black handwritten "Wade"
D. Black ink stamp "Wade England"
E. Black transfer print "Wade England"

No.	Name	Colourways	Size	U.S.$	Can.$	U.K.£
A-57a	Lamb, tail in, legs apart	Dark brown; black/brown markings	53	90.00	130.00	45.00
A-57b	Lamb, tail in, legs apart	Off white; grey markings	53	90.00	130.00	45.00
A-57c	Lamb, tail in, legs apart	Beige; cream markings	53	70.00	90.00	35.00
A-58	Lamb, tail in, legs together	Beige; cream markings	53	90.00	130.00	45.00
A-59a	Lamb, tail out	Off white; grey markings	53	90.00	130.00	45.00
A-59b	Lamb, tail out	Beige; cream markings	53	90.00	130.00	45.00

LIONS

Lion Cubs, 1939

Photograph not available
at press time

No.	Name	Colourways	Size	U.S.$	Can.$	U.K.£
A-60	Lion Cub, paw raised	Brown; white tail tip	135	200.00	275.00	100.00
A-61	Lion Cub, crouching	Brown; white tail tip	135	200.00	275.00	100.00

MONKEY

Monkeys, c.1930

Two monkeys are illustrated in Wade's "Porcelain Figures" brochure. One is a "Miniature Seated Monkey," with his arms at his sides, the second model is much larger and the monkey is crouched in a sleeping position. There is no other information available on these models at press time. We would appreciate hearing from anyone with further information.

Monkey on Tree, 1939

This is a Faust Lang model.

Photograph not available at press time

Backstamp: Blue handwritten "Wade England 1939 Horse" and the incised signature of Faust Lang

No.	Name	Colourways	Size	U.S.$	Can.$	U.K.£
A-62	Monkey on Tree	Light brown; green/brown tree stump	250	455.00	625.00	250.00

OTTER, 1939

Photograph not available at press time

No.	Name	Colourways	Size	U.S.$	Can.$	U.K.£
A-63	Otter	Brown; light brown paws	102 x 275	330.00	450.00	175.00

PANDAS, c.1939

Panda, Sitting

Backstamp: **A.** Black handwritten "Baby Panda 2 Wade Made in England"
B. Black hand written "Wade England"

No.	Name	Colourways	Size	U.S.$	Can.$	U.K.£
A-64	Panda, walking	White; black markings	40	95.00	130.00	50.00
A-65	Panda, sitting	White; black markings	50	95.00	130.00	50.00
A-3b	Panda	Black/white	165	142.00	195.00	75.00

Note: The Panda (A-3b) was also produced with a cellulose glaze see page 72.

PANTHER, 1939

The "Panther" was modelled by Faust Lang.

Backstamp: Blue handwritten "Wade England 1939 Panther" and the incised signature of Faust Lang

No.	Name	Colourways	Size	U.S.$	Can.$	U.K.£
A-66	Panther	Light brown; blue eyes; green tree trunk base	215	325.00	400.00	175.00

POLAR BEAR, 1939

The "Polar Bear" was modelled by Faust Lang.

Photograph not available
at press time.

Backstamp: Blue handwritten "Wade England 1939 Polar Bear" and the incised signature of Faust Lang

No.	Name	Colourways	Size	U.S.$	Can.$	U.K.£
A-67	Polar Bear	White; pink ears/mouth	195	325.00	400.00	175.00

RABBITS, c.1930 -c.1955

This series was first produced in the early 1930s, and due to its popularity, it was reissued in the late 1940s and again in the early 1950s. The reissued figures show very slight variations in colour and sizes.

The original price for the "Miniature Bunny" was 6d, the small "Double Bunnies" was 9d, the medium "Double Bunnies" sold for 1/-, and the large "Double Bunnies" cost 3/-.

Miniature, Double and Large Bunnies

Backstamp: **A.** Black handwritten "Wade Made in England"
B. Black ink stamp "Made in England"
C. Brown ink stamp "Wade England"
D. Black transfer "Wade England"

No.	Name	Colourways	Size	U.S.$	Can.$	U.K.£
A-68a	Bunny	White; light brown patches	Miniature /23	50.00	70.00	25.00
A-68b	Bunny	Brown; white patches	Miniature /23	50.00	70.00	25.00
A-68c	Bunny	White; light grey patches	Miniature /23	50.00	70.00	25.00
A-69a	Double Bunnies	White; grey patches	Small/21	50.00	70.00	25.00
A-69b	Double Bunnies	Brown; white patches	Small/21	50.00	70.00	25.00
A-69c	Double Bunnies	White; pale grey patches	Small/21	50.00	70.00	25.00
A-70	Double Bunnies	White; grey patches	Medium/32	120.00	150.00	60.00
A-71a	Double Bunnies	White; grey patches	Large/45	120.00	150.00	60.00
A-71b	Double Bunnies	White; grey patches, ears	Large/45	120.00	150.00	60.00
A-71c	Double Bunnies	White; grey patches; pink ears	Large/45	120.00	150.00	60.00
A-71d	Double Bunnies	White; dark grey tail;	Large/45	95.00	135.00	50.00

SQUIRRELS, c.1930–c.1955

Both versions were first produced in the 1930s, the smaller model being reissued in the 1940s and 1950s, and the larger squirrel reissued in the 1940s. The original price for the "Squirrel, sitting" was 1/-. The "Squirrel, lying" was recoloured and produced as a posy bowl.

Squirrel, Sitting

Squirrel, Lying

Backstamp:
A. Black handwritten "Wade England"
B. Brown ink stamp "Wade England"
C. Black ink stamp "Wade England"
D. Black transfer "Wade England"

No.	Name	Colourways	Size	U.S.$	Can.$	U.K.£
A-72a	Squirrel, sitting	Red-brown all over	40	80.00	110.00	40.00
A-72b	Squirrel, sitting	Light brown; dark brown acorn	40	80.00	110.00	40.00
A-72c	Squirrel, sitting	Light grey; white markings, brown claws	40	80.00	110.00	40.00
A-72d	Squirrel, sitting	Light grey all over	40	80.00	110.00	40.00
A-73a	Squirrel, lying	Red-brown; black eyes; white back of tail; brown acorn	65	90.00	130.00	45.00
A-73b	Squirrel, lying	Beige; black eyes; white back of tail; green acorn	65	90.00	130.00	45.00

Derivative

Squirrel Posy Bowl, c.1948–1953

The multi-coloured "Squirrel Bramble Ware Mustard Pot Posy Bowl" was made from the model "Squirrel, lying" and had a moulded porcelain flower attached to it. All posy bowls were produced in the Wade Heath Pottery.

Photograph not available
at press time

Backstamp: Green-brown ink stamp "Wade England"

No.	Name	Colourways	Size	U.S.$	Can.$	U.K.£
A-73a1	Mustard Pot	Red-brown squirrel; green/pink/yellow flower	70 x 97	70.00	90.00	35.00

STAG, 1939

The "Stag" was modelled by Faust Lang.

Backstamp: Blue handwritten "Wade England 1939 Highland Stag" and the incised signature of Faust Lang

No.	Name	Colourways	Size	U.S.$	Can.$	U.K.£
A-74	Stag	Beige; blue/green rocky base	245	450.00	525.00	250.00

TORTOISES, c.1930

Backstamp: Black handwritten "Wade England"

No.	Name	Colourways	Size	U.S.$	Can.$	U.K.£
A-75a	Tortoise	Beige; blue grey patches on shell	55	100.00	145.00	55.00
A-75b	Tortoise	Fawn all over	55	100.00	145.00	55.00

WALRUS, c.1978

The "Walrus" was produced by Wade Ireland as part of a set that included a koala bear, polar bear and rhinocerous. We have no other data on these three pieces and would appreciate hearing from anyone who could supply information.

Backstamp: Red and gold label "Wade Ireland"

No.	Name	Colourways	Size	U.S.$	Can.$	U.K.£
A-76	Walrus	Mottled brown/black; white tusks	85	200.00	275.00	100.00

WEASEL, 1939

The "Weasel" was modelled by Faust Lang. This mould was later used to make the model "Ermine."

Photograph not available
at press time

Backstamp: Blue handwritten "Wade Weasel designed in 1939 by Faust Lang"

No.	Name	Colourways	Size	U.S.$	Can.$	U.K.£
A-77	Weasel	Fawn; black eyes; blue/green rock base	220	325.00	400.00	175.00

FLAXMAN WARE
1935-1940

The following models were made in the Wade Heath Pottery in Flaxman Ware matt glazes.

DOGS, 1935-1939

Alsatians, 1935-1939

The models of a resting Alsatian were produced with and without glass eyes.

Backstamp: A. Black ink stamp "Flaxman ware hand made Pottery by Wadeheath England"
B. Black ink stamp "Flaxman Wade Heath England"

No.	Name	Colourways	Size	U.S.$	Can.$	U.K.£
A-78a	Alsatian, glass eyes	Green; black/yellow glass eyes	120	90.00	130.00	45.00
A-78b	Alsatian, glass eyes	Beige; black/yellow glass eyes	120	90.00	130.00	45.00
A-78c	Alsatian	Pale orange	120	80.00	110.00	40.00
A-78d	Alsatian	Orange	120	80.00	110.00	40.00
A-78e	Alsatian	Beige	120	80.00	110.00	40.00
A-78f	Alsatian	Green	120	80.00	110.00	40.00

Long-Haired Dachshund, 1937-1939

Backstamp: Black ink stamp "Wadeheath Ware England"

No.	Name	Colourways	Size	U.S.$	Can.$	U.K.£
A-79	Long-Haired Dachshund	Orange	95	80.00	110.00	40.00

Puppy in a Basket, 1937-1939

Backstamp: Black ink stamp "Flaxman Wade Heath England"

No.	Name	Colourways	Size	U.S.$	Can.$	U.K.£
A-80	Puppy in a Basket	Orange	155	90.00	125.00	45.00

Scotties, 1937-1939

Backstamp: **A.** Embossed "327" in a square
B. Black ink stamp "Flaxman Wade Heath England," impressed "327"

No.	Name	Colourways	Size	U.S.$	Can.$	U.K.£
A-81a	Scottie, sitting	Brown	140	60.00	80.00	30.00
A-81b	Scottie, sitting	Light brown	140	60.00	80.00	30.00
A-81c	Scottie, sitting	Orange	140	60.00	80.00	30.00
A-81d	Scottie, sitting	Light blue	140	60.00	80.00	30.00
A-81e	Scottie, sitting	Dark blue	140	60.00	80.00	30.00
A-82	Scottie, walking	Unknown	115	—	—	—

Terriers, 1935-1937

The sitting terrier has glass eyes.

Terrier, sitting

Backstamp: Black ink stamp"Flaxman Ware Hand Made Pottery By Wadeheath England"

No.	Name	Colourways	Size	U.S.$	Can.$	U.K.£
A-83a	Terrier, sitting	Beige; dark brown glass eyes	160	80.00	110.00	40.00
A-83b	Terrier, sitting	Blue; dark brown glass eyes	160	80.00	110.00	40.00
A-84	Terrier, standing	Brown	125	80.00	110.00	40.00

PANTHER, 1937–1939

In this figure a slender, stylised panther is leaping over a rock base.

Photograph not available
at press time.

Backstamp: Black ink stamp "Flaxman Wade Heath England"

No.	Name	Colourways	Size	U.S.$	Can.$	U.K.£
A-85	Panther	Matt orange	190	150.00	225.00	75.00

RABBITS, 1935-c.1940

The crouching rabbit has its ears apart, and the ears of the sitting rabbit are close together.

Rabbit, crouching

Rabbits, seated

Backstamp: **A.** Black ink stamp "Flaxman Wadeheath England, impressed "337"
B. Black ink stamp "Flaxman Ware Hand Painted Pottery by Wadeheath England"
C. Black ink stamp "Flaxman Wadeheath England"
D. Black ink stamp "Made in England"

No.	Name	Colourways	Size	U.S.$	Can.$	U.K.£
A-86	Rabbit, crouching	Orange-brown; dark brown eyes	110 x 145	70.00	90.00	35.00
A-87a	Rabbit, seated	Light brown	Miniature/75 x 60	50.00	70.00	25.00
A-87b	Rabbit, seated	Light green	Miniature/75 x 60	50.00	70.00	25.00
A-87c	Rabbit, seated	Orange	Miniature/75 x 60	50.00	70.00	25.00
A-88a	Rabbit, seated	Brown	Small/105 x 88	60.00	80.00	30.00
A-88b	Rabbit, seated	Light brown	Small/105 x 88	60.00	80.00	30.00
A-88c	Rabbit, seated	Light green	Small/105 x 88	60.00	80.00	30.00
A-88d	Rabbit, seated	Orange	Small/105 x 88	60.00	80.00	30.00
A-88e	Rabbit, seated	Yellow	Small/105 x 88	60.00	80.00	30.00
A-89a	Rabbit, seated	Brown	Medium/135 x 115	70.00	90.00	35.00
A-89b	Rabbit, seated	Light brown	Medium/135 x 115	70.00	90.00	35.00
A-89c	Rabbit, seated	Green	Medium/135 x 115	70.00	90.00	35.00
A-89d	Rabbit, seated	Orange	Medium/135 x 115	70.00	90.00	35.00
A-89e	Rabbit, seated	Turquoise	Medium/135 x 115	70.00	90.00	35.00
A-90a	Rabbit, seated	Brown	Large/152 x 130	80.00	110.00	40.00
A-90b	Rabbit, seated	Light green	Large/152 x 130	80.00	110.00	40.00
A-90c	Rabbit, seated	Orange	Large/152 x 130	80.00	110.00	40.00
A-90d	Rabbit, seated	Blue	Large/165 x 135	80.00	110.00	40.00
A-91a	Rabbit, seated	Brown	Extra Large/190 x 160	80.00	110.00	40.00
A-91b	Rabbit, seated	Light green	Extra Large/190 x 160	80.00	110.00	40.00
A-91c	Rabbit, seated	Orange	Extra Large/190 x 160	80.00	110.00	40.00

Derivative

Matchbox Holder, 1937–1939

Backstamp: Black ink stamp "Wadeheath Ware England"

No.	Name	Colourways	Size	U.S.$	Can.$	U.K.£
A-88c1	Matchbox Holder	Light green	105 x 85	95.00	135.00	50.00

SQUIRRELS

Backstamp: Black ink stamp "Flaxman Wadeheath England"

No.	Name	Colourways	Size	U.S.$	Can.$	U.K.£
A-92a	Squirrel feeding	Light green	165 x 135	80.00	110.00	40.00
A-92b	Squirrel feeding	Light blue	165 x 135	80.00	110.00	40.00
A-92c	Squirrel feeding	Light brown	165 x 135	80.00	110.00	40.00
A-93	Squirrel with Glass Eyes	Light green	145 x 155	80.00	110.00	40.00

SERIES AND SETS
1975-1991

CHAMPIONSHIP DOGS, 1975–1981

Championship Dogs is a set of five dogs, all standing on green, oval bases. When produced, a bright orange label that reads "Wade England" was affixed to the base; some models still have them. This is the first issue of solid animals, except for the *Whimsies*. The original price was £2.65 per model.

Backstamp: Raised "Wade England"

No.	Name	Colourways	Size	U.S.$	Can.$	U.K.£
A-94	Afghan Hound	Beige/white; light brown face, paws	85 x 90	80.00	110.00	40.00
A-95	Cocker Spaniel	Beige/off white; black patches	80 x 90	95.00	135.00	50.00
A-96	Collie	Honey/dark brown	85 x 85	95.00	135.00	50.00
A-97	English Setter	Beige/off white; black patches	80 x 90	95.00	135.00	50.00
A-98	Old English Sheepdog	Grey/white	85 x 90	95.00	135.00	50.00

THE WORLD OF SURVIVAL SERIES, 1976–1982

British Anglia Television's *World of Survival* film series has won world-wide acclaim. Naturalists and film makers have praised these documentaries featuring many endangered species. George Wade and Son Ltd. collaborated with Anglia Television to produce two sets of six models. The figures are perfect in every detail. They are slip cast and open cast (standing on their feet, not on a base). Produced in a biscuit porcelain, they are matt and rough to the touch and completely unlike any other Wade models.

Due to their expensive retail prices, necessitated by high production costs, only a limited number of models were released. Their original prices started from £45 to £65.

SET 1

African Elephant

American Bison

Polar Bear

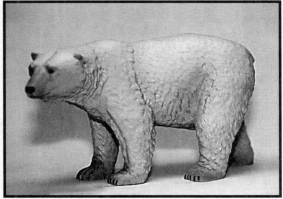

Tiger

Backstamp: **A.** Black transfer print "World of Survival Series, by Wade of England. Copyright Survival Anglia Limited. 1976 All rights reserved"
  B. White transfer print on brown label "World of Survival Series, by Wade of England. Copyright Survival Anglia Limited. 1976 All rights reserved"

No.	Name	Colourways	Size	U.S.$	Can.$	U.K.£
A-99	African Elephant	Grey; white tusks	160 x 260	325.00	400.00	175.00
A-100	African Lion	Biscuit brown; dark brown mane	110 x 200	290.00	325.00	150.00
A-101	American Bison	Dark brown body; charcoal-grey mane	120 x 190	290.00	325.00	150.00
A-102	Black Rhinoceros	Light grey; white horns	110 x 240	290.00	325.00	150.00
A-103	Polar Bear	White; black eyes, nose	110 x 210	240.00	290.00	120.00
A-104	Tiger	Orange/yellow/white/black	95 x 190	240.00	290.00	120.00

SET 2

African Cape Buffalo

American Cougar

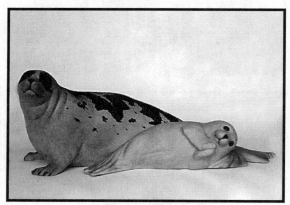

Harp Seal and Pup

Hippopotamus

Backstamp: Black transfer print "World of Survival Series, by Wade of England. Copyright Survival Anglia Limited. 1976 All rights reserved"

No.	Name	Colourways	Size	U.S.$	Can.$	U.K.£
A-105	African Cape Buffalo	Dark brown; grey/white horns	170 x 240	375.00	475.00	200.00
A-106	American Brown Bear	Dark brown; black nose	105 x 145	290.00	325.00	150.00
A-107	American Cougar	Beige; dark grey muzzle	150 x 225	375.00	475.00	200.00
A-108	Harp Seal and Pup	Off white; light grey/black markings	85 x 220	375.00	475.00	200.00
A-109	Hippopotamus	Chocolate brown/pink; pink mouth	105 x 220	375.00	475.00	200.00
A-110	Mountain Gorilla	Black body; silver grey mane; copper head	150 x 150	375.00	475.00	200.00

CHEETAH AND GAZELLE, 1991

Only five copies of the beautifully sculptured "Cheetah and Gazelle" are known to have been produced. This figure of a cheetah chasing a Grants gazelle was modelled by Alan Maslankowski and made of biscuit porcelain. Each model was sold with a signed and numbered limited-edition certificate. The original price direct from the Wade Pottery was £1,200.

Cheetah and Gazelle, front view

Cheetah and Gazelle, back view

Backstamp: The model is unmarked, but a gold-coloured metal plaque on the front of the wooden base is inscribed "Survival" with the model number

No.	Colourways	Size	U.S.$	Can.$	U.K.£
A-111	Orange yellow/black cheetah; orange/white/black gazelle	240 x 200		Extremely rare	

BIRDS
c.1930 to the present

Wade bird models created from the early 1930s to 1939 and from the late 1940s up to the early 1950s are slip-cast. Beginning in the early 1950s, Wade produced some solid models, and afterwards all the models were solid.

The glazes used from the 1930s to the early 1950s are in delicate pastel and natural colours and are very different from the darker colours used from the late 1950s. Many of the models that were first produced in the early 1930s proved to be popular and were reissued in the late 1940s and early 1950s.

BACKSTAMPS

These bird models were produced in both the Wade Heath and the George Wade potteries, which accounts for the various backstamps used in the same time spans.

Handwritten Backstamps

Handwritten marks are found on models produced from the early 1930s to the 1940s.

Black handwritten, early 1930s-1940s

Blue handwritten, 1939-1940s

Blue handwritten, 1939-1940s

Ink Stamps

Ink stamps were used from the late 1940s to 1953.

The size of the mark has no relevance to the date; large ink stamps were used on models with large bases, small ink stamps on small bases. Many of the smaller models are unmarked

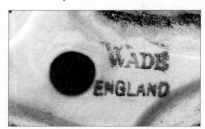

Black, brown or green ink stamp, late 1940s-1953

Transfer Prints

Transfer prints have been used from 1953 to the present.

Transfer print, 1978-1982

HIGH-GLOSS MODELS
c.1930-c.1955

BLUEBIRD ON FLORAL STUMP, c.1930

Backstamp: Black handwritten "Wade 9 England No 124"

No.	Name	Colourways	Size	U.S.$	Can.$	U.K.£
B-1	Bluebird	Blue/white/yellow bird; maroon/ yellow/pink/blue flowers	90	120.00	150.00	60.00

BUDGERIGARS, 1939-c.1955

The budgerigar figures listed on this page were modelled by Faust Lang and have a 1939/1941 date incised on the base. The original price for the "Budgerigar, Style One" was 10/-.

Budgerigar, Style One　　　　**Bugerigar, Style Two**　　　　**Budgerigars**

Backstamp: A. Blue handwritten "Wade England," date, name of model
　　　　　　　B. Green-brown ink stamp "Wade England"
　　　　　　　C. Black ink stamp "Wade England"

No.	Name	Colourways	Size	U.S.$	Can.$	U.K.£
B-2a	Budgerigar, Style One	Pale blue; yellow head; fawn branch, pale blue/green mottled base	190	200.00	275.00	100.00
B-2b	Budgerigar, Style One	Yellow; dark green tail, markings; dark brown stump; brown/green mottled base	190	200.00	275.00	100.00
B-2c	Budgerigar, Style One	Yellow; green wings, tail; dark brown stump; brown/green mottled base	190	200.00	275.00	100.00
B-3a	Budgerigar, Style Two	Pale green; black wing markings; light brown tree branch; dark blue flower; brown/green mottled base	175	250.00	300.00	125.00
B-3b	Budgerigar, Style Two	Pale blue /grey; yellow head; light green tree branch; pink flower, brown/green base	175	250.00	300.00	125.00
B-4a	Budgerigars	Yellow/blue/green bird; all green bird; fawn branch; pale blue/grey/green mottled base	195	250.00	300.00	125.00
B-4b	Budgerigars	Yellow bird with green tail; all green bird; fawn branch; pale blue/grey/green mottled base	195	250.00	300.00	125.00

CHICK, c.1940-1953

The "Chick," version 5c, is a reissue of the earlier models.

Backstamp: **A.** Brown handwritten "Wade Made in England"
B. Brown ink stamp "Wade England"

No.	Name	Colourways	Size	U.S.$	Can.$	U.K.£
B-5a	Chick	Pastel blue/grey; pink beak	55	80.00	110.00	40.00
B-5b	Chick	Light/dark grey; yellow eyes; pink beak	55	80.00	110.00	40.00
B-5c	Chick	Light/dark blue; black eyes; grey beak	55	80.00	110.00	40.00

COCKATOO, 1939-1955

This is a Faust Lang model. The original issue price for the "Cockatoo" was 5/9.

Backstamp: **A.** Blue handwritten "Wade England," date, name of model
B. Green-brown ink stamp "Wade England"
C. Black ink stamp "Wade England"

No.	Name	Colourways	Size	U.S.$	Can.$	U.K.£
B-6a	Cockatoo	White; bright yellow crest; beige-pink eyes, beak	160	290.00	325.00	150.00
B-6b	Cockatoo	White; bright pink crest, beak, wing tips; yellow feet	160	290.00	325.00	150.00
B-6c	Cockatoo	White; bright pink crest, beak; grey wing tips; yellow feet	160	290.00	325.00	150.00

COCKEREL, c.1940

Cockerel (B-7a)

Cockerel Posy Bowl (B-7c1)

Backstamp: Black handwritten "Wade Made in England"

No.	Name	Colourways	Size	U.S.$	Can.$	U.K.£
B-7a	Cockerel	Off white; pink comb, eyes, beak, legs; pale green base	90	90.00	130.00	45.00

Derivatives

Cockerel Posy Bowls, c.1940

A single "Cockerel" model was mounted on a base with a bramble ware mustard pot to make a posy bowl.

Backstamp: Green-brown ink stamp "Wade England"

No.	Name	Colourways	Size	U.S.$	Can.$	U.K.£
B-7b1	Cockerel Posy Bowl	Brown; pink comb, beak; multi-coloured tail; green/pink/yellow posy	95	70.00	90.00	35.00
B-7c1	Cockerel Posy Bowl	Creamy beige/orange all over	95	70.00	90.00	35.00

DRAKE AND DADDY, c.1938–1953

The original price of this model was 2/6d.

Backstamp: **A.** Black handwritten "Wade England"
B. Brown ink stamp "Wade England"

No.	Name	Colourways	Size	U.S.$	Can.$	U.K.£
B-8a	Drake and Daddy	Daddy — white/brown; blue head; pink beak, feet Drake — white; grey wings; pink beak, feet	90	60.00	80.00	30.00
B-8b	Drake and Daddy	Daddy — blue head; beige/white body; grey wings; yellow beak/feet Drake — white; grey wings; yellow beak, feet	90	60.00	80.00	30.00

DUCKS, c.1932-1953

Duck, head forward, small; Duck, pecking, medium

Duck, head back; Duck, preening, medium

Backstamp: **A.** Black handwritten "Wade Made in England"
B. Black handwritten "Wade England"
C. Brown ink stamp "Wade England"
D. Black transfer "Wade England"

No.	Name	Colourways	Size	U.S.$	Can.$	U.K.£
B-9a	Duck, head forward	Beige/white; blue-grey head; dark grey wings; pink beak, feet; grey base	Large/90	80.00	110.00	40.00
B-10a	Duck, head forward	Beige/white; grey head; grey wings; pink beak, feet; grey base	Small/75	60.00	80.00	30.00
B-10b	Duck, head forward	White/beige; grey head; grey wings; pink beak, feet; white base	Small/75	60.00	80.00	30.00
B-10c	Duck, head forward	Beige/white; blue head; grey wings; yellow beak, feet; grey base	Small/75	60.00	80.00	30.00
B-10d	Duck, head forward	White; blue/green head, wings; yellow beak, feet; grey base	Small/70	60.00	80.00	30.00
B-11	Duck, preening	Beige/white; blue/grey head; dark blue wings; pink beak, feet; grey base	Large/85	60.00	80.00	30.00
B-12a	Duck, preening	White /beige; grey head, wings; pink beak, feet; grey base	Medium/80	60.00	80.00	30.00
B-12b	Duck, preening	White/grey; grey blue head; blue/green wings; yellow beak, feet; grey base	Medium/80	60.00	80.00	30.00
B-12c	Duck, preening	White; blue/green head, wings; yellow beak, feet; dark grey base	Small/70	60.00	80.00	30.00
B-12d	Duck, preening	White; light grey head, wings, base; yellow beak, feet	Small/70	60.00	80.00	30.00
B-13a	Duck, head back	White; grey head, wings; pink beak, feet; grey base	74	60.00	80.00	30.00
B-13b	Duck, head back	Beige/white; grey head; blue wings; yellow beak, feet; blue base	74	60.00	80.00	30.00
B-13c	Duck, head back	White; blue/green head, wings; yellow beak, feet; dark grey base	74	60.00	80.00	30.00
B-14a	Duck, pecking	White /light grey body, head; blue wings; pink feet, beak; white base	44	60.00	80.00	30.00
B-14b	Duck, pecking	Dark grey /white body, head; blue/black wings; pink beak, feet; white base	44	60.00	80.00	30.00
B-14c	Duck, pecking	White; light grey head; deep blue wings, base; yellow beak, feet	44	60.00	80.00	30.00
B-14d	Duck, pecking	White/beige; grey blue head; blue wings; yellow beak, feet; grey base	44	60.00	80.00	30.00
B-14e	Duck, pecking	White; blue/green head, wings; yellow beak, feet; grey base	44	60.00	80.00	30.00

Derivatives

Duck Posy Bowls, c.1948–1953

The multi-coloured posy bowls have a moulded porcelain flower attached to the rim of the bowl. One-colour posy bowls are rarely found with the added flower decoration.

Duck, pecking, Posy Bowl

Backstamp: Green-brown ink stamp "Wade England"

No.	Name	Colourways	Size	U.S.$	Can.$	U.K.£
B-9b1	Duck, head forward	White; pale grey head, wings; yellow beak, feet; green/pink/yellow bowl	80	70.00	90.00	35.00
B-12e1	Duck, preening	White; grey head, wings; yellow beak, feet; multi-coloured bowl	Medium/85	70.00	90.00	35.00
B-12f1	Duck, preening	Pale yellow all over	Medium/85	60.00	80.00	30.00
B-12g1	Duck, preening	Light green all over	Medium/85	60.00	80.00	30.00
B-12h1	Duck, preening	Dark blue all over	Medium/85	60.00	80.00	30.00
B-14f1	Duck, pecking	White; grey head, wings, yellow beak, feet; multi-coloured bowl	55	70.00	90.00	35.00
B-14g1	Duck, pecking	Dark blue all over	55	60.00	80.00	30.00

Ducks, Open Wings, 1935-1953

All three ducks have open wings. The "Duck, preening" has turned its head over its back, beak open, as though preening a wing. The "Duck, head forward" has its head tilted, beak closed. The "Duck, head up" has its head up and its beak closed.

Duck, head forward

Backstamp: A. Black handwritten "Wade England"
B. Black transfer "Wade England"

No.	Description	Colourways	Size	U.S.$	Can.$	U.K.£
B-15a	Duck, preening	White; light brown head, wings; pink feet	35	60.00	80.00	30.00
B-15b	Duck, preening	White; blue-grey head, wings; black beak; pink feet	35	60.00	80.00	30.00
B-16	Duck, head forward	White; blue-grey head, wings; black beak; pink feet	45	60.00	80.00	30.00
B-17	Duck, head up	White body; blue-grey head, wings; black beak; pale pink feet	45	60.00	80.00	30.00

FLICKER, 1946-1953

Backstamp: Blue handwritten "Wade England Flicker"

No.	Name	Colourways	Size	U.S.$	Can.$	U.K.£
B-18	Flicker	Off white; blue head, wings, tail; orange beak	115	135.00	185.00	70.00

GOLDFINCHES, 1946-1953

The original price of these models was 6/6d each.

Photograph not available
at press time

Backstamp: Green-brown ink stamp "Wade England"

No.	Name	Colourways	Size	U.S.$	Can.$	U.K.£
B-19	Goldfinch, wings closed	Yellow; black wings, tail, head patch; brown beak; mottled green/brown tree branch	100	135.00	175.00	70.00
B-20	Goldfinch, wings open	Yellow; black wings, tail, head patch; brown beak; mottled green/brown tree branch	100	135.00	175.00	70.00

GREBE, 1939

This is a Faust Lang model.

Backstamp: **A.** Blue handwritten "Wade England," date, name of model
B. Blue handwritten "Wade England," name of model

No.	Name	Colourways	Size	U.S.$	Can.$	U.K.£
B-21	Grebe	White/grey; dark grey crest; yellow beak; blue fish; blue/green/white mottled base	235	325.00	400.00	175.00

HERON, 1946-1953

Backstamp: Green-brown ink stamp "Wade England"

No.	Name	Colourways	Size	U.S.$	Can.$	U.K.£
B-22	Heron	Dark blue/grey; pink breast; orange legs; mottled brown/green tree stump, rock base	190	250.00	300.00	125.00

INDIAN RUNNER DUCKS, c.1932–1953

These three Indian Runner or Peking-type ducks were first produced in the early 1930s and reissued in the late 1940s to 1953. They have long thin bodies; the mother is looking down at her two ducklings, one with its head up the other with the head down. The original selling price was 9d for a set of three.

Duckling, head up, Duckling, head down

Backstamp: **A.** Black handwritten "Wade England"
B. Black transfer print "Wade England"

No.	Name	Colourways	Size	U.S.$	Can.$	U.K.£
B-23	Mother Duck	Blue/grey/white; light brown head; yellow beak, feet; pale blue base	95	60.00	80.00	30.00
B-24	Duckling, head down	White; yellow beak, feet; pale blue base	53	70.00	90.00	35.00
B-25	Duckling, head up	White; yellow beak, feet; pale blue base	55	70.00	90.00	35.00

OWL, 1940

Backstamp: Black handwritten "Wade Made in England," date and name of model

No.	Name	Colourways	Size	U.S.$	Can.$	U.K.£
B-26	Owl	Brown/white; black markings; pale blue log	146	240.00	290.00	125.00

PARROT, 1939

This is a Faust Lang model.

Backstamp: Blue handwritten "Wade England," date and name of model

No.	Name	Colourways	Size	U.S.$	Can.$	U.K.£
B-27	Parrot on Stump	Blue head, wings; green body; peach face, breast; fawn stump	267	325.00	400.00	175.00

PELICAN, 1946-1953

The original price of this model was 6/6d.

Backstamp: **A.** Blue handwritten "Wade England," date and name of model
B. Green-brown ink stamp "Wade England"
C. Black ink stamp "Wade England"

No.	Name	Colourways	Size	U.S.$	Can.$	U.K.£
B-28a	Pelican	White; bright yellow beak; pale green feather tips; brown/orange feet; black claws	170	250.00	300.00	125.00
B-28b	Pelican	White; yellow beak; brown feet; black claws	170	250.00	300.00	125.00

SEAGULL ON ROCK, c.1948–1953

This rarely found model was produced in the late 1940s and reissued in 1953. The original price of the reissue was 3/-.

Backstamp: **A.** Black ink stamp "Wade Made in England"
B. Black transfer "Wade England," 1953

No.	Name	Colourways	Size	U.S.$	Can.$	U.K.£
B-29a	Seagull	White; grey head; blue rock	40	95.00	135.00	50.00
B-29b	Seagull	Grey/white; pale blue rock	40	95.00	135.00	50.00

TOUCAN, 1946-1953

The original issue price for the "Toucan" was 10/-.

Photograph not available
at press time

Backstamp: A. Green-brown ink stamp "Wade England"
        B. Black ink stamp "Wade England"

No.	Name	Colourways	Size	U.S.$	Can.$	U.K.£
B-30	Toucan on Stump	White; dark grey head; black wings; orange beak; brown tree stump	175	290.00	325.00	150.00

WOODPECKER, 1946-1953

The original issue price for the "Woodpecker" was 10/-.

Backstamp: A. Green-brown ink stamp "Wade England"
        B. Black ink stamp "Wade England"

No.	Name	Colourways	Size	U.S.$	Can.$	U.K.£
B-31	Woodpecker	Off white; maroon head; grey-blue beak, feet; light green/brown wings, tail; green/brown trunk	175	160.00	240.00	80.00

SETS AND SERIES
1978 to the present

THE CONNOISSEUR'S BIRD COLLECTION, 1978-1982

This series of 12 British birds was made in the same biscuit porcelain as that used for the *World of Survival Animals*. The models are all slip cast and produced in their natural colours and settings. Their original retail prices ranged from £20 to £45. Set 1 was issued without plinths while Set 2 was issued with circular polished wooden plinths.

Set 1 —Without Plinths

Goldcrest

Nuthatch

Robin

Wren

Backstamp: Black transfer "The Connoisseur's Collection by Wade of England," model name and number

No.	Description	Colourways	Size	U.S.$	Can.$	U.K.£
B-32	Bullfinch	Black head; brown body; pink breast; yellow caterpillar	185	350.00	450.00	190.00
B-33	Coaltit	Black/grey bird; green holly; red berries	145	350.00	450.00	190.00
B-34	Goldcrest	Yellow stripe on head; off-white body; brown branch	135	350.00	450.00	190.00
B-35	Nuthatch	Grey/white bird; yellow/brown log	125	350.00	450.00	190.00
B-36	Robin	Brown body; red breast; orange mushrooms	125	350.00	450.00	190.00
B-37	Wren	Brown bird; grey stones	115	350.00	450.00	190.00

Set 2 - With Plinths

Four of the illustrations are shown without their base due to adhesive failure over time.

Bearded Tit

Kingfisher

Woodpecker (on plinth)

Dipper

Yellow Wagtail

Backstamp: Stamped on metal disk set in base "The Connoisseurs Collection by Wade of England," model name and number

No.	Description	Colourways	Size	U.S.$	Can.$	U.K.£
B-38	Bearded Tit	Reddish brown; grey head	165	350.00	450.00	190.00
B-39	Dipper	Light brown/pale brown bird; grey pebbles	140	350.00	450.00	190.00
B-40	Kingfisher	Blue/grey/white/orange; grey stump	180	350.00	450.00	190.00
B-41	Redstart	Grey/black/reddish brown	180	350.00	450.00	190.00
B-42	Woodpecker	Red/white/black/yellow; brown/yellow stump	165	350.00	450.00	190.00
B-43	Yellow Wagtail	Pale yellow/grey/black; grey/brown pebbles	115	350.00	450.00	190.00

COMMEMORATIVE WARE
1935-1990

The Wade potteries, primarily Wadeheath, have issued a large line of commemoratives. In 1935 Wade began its range of commemorative ware with items marking the silver jubilee of King George V and Queen Mary. Since then Wade has issued commemoratives for coronations, the silver jubilee of Queen Elizabeth, royal birthdays, royal weddings and royal births, as well as for less regal occasions.

The models are listed according to the event they commemorate, which appear here in chronological order.

BACKSTAMPS

Ink Stamps

From 1935 to 1953, the backstamps used on commemorative items were black ink stamps that included the name Wadeheath. A green ink stamped "Wade England" was introduced on some of the 1953 coronation ware.

Black ink stamp, 1937

Green ink stamp, 1953

Embossed Stamps

Also beginning in 1953, the Wade backstamp was either embossed on the model or applied on a transfer print.

Embossed, 1981

Transfer Prints

Transfer print, 1981-1990

KING GEORGE V AND QUEEN MARY

SILVER JUBILEE, 1935

To celebrate the silver jubilee of George V and Queen Mary in May 1935, Wadeheath produced a set of *Jubilee Ware*. These items have transfer prints of King George V and Queen Mary on the front.

Photograph not available
at press time

Backstamp: Black ink stamp "Wadeheath England" with a lion

No.	Description	Colourways	Shape/Size	U.S.$	Can.$	U.K.£
C-1	Child's Beaker	Cream; multi-coloured print	75	95.00	135.00	50.00
C-2	Child's Dish	Cream; multi-coloured print	165	95.00	135.00	50.00
C-3	Cup	Cream; multi-coloured print	65	95.00	135.00	50.00
C-3	Saucer	Cream; multi-coloured print	140	See above		
C-4	Mug	Cream; multi-coloured print	Footed/135	120.00	150.00	60.00
C-5	Plate	Cream; multi-coloured print	Octagonal/165	95.00	135.00	50.00

EDWARD VIII

CORONATION, 1937

Wade produced a small amount of commemorative pottery for the coronation of King Edward VIII. Some of the pottery was adapted from miniature jug designs already in production at the Wade Heath Pottery. A limited supply of these jugs was produced with a multi-coloured transfer print of Edward on the front and a design of flags and a scroll with the words "Long May He Reign" on the back. With the abdication of Edward, the jugs were withdrawn from sale and the transfers replaced with those of George VI and Queen Elizabeth.

The jugs are miniature and come with short- and long-loop handles and a handle of three rings. They have V-shaped moulded spouts and bright orange and blue bands around their bases and handles. The loving cup has a musical box in the base, held in place by a wooden disc, which plays "God Save the King" when lifted. The words "Long May He Reign" are printed on a gold band across the front and "Coronation King Edward VIII May 12th 1937" is on the back.

Jug, long-loop handle

Jug, short-loop handle

Loving Cup, musical

Backstamp: **A.** Black ink stamp "Wadeheath Ware England" and impressed "88M"
B. Black ink stamp "Wadeheath Ware England" and impressed "106M"
C. Black ink stamp "Wadeheath England" with a lion and impressed "113M"
D. Black ink stamp "Wadeheath Ware England"

No	Description	Colourways	Size	U.S.$	Can.$	U.K.£
C-6	Jug, long-loop handle	Cream; orange/blue bands; multi-coloured print	140	125.00	150.00	65.00
C-7	Jug, short-loop handle	Cream; orange/blue bands; multi-coloured print	140	125.00	150.00	65.00
C-8	Jug, three-rings handle	Cream; orange/blue bands; multi-coloured print	135	125.00	150.00	65.00
C-9	Loving Cup, musical	Cream; red/white/blue striped handles; red/blue/green print	125	550.00	625.00	300.00

KING GEORGE VI AND QUEEN ELIZABETH

CORONATION, 1937

To commemorate the coronation on May 12, 1937, Wade issued several new items as well as reissuing the Edward VIII commemorative ware by replacing the original transfer prints of Edward with prints of George VI and Queen Elizabeth.

BOWLS

This was a limited edition of approximately 250 bowls. They were issued in all-over glazes of royal blue, orange and light green. A signed, limited edition of 25 bowls was issued in white with gold edging.

Backstamp: **A.** Black ink stamp "Manufactured in England by Wadeheath and Co Ltd to Commemorate the Coronation of King George VI and Queen Elizabeth—May 12th 1937. 'Long May They Reign'" and the signature of Robert R. Barlow
B. Black ink stamp "Wadeheath England" and a lion

No.	Description	Colourways	Size	U.S.$	Can.$	U.K.£
C-10a	Bowl	White and gold	110	550.00	625.00	300.00
C-10b	Bowl	Mottled orange	110	375.00	475.00	200.00
C-10c	Bowl	Light green	110	375.00	475.00	200.00
C-10d	Bowl	Royal blue	110	375.00	475.00	200.00

CHILDREN'S WARE

The beaker and dish are the same shapes as those used for the silver jubilee of George V. Both have a multi-coloured transfer print of George VI and Queen Elizabeth, but on the dish it is set inside a Canadian maple leaf.

Photograph not available
at press time

Backstamp: Black ink stamp "Wadeheath Ware England"

No.	Description	Colourways	Size	U.S.$	Can.$	U.K.£
C-11	Beaker	White; multi-coloured print	75	95.00	135.00	50.00
C-12	Dish	White; multi-coloured print	165	95.00	135.00	50.00

CORONATION NURSERY WARE

This unusual child's tea set was from the same mould as the Wadeheath Walt Disney children's tea sets. The boxed set comprised 12 pieces—four cups, four saucers, a teapot and lid, a milk jug and a sugar bowl. Each piece, except for the teapot lid, has a multi-coloured portrait on it of King George VI and Queen Elizabeth, surrounded by flags. There is a portrait of Princess Elizabeth on the milk jug and sugar bowl. The original box is blue, with a label that reads, "Coronation Nursery Ware," along with portraits of the King and Queen.

Backstamp: Black transfer "Wadeheath England"

No.	Description	Colourways	Size	U.S.$	Can.$	U.K.£
C-13	Cup and Saucer	Cream; multi-coloured print	48	60.00	80.00	30.00
C-14	Milk Jug	Cream; multi-coloured print	49	20.00	30.00	10.00
C-15	Sugar Bowl	Cream; multi-coloured print	37	20.00	30.00	10.00
C-16	Teapot	Cream; multi-coloured print	83	60.00	80.00	30.00

JUGS, LOVING CUP, AND PLATE

The same three shapes used for the Edward VIII coronation jugs and loving cup were reused here, with the transfer prints changed to show King George VI and Queen Elizabeth. On the back of the jugs is a portrait of Princess Elizabeth. The "Coronation Musical Loving Cup" plays "God Save the King" and has the words "Long May They Reign" on a gold band across the front and the initials GR on the back. The square-cornered plate is the same shape used for the silver jubilee of George V, with a dark red and gold transfer print of the profiles of George VI and Queen Elizabeth set in a gold laurel wreath.

Jug, three-ring handle; Jug, long-loop handle

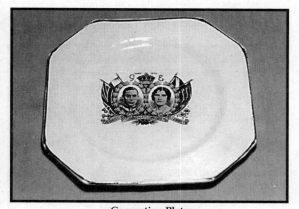

Coronation Plate

Backstamp:
  A. Black ink stamp "Wadeheath England" and a lion
  B. Black ink stamp "Wadeheath Ware England" and an impressed "88M"
  C. Black ink stamp "Wadeheath England," a lion and an impressed "106M"
  D. Black ink stamp "Wadeheath Ware England" and an impressed "106M"
  E. Black ink stamp "Wadeheath England," a lion and an impressed "113M"
  F. Black ink stamp "Wadeheath Ware"
  G. Black ink stamp "Wadeheath Ware England"

No.	Description	Colourways	Shape/Size	U.S.$	Can.$	U.K.£
C-17	Jug, short-loop handle	Cream; orange/blue bands; multi-coloured print	140	95.00	135.00	50.00
C-18	Jug, long-loop handle	Cream; orange/blue bands; multi-coloured print	140	95.00	135.00	50.00
C-19	Jug, three-ring handle	Cream; orange/blue bands; multi-coloured print	135	95.00	135.00	50.00
C-20	Loving Cup, musical	Cream; red/white/blue striped handles; multi-coloured print	125	450.00	525.00	250.00
C-21	Milk Jug	Cream; orange spout, handle; multi-coloured print	108	80.00	110.00	40.00
C-22	Plate	Cream; multi-coloured print	Octagonal/155	95.00	135.00	50.00

QUEEN ELIZABETH II

CORONATION, 1953

Commemorative items with multi-coloured transfer prints were produced by Wade England and Wade Ireland to celebrate the coronation of Queen Elizabeth II on June 2, 1953.

BEAKERS, CUPS AND SAUCERS

Child's Beaker   Fluted Cup

Backstamp: **A.** Large green ink stamp "Wade England"
B. Small green ink stamp "Wade England"
C. Multi-coloured transfer print "Coronation of Her Majesty Queen Elizabeth II Wade England"

No.	Description	Colourways	Size	U.S.$	Can.$	U.K.£
C-23	Child's Beaker	White; gold rim, multi-coloured print	72	70.00	90.00	35.00
C-24	Child's Tea Plate	White; gold rim, multi-coloured print	170	70.00	90.00	35.00
C-25	Cup, fluted	White; gold rim; multi-coloured print	67	70.00	90.00	35.00
C-25	Saucer, fluted	White; gold rim; multi-coloured print	140	See above		
C-26	Cup, plain	White; gold rim; multi-coloured print	72	70.00	90.00	35.00
C-26	Saucer, plain	White; gold rim; multi-coloured print	140	See above		

JUGS

The round milk jug is the same jug as that produced for the 1937 coronation of King George and Queen Elizabeth, except that the transfer print is of Queen Elizabeth II.

Photograph not available
at press time

Backstamp: Large green ink stamp "Wade England"

No.	Description	Colourways	Size	U.S.$	Can.$	U.K.£
C-27	Milk Jug	White; gold rim; multi-coloured print	108	70.00	90.00	35.00

PLATES AND TANKARD

Tea Plate

Wall Plate

Tankard

Backstamp: **A.** Large green ink stamp "Wade England"
B. Green ink stamp "Wade England"

No.	Description	Colourways	Size	U.S.$	Can.$	U.K.£
C-28	Tea Plate, fluted	White; multi-coloured print	170	40.00	55.00	20.00
C-29	Wall Plate	Maroon; white centre; gold edges; multi-coloured print	235	90.00	110.00	45.00
C-30	Tankard	White; gold/red/blue bands; multi-coloured print	Pint/125	70.00	90.00	35.00

DISHES AND BOWLS

The "Coronation Dish" was a scaled-down replica of the 1937 "Coronation Bowl."

The "Coronation Fruit Bowl" has a fluted body and a multi-coloured transfer print of the coat of arms of Queen Elizabeth in the centre. The first "Coronation Dessert Bowl" has gold emblems around the rim and the royal coat of arms in the centre; the second has a fluted body and a portrait of Queen Elizabeth in the centre.

Dish

Backstamp: **A.** Raised "Wade England Coronation 1953"
B. Green transfer print "Wade England"
C. Small green ink stamp "Wade England"

No.	Description	Colourways	Size	U.S.$	Can.$	U.K.£
C-31a	Dish	Dark green	120	40.00	55.00	20.00
C-31b	Dish	Turquoise	120	40.00	55.00	20.00
C-31c	Dish	Beige	120	40.00	55.00	20.00
C-31d	Dish	Dark blue	120	40.00	55.00	20.00
C-31e	Dish	Honey brown	120	40.00	55.00	20.00
C-31f	Dish	Light green	120	40.00	55.00	20.00
C-32	Fruit Bowl, fluted	White; gold rim; multi-coloured print	190	60.00	80.00	30.00
C-33	Dessert Bowl	White; gold band; multi-coloured print	165	45.00	55.00	20.00
C-34	Dessert Bowl, fluted	White; gold band, emblems; multi-coloured print	165	45.00	55.00	20.00

ULSTER WARE GOBLETS AND TANKARDS

In early 1953 Wade (Ulster) Ltd. produced a very limited range of coronation ware goblets and tankards. The enamelled decoration was known as "Coronation" and the design of crossed bands and raised dots was known as "Ulster Ware." The goblets were hand turned, so there are slight variations in sizes. The print on the front of the goblets is of the royal crest. Although the Ulster Ware design were in production for over thirty years, the "Coronation" colours were never used again.

Goblet

Tankard

Backstamp: Unknown

No.	Description	Colourways	Size	U.S.$	Can.$	U.K.£
C-35a	Goblet	Ivory; yellow print	120	80.00	110.00	40.00
C-35b	Goblet	Grey/blue/green; yellow print	120	80.00	110.00	40.00
C-36a	Tankard	Orange/lilac; multi-coloured arms	Pint/118	70.00	90.00	35.00
C-36b	Tankard	Grey/blue; multi-coloured crest	Pint/118	50.00	70.00	25.00
C-37a	Tankard	Orange/grey; multi-coloured arms	1/2 pint/98	70.00	90.00	35.00
C-37b	Tankard	Grey/blue; multi-coloured crest	1/2 pint/98	50.00	70.00	25.00

1953 ADVERTISING COMMEMORATIVES

BURROWS AND STURGESS DISH

Commissioned by Burrows and Sturgess, which produced Spa Table Waters, this dish has "Burrows and Sturgess Ltd" embossed on the top rim and "Spa Table Waters" on the lower rim. In the centre is an embossed design of a shield and laurel wreath, with the initials *ER*. Encircling the dish are embossed animals and the embossed names of some of the members of the British Empire—a lion (Great Britain), kangaroo (Australia), kiwi (New Zealand), beaver (Canada), sea lion (Newfoundland), elephant (India) and springbok (South Africa).

Photograph not available
at press time

Backstamp: Raised "Wade England Coronation 1953" in hollow of base

No.	Description	Colourways	Size	U.S.$	Can.$	U.K.£
C-38a	Dish	Dark green	120	20.00	30.00	12.00
C-38b	Dish	Turquoise	120	20.00	30.00	12.00
C-38c	Dish	Mint green	120	20.00	30.00	12.00
C-38d	Dish	Amber brown	120	20.00	30.00	12.00

REGINALD CORFIELD LTD.

The water jug is a large round-bodied jug, with a portrait of Queen Elizabeth and "June 2nd 1953" on it. Produced in collaboration with Reginald Corfield Ltd., it was intended for use in public houses. (This is the same style jug as that used for Trumans Beer.)

Photograph not available
at press time

Backstamp: Black transfer print "Wade Regicor England"

No.	Description	Colourways	Size	U.S.$	Can.$	U.K.£
C-39	Water Jug	White; multi-coloured print	115	60.00	80.00	30.00

SHELL MEX AND BRITISH PETROLEUM DISH

This dish is the same as that for Burrows and Sturgess, with the words "Shell Mex and British Petroleum" added to the upper rim and "North Eastern Division" on the lower rim.

Photograph not available
at press time

Backstamp: Raised "Wade England 1953"

No.	Description	Colourways	Size	U.S.$	Can.$	U.K.£
C-40a	Dish	Dark green	120	20.00	30.00	12.00
C-40b	Dish	Maroon	120	20.00	30.00	12.00

TRUMANS BEER

Backstamp: Black transfer print "Wade Regicor England"

No.	Description	Colourways	Size	U.S.$	Can.$	U.K.£
C-41	Jug	White; gold rim; multi-coloured print; blue lettering	108	70.00	90.00	35.00

LORD BADEN POWELL, 1957

PLATE

A plate with a portrait of Lord Baden Powell in the centre was produced in 1957 to commemorate the 50th anniversary of the first Scout camp on Brownsea Island, near Poole, in Dorset, England.

Photograph not available
at press time

Backstamp: Black transfer "Wade England"

No.	Description	Colourways	Size	U.S.$	Can.$	U.K.£
C-42	Plate	White; multi-coloured print	155	50.00	70.00	25.00

BASS, 1977

200TH ANNIVERSARY JUG

In 1977 Wade PDM produced a traditional-style water jug to commemorate the 200th anniversary of the building of the first brewery in Burton-upon-Trent by William Bass & Company. The jug is decorated with a print of the beer label and golden yellow prints of barley and hops.

Photograph not available
at press time

Backstamp: Black print "This jug was produced in 1977 to celebrate the two hundred years that have passed since William Bass first brewed in Burton-upon-Trent—Supplied by Wade (PDM) Limited, England"

No.	Description	Colourways	Size	U.S.$	Can.$	U.K.£
C-43	Jug	White; multi-coloured prints	160	50.00	70.00	25.00

SILVER JUBILEE OF QUEEN ELIZABETH II, 1977

Only a very limited quantity of commemorative ware was produced by Wade for the silver jubilee of Queen Elizabeth II on June 2, 1977.

The unusual "Silver Jubilee Beer Stein" has a pewter lid, which is lifted by pressing down on a thumb lever on the top of the handle. The tankard has a transfer print of Queen Elizabeth and Prince Philip on the front and the words "1952–1977 The Queen's Silver Jubilee."

The "Silver Jublee Dish" is from the same mould as the 1953 "Coronation Dish." The centre design has been changed to show a crown and a scroll, with the words "The Queen's Silver Jubilee," and the names of the countries above the animals have been omitted. The back of the rim is embossed with the words "Part of the proceeds from the sale of this souvenir will be donated to the Queen's Silver Jubilee Appeal." The original price was 90p.

The decanter, in the shape of the royal coach, has the words "Royal Jubilee" on the top and "25 year old Pure Malt Whisky" on the front. The cork is in the shape of a royal crown.

Backstamp: **A.** Red transfer print "Wade England"
B. Red transfer print "Wade Ireland"
C. Raised "Wade England"

No.	Description	Colourways	Size	U.S.$	Can.$	U.K.£
C-44	Beer Stein	Dark grey; gold crest	227	90.00	130.00	45.00
C-45a	Dish	Honey brown	120	25.00	30.00	12.00
C-45b	Dish	Dark green	120	25.00	30.00	12.00
C-45c	Dish	Light green	120	25.00	30.00	12.00
C-45d	Dish	Dark blue	120	25.00	30.00	12.00
C-46	Royal Coach Decanter	White; red cork; red/black/gold decoration	165	800.00	1,100.00	475.00
C-47a	Tankard	Amber; gold band; multi-coloured print	Pint/115	70.00	90.00	35.00
C-47b	Tankard	White; gold band; multi-coloured print	Pint/115	70.00	90.00	35.00

TAUNTON CIDER LOVING CUPS

A limited edition of 2,500 loving cups was produced by Wade for Taunton Cider for the 1977 Silver Jubilee. Unfortunately the first run of the cups had a mistake in the inscription. It read "Her Royal Highness Queen Elizabeth" instead of the correct title of "Her Majesty Queen Elizabeth II." The cups were immediately recalled and destroyed. Only one cup with the wrong title is known to exist. On the reverse side of the cups is a transfer print of a Taunton Dry Blackthorn Cider label.

| Loving Cup, front | Loving Cup, back "Her Royal" | Loving Cup, back "Her Majesty" |

No.	Description	Colourways	Size	U.S.$	Can.$	U.K.£
C-48a	Loving Cup	White; black lettering "Her Royal Highness Queen Elizabeth"	90		Rare	
C-48b	Loving Cup	White; black lettering "Her Majesty Queen Elizabeth II"	90	40.00	55.00	20.00

ROYAL WEDDING OF PRINCE CHARLES AND LADY DIANA, 1981

To commemorate the marriage of Prince Charles and Lady Diana Spencer on July 29, 1981, George Wade & Son Ltd. produced a quantity of commemorative ware.

Although the backstamp on the "Royal Wedding Candlesticks" only says "Wade," they were produced by Wade Ireland. They are decorated with transfer printed portraits of the couple within a floral garland.

For many years Wade Ceramics has collaborated with Arthur Bell & Sons Ltd. to produce decanters, in the shape of hand bells, to commemorate royal occasions. The first such decanter was created for the royal wedding. The multi-coloured print on this 75-centilitre decanter is of a portrait of Prince Charles and Lady Diana at the time of their engagement. A limited edition of 2,000 miniature "Royal Wedding Decanters" was made to present to the staffs of the George Wade Pottery and Bell's Whisky in commemoration of the event.

The "Royal Wedding Goblet" was produced by Wade Ireland, although the backstamp only says "Wade." It is white on the outside and glazed inside with gold.

The two-handled "Royal Wedding Loving Cup" is decorated on the front with a multi-coloured transfer print of Charles and Diana within two hearts, as well as the royal coat of arms. The miniature version has gold-leaf silhouettes of the heads of the couple facing each other. On the back is the inscription, "To Commemorate the Wedding of H.R.H. Prince Charles and Lady Diana Spencer at St Pauls Cathedral 29th of July 1981." The original price was £1.50.

The "Royal Wedding Napkin Ring" has gold-leaf silhouettes of the heads of the bride and groom facing each other. On the back of the ring is the inscription "To Commemorate the Wedding of H.R.H. Prince Charles and Lady Diana Spencer at St Pauls Cathedral 29th of July 1981." It was manufactured in alumina ceramic, a material usually associated with the electronics and space industries and well known for its durability. The original price for the napkin ring was £1.50.

On the front of the "Royal Wedding Tankard" there is a transfer print of the couple within two hearts, as well as the royal coat of arms. On the back is the Welsh dragon, Scottish thistle, Irish shamrock and English rose. It was produced by Wade Ireland but the backstamp reads "Wade England."

Only a small number of teapots were produced. They had a transfer print of the couple within two hearts and the royal coat of arms on the front.

GIFTWARE

Backstamp: **A.** Black transfer print "Wade"
   B. Black transfer print "Wade—Commemorative Porcelain Decanter From Bell's Scotch Whisky Perth Scotland—75cl Product of Scotland 40% vol"
   C. Black transfer print "Wade—Commemorative Porcelain Decanter From Bell's Scotch Whisky Perth Scotland—Product of Scotland"
   D. Black transfer print "Wade England"
   E. Black transfer print "Wade Made in England"
   F. Black transfer print "Genuine Wade Porcelain"

No.	Description	Colourways	Shape/Size	U.S.$	Can.$	U.K.£
C-49	Candlesticks (pair)	White; multi-coloured print	145	80.00	110.00	40.00
C-50	Decanter	White; gold rim; multi-coloured print	250	250.00	300.00	125.00
C-51	Decanter	White; gold rim; multi-coloured print	Miniature/105	550.00	625.00	300.00
C-52	Goblet	White/gold; multi-coloured print	145	50.00	70.00	25.00
C-53	Loving Cup	White; multi-coloured print	85	50.00	70.00	25.00
C-54	Loving Cup	White; gold silhouettes	Miniature/50	30.00	35.00	15.00
C-55	Napkin Ring	White; gold silhouettes	45	30.00	35.00	15.00
C-56	Tankard	White; gold band; multi-coloured print	Pint/95	50.00	70.00	25.00
C-57	Teapot	White; multi-coloured print	120	80.00	110.00	40.00

Derivative

Napkin Ring with Base and Lid

A napkin ring has been found positioned on a polished turned-wood stand with a polished wood lid. In this form it resembles a mustard pot, although the ring is not attached to the top or base.

Photograph not available
at press time

Backstamp: Black transfer print "Wade Made in England"

No.	Description	Colourways	Size	U.S.$	Can.$	U.K.£
C-55a1	Napkin Ring	White ring; gold silhouettes; wood base, lid	43	35.00	50.00	15.00

DECORATIVE WARE

The ashtray is square, with a multi-coloured transfer print of Charles and Diana within two hearts and the royal coat of arms in the centre.

Although the "Royal Wedding Bell" was backstamped "Wade," it was produced by Wade Ireland. It is decorated with a gold band around the base and transfer-printed portraits of Charles and Diana within a floral wreath.

The "Royal Wedding Plaque" was produced by Wade Ireland, although the backstamp reads only "Wade." It is white with a transfer print of Prince Charles and Lady Diana Spencer inside a garland. There is a supporting foot on the back.

In the centre of the heart-shaped trinket box is a transfer print of Charles and Diana within a two hearts and the royal coat of arms. The original price was £2.50.

Version one (62a) of the "Royal Wedding Vase" has a red Welsh dragon over the royal portraits, which are in a yellow circular design. Version two (62b) was produced by Wade Ireland, even though the backstamp says "Wade." On the front it has a transfer print of the royal portraits within two hearts and the royal coat of arms.

Backstamp: **A.** Black transfer print "Wade"
B. Black transfer print "Wade England"
C. Raised "Wade Porcelain Made in England"

No.	Description	Colourways	Size	U.S.$	Can.$	U.K.£
C-58	Ashtray	White; multi-coloured print	110	15.00	20.00	8.00
C-59	Bell	White; multi-coloured print	145	50.00	70.00	25.00
C-60	Plaque	White; multi-coloured print	100	50.00	70.00	25.00
C-61	Trinket Box	White; multi-coloured print	40	30.00	35.00	15.00
C-62a	Vase	White; red dragon; multi-coloured print	220	50.00	70.00	25.00
C-62b	Vase	White; multi-coloured print	220	50.00	70.00	25.00

RACING CAR SHOW, 1961

JACK BRABHAM RACING CAR DISH AND TANKARD

Produced to commemorate the 1961 Racing Car Show, this dish is from the same mould as the *Veteran Car Tire Dishes*, with details of the champion racing car on the base.

Photograph not available
at press time

Backstamp: Black transfer print "Racing Car Show 1961 Jack Brabham Cooper Climax 1960 World Champions, Wade England"

No.	Description	Colourways	Size	U.S.$	Can.$	U.K.£
C-63	Dish	White; grey rim; green car print	125	35.00	30.00	10.00
C-64	Tankard	Amber; green print	1/2 pint/90	25.00	30.00	10.00

POPE JOHN PAUL II, 1982

DISH

This square dish was produced to commemorate the visit to England of His Holiness Pope John Paul II on May 28, 1982.

Backstamp: Brown transfer print "Wade England"

No.	Description	Colourways	Size	U.S.$	Can.$	U.K.£
C-65	Dish	White; gold rim; multi-coloured print	135	20.00	28.00	8.00

COMPASITE ORDNANCE DEPOT, 1982

TANKARD

The Compasite Ordnance Depot (COD) in Donnington, Shropshire, England, is one of two locations where all British military equipment is stored. This pint-sized traditional tankard, with a rolled rim, was decorated with coats of arms and bears the inscription "To commemorate the Royal Visit of Her Majesty to COD Donnington on the 4th June 1982." The tankards were presented to the staff.

Photograph not available
at press time

Backstamp: Red transfer print "Royal Victoria Pottery Staffordshire Wade England"

No.	Description	Colourways	Size	U.S.$	Can.$	U.K.£
C-66	Tankard	White; multi-coloured prints	Pint/115	25.00	30.00	12.00

PRINCE WILLIAM, 1982

HAND BELL DECANTER

This decanter was produced in partnership with Bell's Whisky to commemorate the birth of Prince Charles and Princess Diana's first son on June 21, 1982. The 50-centilitre container is in the shape of a hand bell and has a porcelain cap. It is decorated with a blue and gold transfer print of a crown, cherubs and ribbons.

Photograph not available
at press time

Backstamp: Black transfer print "Wade—Commemorative Porcelain Decanter From Bell's Scotch Whisky Perth Scotland—50cl Product of Scotland 40% vol"

No.	Description	Colourways	Size	U.S.$	Can.$	U.K.£
C-67	Decanter	White; gold bands; blue/gold print	205	100.00	145.00	55.00

75TH ANNIVERSARY OF THE FIRST SCOUT CAMP, 1982

Wade produced a series of porcelain items to celebrate the 75th anniversary of the first Scout camp on Brownsea Island, near Poole, in Dorset, England. They have a portrait of Lord Baden Powell in the centre, encircled by "1907–1982 Celebrates the 75th Anniversary of the First Camp—Brownsea Island."

Plate

Tankard

Backstamp: **A.** Black transfer print "Wade England"
B. Black transfer print "Produced by Wade Potteries Ltd"
C. Black transfer print "Produced for Commemorative House by Wade Potteries England"

No.	Description	Colourways	Size	U.S.$	Can.$	U.K.£
C-68	Dish	White; multi-coloured print	140	30.00	35.00	15.00
C-69a	Loving Cup	Amber; black print	85	40.00	55.00	20.00
C-69b	Loving Cup	Amber; multi-coloured print	85	50.00	70.00	25.00
C-69c	Loving Cup	Amber; two-colour Scout flag print	85	40.00	55.00	20.00
C-70	Plate	White; gold rim; multi-coloured print	195	40.00	55.00	20.00
C-71a	Tankard	Amber; multi-coloured print	Pint/115	50.00	70.00	25.00
C-71b	Tankard	Amber; black print	Pint/115	40.00	55.00	20.00
C-71c	Tankard	Amber; multi-coloured print	Pint/115	50.00	70.00	25.00

PRINCE HENRY, 1984

HAND-BELL DECANTER

Bell's Whisky issued this decanter to commemorate the birth of Prince Henry on September 15, 1984, the second son of Prince Charles and Princess Diana.

Backstamp: Black transfer print "Wade—Commemorative Porcelain Decanter From Bell's Scotch Whisky Perth Scotland—50cl Product of Scotland 40% vol"

No.	Description	Colourways	Size	U.S.$	Can.$	U.K.£
C-72	Decanter	White; gold bands; red/gold print	200	100.00	145.00	55.00

QUEEN ELIZABETH'S 60TH BIRTHDAY, 1986

This decanter was produced by Bell's Whisky to commemorate the 60th birthday of Queen Elizabeth on April 21, 1986.

HAND-BELL DECANTER

Backstamp: Black transfer print "Wade—Commemorative Porcelain Decanter from Bell's Scotch Whisky Perth Scotland—75cl product of Scotland 43% GL"

No.	Description	Colourways	Size	U.S.$	Can.$	U.K.£
C-73	Decanter	White; gold bands; multi-coloured print	250	95.00	135.00	50.00

PRINCE ANDREW AND SARAH FERGUSON, 1986

WEDING HAND-BELL DECANTER

This decanter, shaped like a hand bell, was issued by Bell's Whisky to commemorative the royal wedding of Prince Andrew and Sarah Ferguson on July 23, 1986.

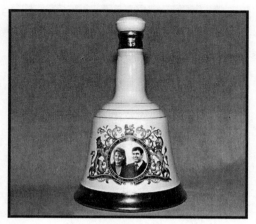

Backstamp: Black transfer print "Wade—Commemorative Porcelain Decanter from Bell's Scotch Whisky Perth Scotland—75cl product of Scotland 43% GL"

No.	Description	Colourways	Size	U.S.$	Can.$	U.K.£
C-74	Decanter	White; gold bands; multi-coloured print	250	95.00	135.00	50.00

PRINCESS BEATRICE, 1988

CHURCH-BELL DECANTER

In 1988 Wade and Bell's Whisky produced this decanter to commemorate the birth of Princess Beatrice on August 8, 1988, the first child of Prince Andrew and the Duchess of York.

Backstamp: Black transfer print "Genuine Wade Porcelain—Commemorative Porcelain Decanter From Bell's Scotch Whisky Perth Scotland—50cl Product of Scotland 40% vol"

No.	Description	Colourways	Size	U.S.$	Can.$	U.K.£
C-75	Decanter	White; gold/red/blue bands; blue/gold/brown print	200	70.00	90.00	35.00

PRINCESS EUGENIE, 1990

CHURCH-BELL DECANTER

Wade and Bell's Whisky issued this decanter to commemorate the birth of Princess Eugenie on March 23, 1990, the second daughter of Prince Andrew and the Duchess of York.

Backstamp: Black transfer print "Genuine Wade Porcelain—Commemorative Porcelain Decanter From Bell's Scotch Whisky Perth Scotland—50cl Product of Scotland 40% vol"

No.	Description	Colourways	Size	U.S.$	Can.$	U.K.£
C-76	Decanter	White; gold/red/blue bands; blue/gold/brown print	200	70.00	90.00	35.00

90TH BIRTHDAY OF QUEEN ELIZABETH, THE QUEEN MOTHER, 1990

The "Church-Bell Decanter" was issued by Bell's Whisky to commemorate the Queen Mother's 90th birthday on August 4, 1990. Wade also produced 10,000 circular dishes and 10,000 circular trinket boxes for Ringtons Teas Ltd.

Backstamp: **A.** Black /red/blue transfer print "Genuine Wade Porcelain Commemorative Decanter from Arthur Bell and Son Perth Scotland—Product of Scotland 75cl—43% proof"
B. Red transfer print "Wade Ceramics"

No.	Description	Colourways	Size	U.S.$	Can.$	U.K.£
C-77	Decanter	White; gold/blue bands; multi-coloured print	200	90.00	130.00	45.00
C-78	Dish	White; multi-coloured print	110	10.00	15.00	5.00
C-79	Trinket Box	White; multi-coloured print	44 x 95	20.00	30.00	10.00

FIGURES
1927 to the present

The production of Wade figures began in late 1927. In 1930 a talented modeller, Jessie Van Hallen, was employed by the company to increase their production. With her input Wade figures started to appear in large numbers at various trade shows and retail outlets.

All Wade figures are slip cast and therefore hollow, with a circular casting hole in the base. Initially they were glazed with what was at that time a new Scintillite cellulose glaze. In 1939 and again in the late 1940s to the mid 1950s, a number of models were produced in high-gloss glaze. These figures command a much higher price than the cellulose-glazed figures and are considered extremely rare.

The figures are divided into three sections—Cellulose Figures, 1927-1939; High-Gloss Figures, 1939 to the the mid 1950s and Sets and Series, c.1948 to the present. The models are listed alphabetically within the cellulose and high-gloss sections. The sets and series are presented in chronological order.

Care and Handling

The Scintillite glaze easily chips and flakes off models that have been kept in direct sunlight or in damp conditions. Most of these figures now have varying degrees of flaking. On no account should the collector try to touch up these models as it will detract from their value. If models have more white porcelain exposed than glazing, the job of restoration should be done by a professional.

Pricing

The degree of flaking on the cellulose figures will affect the price. Prices in this catalogue are for figures with a moderate degree of flaking. Mint figures with no flaking will command higher prices than those listed here, while figures with excessive flaking will be worth much less.

BACKSTAMPS

Cellulose Figures

The earliest Wade figures were produced with a rarely seen backstamp that included a grey ink-stamped owl. Because some models were reissued once or twice, they can be found with two or three different backstamps on the base. The following backstamps can be found on the cellulose figures:

1927-1930: Paper label "Scinitillite Ware," grey ink stamp "BCM/OWL Made in England" and owl's head, with the name of the model hand painted in red

1927-1930: Grey ink stamp of an owl over "British Scintillite REGD" and "Made in England" (or "British Make") with the name of the model hand painted in red (some include "Red - Ashay" and registration number)

1930-c.1935: Grey ink stamp of an owl over "British Scintillite REGD," black handwritten "Wade Figures," black ink stamp "Made in England" and the name of the model hand painted in black (with and without Jessie Van Hallen's signature hand painted in black)

Mid 1930s: Black hand painted "Wade Figures," a red ink stamp of a leaping deer with "Made in England" and the name of the figure handwritten in black

c.1930-c.1939: Black hand painted "Wade," a red ink stamp of a leaping deer over "Made in England" and the name of the figure handwritten in black

1938-1939: 1) Black hand painted "Wade," black ink stamp" Made in England" (may include "Great Britain") and the name of the figure handwritten in black
2) Black handwritten "Pageant Made in England" and black handwritten name of the figure

1939: 1) Black hand painted "Wade England" with the name of the figure handwritten in black
2) The name of the figure handwritten in black

Numbers or a letter written in black on the base along with the backstamp, do not signify the order in which the models were produced. Instead, they identify the decorator or that it is a second version of the model.

High-Gloss Figures

The following backstamps are found on the high-gloss figures:

1939: 1) Blue handwritten "Wade England 1939" and the figure name
2) Black handwritten "Wade England"

c.1948-c.1952: Blue handwritten "Wade England" and the figure name

c.1948-c.1955: Black or green ink stamp "Wade England" (sometimes includes the name of the figure)

Sets and Series

The figures of the sets and series were backstamped as follows:

c.1945-c.1952: Black ink stamp "Wade England"

1962-1963: Black transfer print "Irish Porcelain Made in Ireland"

1977: Black ink stamp "Made in Ireland"

1977-1986: Black transfer print "Irish Porcelain Made in Ireland" with shamrock or inside Irish-knot wreath

1986: 1) Black transfer print "Irish Porcelain Made in Ireland"
2) Black transfer print "Irish Porcelain Figures Made in Ireland" inside an Irish-knot wreath

1990-1992: Red or grey transfer print "My Fair Ladies, fine porcelain, Wade Made in England" with the figure name

1991: 1) Red transfer print "Wade England"
2) Green ink stamp "Seagoe Ceramics Wade Ireland 1991"

CELLULOSE FIGURES
1927-1939

Alfie and Peggy

Anita

Ann

Anton

Argentina, no bracelets

Argentina, with bracelets

No.	Name	Colourways	Size	U.S.$	Can.$	U.K.£
F-1a	Alfie and Peggy	Grey wall; green shawl; yellow clothes	150	350.00	450.00	190.00
F-1b	Alfie and Peggy	Green wall, shawl; yellow clothes	150	350.00	450.00	190.00
F-1c	Alfie and Peggy	Green wall; red shawl; green clothes	150	350.00	450.00	190.00
F-2a	Anita	Grey ruff; multi-coloured suit; yellow wall	170	290.00	325.00	150.00
F-2b	Anita	Orange ruff; multi-coloured suit; grey wall	170	290.00	325.00	150.00
F-3	Ann	Yellow top; red/brown skirt	145	250.00	300.00	125.00
F-4a	Anna	Black hair band, tutu, ballet slippers	160	290.00	325.00	150.00
F-4b	Anna	Green hair band; yellow/green/orange tutu; black ballet slippers	160	290.00	325.00	150.00
F-5a	Anton	Black cape; black/yellow/red suit; red hat	135	290.00	325.00	150.00
F-5b	Anton	Red cape; black/yellow/pink suit; black hat	135	290.00	325.00	150.00
F-5c	Anton	Red cape, hat; black/yellow/green suit	135	290.00	325.00	150.00
F-5d	Anton	Green cape; black/yellow/red suit; red hat	135	290.00	325.00	150.00
F-6a	Argentina, bracelets	Mauve dress; black scarf	240	325.00	400.00	175.00
F-6b	Argentina, bracelets	Black/red/orange dress; orange scarf	240	325.00	400.00	175.00
F-6c	Argentina, bracelets	Black/red/green/yellow dress; yellow scarf	240	325.00	400.00	175.00
F-6d	Argentina, without bracelets	Yellow/red/orange dress; black/yellow scarf	240	325.00	400.00	175.00
F-6e	Argentina, without bracelets	Red dress; black scarf	240	325.00	400.00	175.00

Note: Condition is important in pricing due to the poor aging of these figurines.

Barbara

Betty, Style One

Betty, Style Two

Bride

Carmen

Carnival

No.	Name	Colourways	Size	U.S.$	Can.$	U.K.£
F-7a	Barbara	Pink/yellow bonnet; pink ribbons; yellow/green dress	210	250.00	300.00	125.00
F-7b	Barbara	Black/pink bonnet; green ribbons, pink/yellow dress	210	250.00	300.00	125.00
F-7c	Barbara	Orange bonnet; black/orange ribbons, pale orange dress	210	250.00	300.00	125.00
F-8	Betty, Style One	Black hair; yellow/orange dress; yellow/black fan	115	200.00	275.00	100.00
F-9a	Betty, Style Two	Black hair; yellow/maroon dress; yellow flowers	125	170.00	250.00	85.00
F-9b	Betty, Style Two	Black hair; pink/red dress; pink/yellow flowers	125	170.00	250.00	85.00
F-9c	Betty, Style Two	Black hair; yellow dress	125	170.00	250.00	85.00
F-10a	Blossoms with Mirror	Black hair; pink shawl	200	420.00	500.00	225.00
F-11	Boy Scout	Beige uniform; green base	Unkn.	290.00	325.00	150.00
F-12a	Bride	Cream dress, lilies; pink garland in hair	190	375.00	475.00	200.00
F-13a	Carmen	Orange dress; red shoes; red/yellow earrings	265	440.00	570.00	220.00
F-13b	Carmen	Orange dress; black shoes; gold earrings;	265	440.00	570.00	220.00
F-13c	Carmen	Green/yellow dress; gold earrings	265	440.00	570.00	220.00
F-13d	Carmen	Red dress, earrings	265	440.00	570.00	220.00
F-13e	Carmen	Yellow/orange/black dress; yellow earrings	265	440.00	570.00	220.00
F-14a	Carnival	Maroon bodice; yellow skirt; brown hat, pompon	245	240.00	290.00	120.00
F-14b	Carnival	Green dress, pompon; black hat	245	240.00	290.00	120.00
F-14c	Carnival	Orange/black dress; black hat; orange pompon	245	240.00	290.00	120.00

Carole

Cherry

Christina

Claude with Coin

No.	Name	Colourways	Size	U.S.$	Can.$	U.K.£
F-15a	Carole	Black/red dress; red shoes	215	250.00	300.00	125.00
F-15b	Carole	Red/yellow dress; red shoes	215	250.00	300.00	125.00
F-16a	Cherry with Cherries	Red dress; yellow/green sash; black hair	250	250.00	300.00	125.00
F-16b	Cherry with Cherries	Red/yellow dress; green sash; black hair	250	250.00	300.00	125.00
F-17a	Choir Boy	White smock; red cassock	190	250.00	300.00	125.00
F-18a	Christina	Black hair; pink shirt; yellow trousers; yellow dog	275	290.00	325.00	150.00
F-18b	Christina	Black hair; yellow shirt; brown trousers; black/brown dog	275	290.00	325.00	150.00
F-18c	Christina	Yellow hair, shirt; gold/brown trousers; grey/yellow dog	275	290.00	325.00	150.00
F-19	Claude with Cards	Green coat, trousers; red waistcoat; brown cloak	200	550.00	625.00	300.00
F-20a	Claude with Coin	Black/brown coat; blond hair; green trousers; maroon/brown cloak	200	550.00	625.00	300.00
F-20b	Claude with Coin	Black/brown coat; brown hair; yellow trousers; black cloak	200	550.00	625.00	300.00
F-20c	Claude with Coin	Black coat; pink waistcoat; yellow trousers; green cloak	200	550.00	625.00	300.00
F-20d	Claude with Coin	Green coat; yellow waistcoat; gold trousers; black cloak	200	550.00	625.00	300.00

Colorado

Conchita

Curls

Curtsey

Cynthia

Daisette

No.	Name	Colourways	Size	U.S.$	Can.$	U.K.£
F-21a	Colorado	Man — red/black jacket; black trousers Woman — red/yellow dress	245	375.00	450.00	200.00
F-21b	Colorado	Man — black suit; yellow waistcoat Woman — yellow dress	245	375.00	450.00	200.00
F-21c	Colorado	Man — black suit; yellow waistcoat Woman — red dress	245	375.00	450.00	200.00
F-22	Conchita	Green/ yellow dress; yellow fan; orange shoes	220	200.00	275.00	100.00
F-23a	Curls	Dark brown hair, puppy	120	250.00	300.00	125.00
F-23b	Curls	Pale yellow hair, puppy; pale green nappy	120	250.00	300.00	125.00
F-23c	Curls	Light brown hair, puppy; blue eyes; yellow/ green nappy	120	250.00	300.00	125.00
F-24a	Curtsey	Yellow bonnet, ribbon; green/yellow dress	125	125.00	155.00	65.00
F-24b	Curtsey	Yellow/red bonnet; yellow ribbon; red/black dress	125	150.00	225.00	75.00
F-24c	Curtsey	Black bonnet; yellow ribbon; pink dress	125	125.00	155.00	65.00
F-24d	Curtsey	Black/yellow bonnet; yellow ribbon; red/yellow dress	125	150.00	225.00	75.00
F-24e	Curtsey	Black bonnet; pink ribbon, dress	125	125.00	155.00	65.00
F-24f	Curtsey	Black/green bonnet; yellow ribbon, bodice; maroon dress	125	125.00	155.00	65.00
F-25a	Cynthia	Yellow bonnet; green ribbon; cream dress	110	165.00	230.00	85.00
F-25b	Cynthia	Green bonnet; red ribbon; cream flowered dress	110	165.00	230.00	85.00
F-25c	Cynthia	Black bonnet; orange ribbons; cream flowered dress	110	165.00	230.00	85.00
F-26	Daisette	Multi-coloured dress; silver petticoat, shoes	250	375.00	450.00	200.00

Dawn, Version One

Dawn, Version Two

Delight

Dolly Vardon

Elf

Ginger

No.	Name	Colourways	Size	U.S.$	Can.$	U.K.£
F-27a	Dawn, Version One	Green dress, scarf	205	290.00	325.00	150.00
F-27b	Dawn, Version One	Yellow dress; maroon scarf	205	325.00	400.00	190.00
F-27c	Dawn, Version One	Yellow dress, scarf	205	290.00	325.00	150.00
F-28b	Dawn, Version Two	Yellow/red dress, scarf	205	290.00	325.00	150.00
F-29	Delight	Yellow hair; multi-coloured flowers; green base	75	365.00	500.00	200.00
F-30a	Dolly Varden	Maroon hat; yellow/orange dress, bows; green shoes	265	290.00	325.00	150.00
F-30b	Dolly Varden	Yellow hat, dress, bows; mauve shoes	265	290.00	325.00	150.00
F-30c	Dolly Varden	Yellow hat, dress; black bows; red shoes	265	290.00	325.00	150.00
F-30d	Dolly Varden	Brown hat; yellow dress, shoes	260	290.00	325.00	150.00
F-30e	Dolly Varden	Brown hat; yellow dress, shoes	260	290.00	325.00	150.00
F-31	Dora	Nude; black hair; long pink/maroon robe	190	375.00	450.00	200.00
F-32a	Elf	Dark green butterfly, base	100	250.00	350.00	125.00
F-32b	Elf	Yellow butterfly; light green base	100	250.00	350.00	125.00
F-32c	Elf	Blue/red butterfly; pink base	100	250.00	350.00	125.00
F-32d	Elf	Pink/yellow butterfly; pink base	100	250.00	350.00	125.00
F-33a	Ginger	Silver hat, shoes; silver/lilac suit	245	550.00	625.00	300.00
F-33b	Ginger	Black hat, suit, shoes	245	550.00	625.00	300.00
F-33c	Ginger	Black hat; orange/yellow suit	245	550.00	625.00	300.00

Gloria

Grace, long-stemmed flowers

Grace, short-stemmed flowers

Greta

Harriet with Flowers

Harriet with Fruit

No.	Name	Colourways	Size	U.S.$	Can.$	U.K.£
F-34a	Gloria	Yellow/orange fan, skirt; black/maroon shawl	135	120.00	150.00	60.00
F-34b	Gloria	Maroon fan, shawl; red/yellow dress	135	120.00	150.00	60.00
F-34c	Gloria	Yellow/red fan; black/yellow shawl; green/orange dress	135	120.00	150.00	60.00
F-34d	Gloria	Maroon fan, shawl; red/black dress	135	120.00	150.00	60.00
F-35	Grace, Version One	Pink hat; yellow dress; long-stemmed pink flowers	245	200.00	275.00	100.00
F-36	Grace, Version Two	Green hat; yellow dress; short-stemmed orange/yellow flowers	245	200.00	275.00	100.00
F-37a	Greta	Green dress, shoes	198	325.00	400.00	190.00
F-37b	Greta	Yellow/green/pink dress; yellow shoes	198	325.00	400.00	190.00
F-38a	Harriet with Flowers	Black hat; red feather, shawl; yellow blouse, apron; green/yellow skirt	210	200.00	275.00	100.00
F-38b	Harriet with Flowers	Black hat; yellow feather; green shawl; yellow blouse, apron; green/yellow skirt	210	200.00	275.00	100.00
F-39a	Harriet with Fruit	Green hat; yellow feather; black shawl; yellow skirt	210	200.00	275.00	100.00
F-39b	Harriet with Fruit	Black hat; red feather, maroon shawl; yellow skirt	210	200.00	275.00	100.00

Helga

Hille Bobbe

Humoresque

Iris

No.	Name	Colourways	Size	U.S.$	Can.$	U.K.£
F-40a	Helga	Yellow hair; yellow/orange dress; black scarf, shoes	230	250.00	300.00	125.00
F-40b	Helga	Yellow hair, scarf, shoes; yellow/red dress	230	250.00	300.00	125.00
F-40c	Helga	Black hair; yellow/green dress, scarf	230	250.00	300.00	125.00
F-40d	Helga	Black hair; red/black dress; black scarf	230	250.00	300.00	125.00
F-41a	Hille Bobbe	Green/yellow/black dress; brown table	255	150.00	225.00	75.00
F-41b	Hille Bobbe	Blue dress; cream collar, apron	255	150.00	225.00	75.00
F-41c	Hille Bobbe	Brown dress; yellow bonnet	255	150.00	225.00	75.00
F-41d	Hille Bobbe	Green dress; yellow bonnet	255	150.00	225.00	75.00
F-42a	Humoresque	Green hat, pompon, shoes, bobbles; yellow/orange dress	200	200.00	275.00	100.00
F-42b	Humoresque	Black hat, shoes, bobbles; red pompon; red dress	200	200.00	275.00	100.00
F-42c	Humoresque	Red hat, bobbles; black pompon, shoes; yellow/green dress	200	200.00	275.00	100.00
F-42d	Humoresque	Black hat, shoes; red pompon, bobbles; black/red dress	200	200.00	275.00	100.00
F-43a	Iris	Black dress with yellow/green/orange splashes; light brown hair	190	290.00	325.00	150.00

Jean

Jeanette

Jose

Joy

No.	Name	Colourways	Size	U.S.$	Can.$	U.K.£
F-44	Jean	Yellow hat; yellow/green dress; black base	170	250.00	300.00	125.00
F-45a	Jeanette	Yellow flowered dress; yellow gloves; black hat	145	250.00	300.00	125.00
F-45b	Jeanette	Yellow/orange/black dress; yellow gloves; black hat	145	180.00	255.00	90.00
F-45c	Jeanette	Green/yellow dress; yellow gloves; black hat	145	180.00	255.00	90.00
F-45d	Jeanette	Red dress; black hat, gloves	145	180.00	255.00	90.00
F-46	Joie Ballerina	Yellow dress, slippers	110	250.00	300.00	125.00
F-47a	Jose	Pink/yellow/lilac dress	110	100.00	145.00	55.00
F-47b	Jose	Green/yellow dress	110	100.00	145.00	55.00
F-47c	Jose	Green/blue dress	110	100.00	145.00	55.00
F-47d	Jose	Yellow/orange dress	110	100.00	145.00	55.00
F-47e	Jose	Yellow dress	110	100.00	145.00	55.00
F-48a	Joy	Yellow/orange dress; orange shoes; floral cap	245	375.00	450.00	200.00
F-48b	Joy	Yellow/red dress; green shoes; floral cap	245	375.00	450.00	200.00
F-48c	Joy	Yellow flowered dress; green shoes; floral cap	245	375.00	450.00	200.00

Joyce

June

Lady Gay

Lotus/Anna May Wong

Lupino Lane

Madonna and Child

No.	Name	Colourways	Size	U.S.$	Can.$	U.K.£
F-49a	Joyce	Yellow/green dress; black hat; red shoes	185	250.00	300.00	125.00
F-49b	Joyce	Black/yellow dress; multi-coloured hat; green shoes	185	250.00	300.00	125.00
F-49c	Joyce	Black/gold dress; black hat; shoes	185	250.00	300.00	125.00
F-50a	June	Yellow hat; maroon suit, shoes	180	250.00	300.00	125.00
F-50b	June	Yellow/green hat, suit; yellow shoes	180	180.00	225.00	90.00
F-50c	June	Green hat; yellow suit; red shoes	180	180.00	225.00	90.00
F-50d	June	Green hat; yellow suit; black shoes	180	180.00	225.00	90.00
F-50e	June	Yellow hat; red suit; green shoes	180	250.00	300.00	125.00
F-51a	Lady Gay	Grey hair; brown hat, muff; yellow dress; red stripe	230	375.00	450.00	200.00
F-51b	Lady Gay	Grey hair; brown hat, muff; red dress; yellow stripe	230	375.00	450.00	200.00
F-51c	Lady Gay	Brown hair; black/green hat; green dress; yellow/brown muff	230	375.00	450.00	200.00
F-51d	Lady Gay	Yellow hair; green hat; yellow/green dress, muff	225	375.00	450.00	200.00
F-52a	Lotus/ Anna May Wong	Orange/green brassiere, skirt; orange shoes	245	325.00	400.00	190.00
F-52b	Lotus/ Anna May Wong	Yellow/green brassiere, skirt; yellow shoes	245	325.00	400.00	190.00
F-53	Lupino Lane	Red/white crown, cloak	100	150.00	225.00	75.00
F-54a	Madonna and Child	Cream scarf; green robe	340	325.00	400.00	190.00

Maria Theresa

Mimi

Pavlova, Large

No.	Name	Colourways	Size	U.S.$	Can.$	U.K.£
F-55	Maria Theresa	Maroon/orange/green dress	195	325.00	400.00	190.00
F-56a	Mimi	Mottled red dress; yellow top; black shoes	190	290.00	325.00	150.00
F-56b	Mimi	Black dress, shoes	190	290.00	325.00	150.00
F-56c	Mimi	Red/yellow dress; red shoes	190	290.00	325.00	150.00
F-56d	Mimi	Green dress; brown shoes	190	290.00	325.00	150.00
F-57a	Pavlova, Large	Orange/yellow dress; orange hat, shoes	240	250.00	300.00	125.00
F-57b	Pavlova, Large	Green/yellow dress; yellow hat, shoes	240	250.00	300.00	125.00
F-57c	Pavlova, Large	Yellow dress; black hat, shoes	240	250.00	300.00	125.00
F-57d	Pavlova, Large	Red dress; black hat, shoes	240	250.00	300.00	125.00
F-57e	Pavlova, Large	Pink dress; black hat, shoes	240	250.00	300.00	125.00
F-57f	Pavlova, Large	Black/orange dress, hat	240	250.00	300.00	125.00
F-57g	Pavlova, Large	Green dress, hat	240	250.00	300.00	125.00
F-57h	Pavlova, Large	Red/yellow dress; black hat, shoes	240	250.00	300.00	125.00
F-57i	Pavlova, Large	Yellow/maroon dress; maroon hat	240	250.00	300.00	125.00
F-58a	Pavlova, Small	Red/yellow dress; yellow hat	110	165.00	230.00	85.00
F-58b	Pavlova, Small	Green dress; black hat	110	165.00	230.00	85.00
F-58c	Pavlova, Small	Pink dress; black hat	110	165.00	230.00	85.00
F-58d	Pavlova, Small	Black dress, hat	110	165.00	230.00	85.00
F-58e	Pavlova, Small	Blue/yellow/orange dress; black hat	110	165.00	230.00	85.00

Peggy

Phyllis

Pompadour

Princess Elizabeth

No.	Name	Colourways	Size	U.S.$	Can.$	U.K.£
F-59a	Peggy	Yellow/pink dress; black hat, shoes	175	250.00	300.00	125.00
F-59b	Peggy	Yellow dress; green hat, shoes	175	250.00	300.00	125.00
F-59c	Peggy	Yellow dress, hat; black shoes	175	250.00	300.00	125.00
F-60a	Phyllis	Yellow/ orange dress; pink/brown/green bustle; black hat, shoes	180	200.00	275.00	100.00
F-60b	Phyllis	Pink dress; brown bustle; black hat, shoes	180	200.00	275.00	100.00
F-61a	Pompadour	Yellow/maroon dress; maroon fan	150	200.00	275.00	100.00
F-61b	Pompadour	Cream/yellow/orange dress; green fan	150	200.00	275.00	100.00
F-61c	Pompadour	Yellow/maroon dress; red fan	150	200.00	275.00	100.00
F-61d	Pompadour	Yellow/orange/black dress; orange fan	150	200.00	275.00	100.00
F-61e	Pompadour	Orange dress; green fan	150	200.00	275.00	100.00
F-62a	Princess Elizabeth	Yellow/orange dress; grey shoes; black stool	150	290.00	325.00	150.00
F-62b	Princess Elizabeth	Pink dress; white shoes; brown stool	150	290.00	325.00	150.00
F-62c	Princess Elizabeth	Green dress; black shoes	150	290.00	325.00	150.00
F-62d	Princess Elizabeth	Yellow dress; green shoes	150	290.00	325.00	150.00

Queenie

Rhythm

Romance

Sadie

No.	Name	Colourways	Size	U.S.$	Can.$	U.K.£
F-63a	Queenie	Pink/yellow dress; green hair band; pink/black fan	100	165.00	230.00	85.00
F-63b	Queenie	Yellow/pink dress; pink hair band; pink fan	100	165.00	230.00	85.00
F-63c	Queenie	Yellow/red dress; green hair band; green/red fan	100	165.00	230.00	85.00
F-64a	Rhythm	Red dress; black hair	230	290.00	325.00	150.00
F-64b	Rhythm	Yellow/green dress; black hair	230	290.00	325.00	150.00
F-64c	Rhythm	Green mottled dress; black hair	230	290.00	325.00	150.00
F-64d	Rhythm	Red/black dress; black hair	230	290.00	325.00	150.00
F-65a	Romance	Yellow/orange/black dress; yellow parasol	165	165.00	230.00	85.00
F-65b	Romance	Yellow/green dress	165	165.00	230.00	85.00
F-65c	Romance	Orange dress, parasol	165	165.00	230.00	85.00
F-65d	Romance	Yellow/green all over	165	165.00	230.00	85.00
F-66a	Sadie	Yellow wall; maroon hat; orange suit	350	290.00	325.00	150.00
F-66b	Sadie	Yellow wall, hat; green suit	350	290.00	325.00	150.00
F-66c	Sadie	Brown wall; red suit	350	290.00	325.00	150.00
F-67	Sandra	Green scarf, bolero, skirt	230	290.00	400.00	150.00
F-68a	Sleepyhead	Yellow pillow; dull yellow all over	140	250.00	300.00	125.00
F-68b	Sleepyhead	Orange/yellow pillow; green/yellow coat	140	250.00	300.00	125.00

Springtime

Strawberry Girl

Sunshine

Susan

Sylvia

No.	Name	Colourways	Size	U.S.$	Can.$	U.K.£
F-69a	Springtime	Red shoes; yellow dress; green/multi-coloured flower base	235	325.00	400.00	190.00
F-69b	Springtime	Yellow shoes, dress; green/multi-coloured flower base	235	325.00	400.00	190.00
F-69c	Springtime	Green shoes; yellow dress; green/multi-coloured flower base	235	325.00	400.00	190.00
F-70a	Strawberry Girl	Red hat; green/yellow dress; brown basket	135	290.00	325.00	150.00
F-70b	Strawberry Girl	Blue hat; orange dress; brown basket	135	290.00	325.00	150.00
F-71a	Sunshine	Green bonnet; orange feather, parasol; green/orange jacket; green/yellow dress	165	165.00	230.00	85.00
F-71b	Sunshine	Black/orange bonnet; green feather; black/green jacket; yellow/orange dress	165	165.00	230.00	85.00
F-71c	Sunshine	Black bonnet; orange feather; maroon jacket; orange/yellow dress; black necklace	165	165.00	230.00	85.00
F-71d	Sunshine	Blue bonnet; red feather; green dress	165	165.00	230.00	85.00
F-71e	Sunshine	Black/orange bonnet; yellow jacket; yellow/orange dress	165	165.00	230.00	85.00
F-72	Susan	Orange/yellow dress; green belt; yellow daffodils	135	290.00	325.00	150.00
F-73a	Sylvia	Yellow/green dress; silver sandals	200	250.00	300.00	125.00
F-73b	Sylvia	Yellow dress; brown sandals	200	250.00	300.00	125.00
F-73c	Sylvia	Black dress with red/yellow/green patches; silver sandals	200	290.00	325.00	150.00
F-73d	Sylvia	Red/yellow dress; gold sandals	200	290.00	325.00	150.00

Tessa

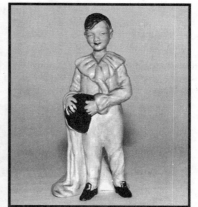

Tony

Trixie

Zena, Large

No.	Name	Colourways	Size	U.S.$	Can.$	U.K.£
F-74a	Tessa	Yellow dress; green bow; black shoes	120	165.00	230.00	85.00
F-74b	Tessa	Green flowered dress; pink bow; black shoes	120	200.00	275.00	100.00
F-74c	Tessa	Green/yellow dress; pink bow; black shoes	120	165.00	230.00	85.00
F-74d	Tessa	Pink dress, bow; black shoes; brown bench	120	165.00	230.00	85.00
F-75	Tony	Cream suit; black hat, shoes	120	200.00	275.00	100.00
F-76	Trixie	Cream/red hat; brown/cream suit; red gloves, shoes	255	290.00	325.00	150.00
F-77a	Zena, Large	Green hat; yellow/orange dress	220	290.00	325.00	150.00
F-77b	Zena, Large	Maroon/green hat; red/yellow dress	220	290.00	325.00	150.00
F-77c	Zena, Large	Black/green hat; black/green/red/yellow dress	220	290.00	325.00	150.00
F-78a	Zena, Small	Yellow hat; yellow/orange dress; red shoes	105	165.00	230.00	85.00
F-78b	Zena, Small	Green hat; green/yellow dress	105	165.00	230.00	85.00
F-78c	Zena, Small	Pink/ yellow hat, dress	105	165.00	230.00	85.00
F-78d	Zena, Small	Blue/green hat, dress	105	165.00	230.00	85.00

Derivatives

Models on Mirrors, c.1935-1939

Some figures have been found mounted on a base with an oval or round mirror. In the 1938 trade papers, Wade advertised the model "Blossoms" attached to a mirror decorated in porcelain flowers. Mirrors that were not incorporated into the design and had no floral decoration were not produced by Wade. Models found mounted with a plain mirror were attached by another company. Backstamps are unavailable on attached figures.

Sunshine and Mirror

No.	Name	Colourways	Size	U.S.$	Can.$	U.K.£
F-24a1	Curtsey	Yellow bonnet, ribbon; green/yellow dress	125	175.00	255.00	90.00
F-57f1	Pavlova, Large	Maroon hat; yellow/maroon dress;	240	400.00	450.00	200.00
F-71f1	Sunshine	Yellow parasol; yellow/green dress	165	200.00	275.00	100.00

Models on Table Lamps, c.1935-1939

Figures have been found mounted on wooden table lamp bases. The wooden bases are usually black.

No.	Name	Colourways	Size	U.S.$	Can.$	U.K.£
F-14d1	Carnival	Black hat; yellow/green balloons, pompon dress	245	240.00	290.00	120.00
F-24d1	Curtsey	Black/yellow bonnet; yellow ribbon; red/yellow dress	125	200.00	275.00	100.00
F-61e1	Pompadour	Orange flowered dress; green fan	150	250.00	300.00	125.00
F-71e1	Sunshine	Black/orange bonnet; yellow jacket; yellow/orange dress	165	200.00	300.00	100.00

Models on Bookends and Floral Bases, c.1939

Wade did not attach models to bookends or floral bases; this was done by an outside company marketing such products.

Photograph not available
at press time

No.	Name	Colourways	Size	U.S.$	Can.$	U.K.£
F-25d1	Cynthia	Porcelain floral base — Green/yellow bonnet; green/yellow/brown dress	110	290.00	325.00	150.00
F-70b1	Strawberry Girl	Bookends — Blue hat; orange dress; brown basket	135	290.00	325.00	150.00

PAGEANT FIGURES, 1938-1939

The *Pageant Figures* series is a small set of models based on historical figures, all hand decorated in the cellulose Scintillite glaze. Advertising material suggests that they were produced and offered for sale at the same time as "Barbara," "Zena," "Rhythm," "Daisette" and others created in the late 1930s.

Henry VIII and Elizabeth I

No.	Name	Colourways	Size	U.S.$	Can.$	U.K.£
F-79	Henry VIII	Black/white hat, cloak; yellow tunic, shoes	115	290.00	325.00	150.00
F-80	James I	Yellow cloak; green suit	115	290.00	325.00	150.00
F-81	Richard the Lionheart	Silver grey chain mail; red cross on white tunic	115	290.00	325.00	150.00
F-82	Robert the Bruce	Silver grey; dark blue	115	290.00	325.00	150.00
F-83	Cardinal Wolsey	Red hat, cloak, tunic	115	290.00	325.00	150.00
F-84	John Knox	Black coat; yellow vest	115	290.00	325.00	150.00
F-85	Mary, Queen of Scots	White hat; black/white dress	110	290.00	325.00	150.00
F-86	Elizabeth I	Green/white dress; yellow fan; gold highlights	110	290.00	325.00	150.00

Note: Condition is important in pricing.

HIGH-GLOSS FIGURES
1939 to the mid 1950s

PINCUSHION DOLLS, 1939

Pincushion dolls are a very popular collectable. They comprise the top half of a lady model, with small holes around the hips with which to attach a dress. The purchaser of the doll sewed, knitted or crocheted a padded dress which formed a pincushion.

The models are hollow and are marked around the rim of the base. Only four varieties of *Pincushion Dolls* have been reported.

Photograph not available
at press time

No.	Name	Colourways	Size	U.S.$	Can.$	U.K.£
F-87	Gypsy Girl	Black hair, shawl; gold earrings	95	95.00	135.00	50.00
F-88	Spanish Lady	Blue dress; pink hair comb	95	95.00	135.00	50.00
F-89	Welsh Lady	Black hat; red shawl	95	95.00	135.00	50.00
F-90	Woman with Bonnet	Yellow bonnet; cream/yellow dress	95	95.00	135.00	50.00

Betty, Style Two

Curtsey

Cynthia

Iris

No.	Name	Colourways	Size	U.S.$	Can.$	U.K.£
F-9d	Betty, Style Two	White/green/yellow dress; pink flowers	125	290.00	325.00	150.00
F-9e	Betty, Style Two	Pink dress; yellow/blue garland, flowers	125	290.00	325.00	150.00
F-12b	Bride	White	190	450.00	525.00	250.00
F-17b	Choir Boy	White smock; red cassock	205	290.00	325.00	150.00
F-24g	Curtsey	Cream bonnet, ribbon; green/yellow dress	125	180.00	255.00	90.00
F-24h	Curtsey	Maroon bonnet, dress; yellow ribbon	125	180.00	255.00	90.00
F-24i	Curtsey	Blue bonnet, dress; pink ribbon	125	180.00	255.00	90.00
F-25d	Cynthia	Black hat, ribbon; pale pink dress with multi-coloured flowers	110	250.00	300.00	125.00
F-25e	Cynthia	Black hat; green ribbon; pale pink dress with multi-coloured flowers	110	250.00	300.00	125.00
F-25f	Cynthia	Yellow hat; pink ribbon; pale pink dress with multi-coloured flowers	110	250.00	300.00	125.00
F-38c	Harriet with Flowers	Green shawl; white apron; yellow dress	210	250.00	300.00	125.00
F-43b	Iris	Pale blue/blue dress; pink/green/gold circles	190	550.00	625.00	300.00
F-43c	Iris	Pale green/pink dress; gold design	190	550.00	625.00	300.00
F-47f	Jose	Cream/yellow dress; pink flowers	110	250.00	300.00	125.00

Joy

Juliet

Old Nannie

Zena, Large

No.	Name	Colourways	Size	U.S.$	Can.$	U.K.£
F-48d	Joy	Pastel blue cap, dress, shoes	245	550.00	625.00	300.00
F-91a	Juliet	Sage green dress with pink/brown flowers	240	550.00	625.00	300.00
F-91b	Juliet	White dress with blue/yellow flowers	240	550.00	625.00	300.00
F-92	Lady in Armchair	Multi-coloured dress; blue chair, stool	185	550.00	625.00	300.00
F-54b	Madonna and Child	Cream scarf; green robe	340	375.00	450.00	200.00
F-54c	Madonna and Child	Cream scarf; pale blue robe	340	375.00	450.00	200.00
F-93	Old Nannie	Pale blue dress; white hat, apron	230	290.00	325.00	150.00
F-57j	Pavlova, Large	Black hat with multi-coloured flowers; mauve dress	240	290.00	325.00	150.00
F-58f	Pavlova, Small	Orange hat with multi-coloured flowers; mauve dress	110	180.00	255.00	90.00
F-63d	Queenie	Cream/pink dress	100	180.00	255.00	90.00
F-65e	Romance	Pale pink/blue dress; blue parasol; white/yellow sofa	170	200.00	275.00	100.00
F-94	The Swan Dancer *	Black hair; white hair band, dress	240	365.00	450.00	200.00
F-77d	Zena, Large	Pastel blue hat; blue/green/pink dress	220	290.00	325.00	150.00
F-77e	Zena, Large	Grey-blue hat, shoes; dark red dress	220	290.00	325.00	150.00
F-77f	Zena, Small	Blue/green hat; lilac dress	100	180.00	255.00	90.00

Note: * "The Swan Dancer" is also known as "Pavlova–The Swan."

Note: We believe three other models were issued — Amy, Joan and The Lady with Two Greyhounds. We would appreciate any information on these pieces.

SETS AND SERIES
c.1948 to the present

CANTERBURY TALES FIGURES, c.1948-c.1952

These four characters from *The Canterbury Tales* were produced in a limited edition of 100 each. The exact date of production is not known, however the backstamp suggests the period indicated above. A paper label was pasted on the front of the base with a short quote from the poem relating to the model. The label on "The Nun's Priest" reads, "Just look what brawn he has this Gentle Priest." Each figure was produced in two sizes.

The Nun's Priest

No.	Name	Colourways	Size	U.S.$	Can.$	U.K.£
F-95a	The Nun's Priest	White hat; pale blue cloak; pink robe; beige horse	150	250.00	300.00	125.00
F-95b	The Nun's Priest	Pink hat, robe; grey/blue cloak; beige horse	150	250.00	300.00	125.00
F-96	The Nun's Priest	White hat; pale blue cloak; pink robe; beige horse	95	250.00	300.00	125.00
F-97	The Prioress	Dark/light brown habit; grey horse	150	250.00	300.00	125.00
F-98	The Prioress	Dark/light brown habit; grey horse	95	250.00	300.00	125.00
F-99a	The Reeve	Grey collar; blue robe; white hair; orange-brown horse	150	250.00	300.00	125.00
F-99b	The Reeve	Pink collar; blue robe; white hair; orange-brown horse	150	250.00	300.00	125.00
F-100	The Reeve	Grey collar; blue robe; white hair; orange-brown horse	95	250.00	300.00	125.00
F-101	The Squire	Dark blue hat; silver-grey tunic; white hose, horse	150	250.00	300.00	125.00
F-102	The Squire	Dark blue hat; silver-grey tunic; white hose, horse	95	250.00	300.00	125.00

IRISH FOLKLORE CHARACTERS, 1962-1986

This series of figures based on Irish folklore, songs and ballads, were produced in two sizes. The eight small figures (125 to 160 mm) were modelled by William K. Harper, and Phoebe Stabler modelled the three larger (220 - 225 mm) figures.

FIRST ISSUE, 1962-63

Little Mickey Mulligan

Molly Malone, Style One

Phil the Fluter

Star of County Down

Widda Cafferty

No.	Name	Colourways	Size	U.S.$	Can.$	U.K.£
F-103a	Bard of Armagh	Light brown jacket, boots, harp; grey trousers	125	200.00	275.00	100.00
F-104a	Dan Murphy	Light grey coat, trousers; dark green hat	220	325.00	400.00	190.00
F-105a	Eileen Oge, Style One	Light grey hair; dark blue dress; white apron	225	325.00	400.00	190.00
F-106a	Irish Emigrant	Light brown suit, hat; blue tie	155	200.00	275.00	100.00
F-107a	Little Crooked Paddy	Grey suit; beige hat; gold coins	135	200.00	275.00	100.00
F-108a	Little Mickey Mulligan	Grey/brown coat, trousers	150	200.00	275.00	100.00
F-109a	Molly Malone, Style One	Blue dress; grey cart; pale yellow/blue/pink flowers	150	200.00	275.00	100.00
F-110a	Mother MacCree, Style One	Light grey shawl, skirt; blue blouse; white apron	225	325.00	400.00	190.00
F-111a	Phil the Fluter, Style One	White shirt; grey waistcoat; blue trousers; silver flute	160	200.00	275.00	100.00
F-112a	Star of County Down	Grey dress; white apron; red/yellow comb on chickens	160	200.00	275.00	100.00
F-113a	Widda Cafferty	Pale blue dress; dark grey shawl, stockings; white apron	160	200.00	275.00	100.00

SECOND ISSUE, 1977–1986

Some variations in colour were used on these reissues; for example, light grey changed to dark grey and grey-blue changed to blue. Unless the first and second issues are side by side, it is difficult to tell them apart.

Bard of Armagh

Dan Murphy

Eileen Oge, Style One

Little Crooked Paddy

Molly Malone

Mother MacCree, Style One

No.	Name	Colourways	Size	U.S.$	Can.$	U.K.£
F-103b	Bard of Armagh	Brown jacket; grey trousers; dark brown boots	125	120.00	150.00	60.00
F-104b	Dan Murphy	Dark brown hat; dark grey trousers	220	250.00	300.00	125.00
F-105b	Eileen Oge, Style One	Dark grey hair; light blue dress; white apron	225	250.00	300.00	125.00
F-106b	Irish Emigrant	Brown hat, suit; blue tie	155	120.00	150.00	60.00
F-107b	Little Crooked Paddy	Grey suit; beige hat; gold coins	135	120.00	150.00	60.00
F-108b	Little Mickey Mulligan	Brown coat, trousers	150	120.00	150.00	60.00
F-109b	Molly Malone, Style One	Pale blue dress; beige cart; dark yellow/blue/pink flowers	160	120.00	150.00	60.00
F-110b	Mother MacCree, Style One	Dark grey shawl, skirt; blue blouse; white apron	225	250.00	300.00	125.00
F-111b	Phil the Fluter, Style One	White shirt; grey waistcoat; blue trousers; grey flute	160	120.00	150.00	60.00
F-112b	Star of County Down	Grey blue dress; white apron; yellow comb on chickens	160	120.00	150.00	60.00
F-113b	Widda Cafferty	Pale blue dress; light grey shawl, stockings; white apron	160	120.00	150.00	60.00

IRISH FOLK-SONG CHARACTERS, 1977-1991

FIRST ISSUE, 1977-1986

This is a set of nine small characters representing well-known Irish folk songs. They were coloured in honey brown and olive-grey glazes. The backstamp washes and wears off easily.

No.	Name	Colourways	Size	U.S.$	Can.$	U.K.£
F-114a	Danny Boy	Light brown cap, shoes; grey scarf, coat, waistcoat; honey-brown trousers	95	30.00	35.00	15.00
F-115a	Eileen Oge, Style Two	Black shawl; blue-grey skirt; honey apron; black shoes	95	30.00	35.00	15.00
F-116a	Kathleen	Grey scarf; dark brown fringe on shawl; honey-brown dress	88	30.00	35.00	15.00
F-117a	Molly Malone, Style Two	Grey scarf; red-brown blouse; grey skirt; honey box of cockles and mussels	88	30.00	35.00	15.00
F-118a	Mother MacCree, Style Two	Honey-brown figure; dark brown shoes; olive-green stool	70	30.00	35.00	15.00

No.	Name	Colourways	Size	U.S.$	Can.$	U.K.£
F-119a	Paddy McGinty	Honey-brown hat; light brown waistcoat, coat; dark brown boots	90	40.00	45.00	20.00
F-120a	Paddy Reilly	Olive-grey hat, coat; blue-grey waistcoat; honey trousers; red-brown dog	95	40.00	45.00	20.00
F-121a	Phil the Fluter, Style Two	Blue waistcoat; olive-grey trousers; dark brown boots	85	40.00	45.00	20.00
F-122a	Rose of Tralee	Blue-grey bonnet; honey dress	100	30.00	35.00	15.00

SECOND ISSUE, 1991 to the present

The reissued models are in a darker honey glaze and have a different backstamp, although it also washes and wears off easily.

Photograph not available
at press time

No.	Name	Colourways	Size	U.S.$	Can.$	U.K.£
F-114b	Danny Boy	Dark brown cap, shoes; honey scarf, coat, trousers; grey waistcoat	95	25.00	30.00	12.00
F-115b	Eileen Oge, Style Two	Dark grey shawl; skirt; dark honey-brown apron; black shoes	95	25.00	30.00	12.00
F-116b	Kathleen	Grey scarf, shawl; honey-brown dress	88	25.00	30.00	12.00
F-117b	Molly Malone, Style Two	Grey scarf, skirt; dark honey-brown blouse, box of cockles and mussels	88	25.00	30.00	12.00
F-118b	Mother MacCree, Style Two	Dark honey-brown figure; grey blouse, honey-brown stool	70	25.00	30.00	12.00
F-119b	Paddy McGinty	Dark brown hat, coat, boots; light brown waistcoat, trousers	90	25.00	30.00	12.00
F-120b	Paddy Reilly	Honey-brown hat, coat; grey waistcoat; honey trousers; red-brown dog	95	25.00	30.00	12.00
F-121b	Phil the Fluter, Style Two	Dark grey waistcoat; dark honey-brown trousers, boots	85	25.00	30.00	12.00
F-122b	Rose of Tralee	Blue-grey bonnet; dark honey-brown dress	100	25.00	30.00	12.00

Derivatives

Pipe Stands, 1991

No.	Name	Colourways	Size	U.S.$	Can.$	U.K.£
F-119b1	Paddy McGinty	Greenish brown stand; honey-brown figure	95	60.00	80.00	30.00
F-121b1	Phil the Fluter	Greenish brown stand; honey-brown figure	95	60.00	80.00	30.00

THE BABY, 1986

No.	Name	Colourways	Size	U.S.$	Can.$	U.K.£
F-123	The Baby	Light brown hair; pale blue suit	110	290.00	325.00	150.00

MY FAIR LADIES, 1990–1991

A series of 16 Victorian-style lady figures was produced in Wade's Royal Victoria Pottery from 1990 to 1991. They were issued in two sets of eight, although only four moulds were used for each set.

A number of these models were also used by Hebrides Scotch Whiskey in late 1992 as decanters (Liquor Products). "Natalie" has been found wrongly named "Belinda."

The grey transfer print backstamp was first used on set one and the red transfer print on set two, but because of firing difficulties with the red transfer, the second set was later produced with the grey backstamp.

SET 1, 1990

"Sarah" is from the same mould as "Marie," "Lisa" is from the same mould as "Hannah," "Rebecca" is from the same mould as "Caroline" and "Kate" is from the same mould as "Rachel."

Marie/Sarah and Hannah/Lisa

Caroline/Rebecca and Rachel/Kate

No.	Name	Colourways	Size	U.S.$	Can.$	U.K.£
F-124	Marie	Dark green hat; dark green/grey-green dress	92	30.00	35.00	15.00
F-125	Sarah	Greenish grey hat; greenish grey/white dress; pink flowers	92	30.00	35.00	15.00
F-126	Hannah	Brown hair; green/grey/white dress	94	30.00	35.00	15.00
F-127	Lisa	Brown hair; pastel blue/white dress	94	30.00	35.00	15.00
F-128	Caroline	Dark blue hat; yellow flower; dark blue bodice; grey-blue skirt; yellow bow	94	30.00	35.00	15.00
F-129	Rebecca	Yellow/beige hat; pink flower; grey bodice; white skirt; pink bow	94	30.00	35.00	15.00
F-130	Rachel	White/grey-blue dress; grey-blue hat	96	30.00	35.00	15.00
F-131	Kate	Off white/grey/white dress with red roses; grey hat	96	30.00	35.00	15.00

SET 2, 1991

"Amanda" is from the same mould as "Melissa," "Anita" is from the same mould as "Belinda," "Natalie" is from the same mould as "Emma" and "Diane" is from the same mould as "Lucy."

Melissa/Amanda and Belinda/Anita

Emma/Natalie and Lucy/Diane

No.	Name	Colourways	Size	U.S.$	Can.$	U.K.£
F-132	Melissa	Light brown hat; dark blue jacket; pale blue skirt; white petticoat	95	30.00	35.00	15.00
F-133	Amanda	Dark brown jacket; pink skirt; white petticoat	95	30.00	35.00	15.00
F-134	Belinda	Pearl/white/yellow dress	90	30.00	35.00	15.00
F-135	Anita	Shell pink dress	90	30.00	35.00	15.00
F-136	Emma	White dress; creamy yellow shawl, ribbons, bows	90	30.00	35.00	15.00
F-137	Natalie	Pale pink dress; light grey scarf, ribbons, bows	90	30.00	35.00	15.00
F-138	Lucy	Grey hat, skirt; dark brown jacket, handbag	90	30.00	35.00	15.00
F-139	Diane	Pale blue/white hat, jacket, handbag; off-white skirt	90	30.00	35.00	15.00

SOPHISTICATED LADIES, 1991

This is a limited edition of four hand-decorated lady figures in the style of *My Fair Ladies*. The same four figures were also issued in an all-over, white porcelain glaze.

Some of the first models were mistakenly marked "My Fair Ladies Fine Porcelain Wade England" using a grey transfer print. Later models have a red transfer print which reads "Wade England."

Emily

Felicity

Roxanne

Susannah

No.	Name	Colourways	Size	U.S.$	Can.$	U.K.£
F-140a	Emily	Blonde hair; pink/white dress; white petticoat	145	120.00	150.00	60.00
F-140b	Emily	White all over	145	60.00	80.00	30.00
F-141a	Felicity	Brown hair; dark green jacket; pale yellow skirt	150	120.00	150.00	60.00
F-141b	Felicity	White all over	150	60.00	80.00	30.00
F-142a	Roxanne	Blonde hair; pale blue/lilac dress	145	120.00	150.00	60.00
F-142b	Roxanne	White all over	145	60.00	80.00	30.00
F-143a	Susannah	Brown hair; orange/yellow dress; white	150	120.00	150.00	60.00
F-143b	Susannah	White all over	150	60.00	80.00	30.00

JUGS, STEINS AND TANKARDS c.1938-1991

Toby jugs are named after an 18th-century drinking character named Toby Philpot. The first toby jug was produced in the early 18th century by the Ralph Wood Pottery of Burslem, Staffordshire. It was modelled after Toby Philpot sitting on a barrel with a glass of ale in his hand and carries his name. The Wadeheath Pottery only produced small quantities of toby jugs, usually in limited numbers of 1,000 of each style. Toby jugs represent the full figure of a person; character jugs depict only the head and shoulders.

Beer steins are replicas of continental-shaped tankards, which are taller and narrower than the British style.

The majority of Wade's tankards were produced in a "traditional" shape, which is wider at the base than the top and has a leaf-shaped thumb rest on top of the handle.

Wade Ireland's Ulster Ware tankards are decorated in characteristic mottled blue, green and grey and come in styles completely different from the English tankards. As with the other Wade tankards, these tankards were in almost constant production, and the replacement of worn dies produced tankards in varying sizes (from 105 to 107 millimetres in the half-pint size and from 160 to 162 millimetres in the pint size). Actual sizes are given when known.

BACKSTAMPS

Ink Stamps

Jugs and tankards produced from the late 1940s to the early 1950s are stamped with some variation of "Wade Heath England" or "Wade England."

Reddish brown ink stamp, c.1948-c.1955

Green ink stamp, c.1948-c.1952

Black ink stamp, c.1938, c.1940, c.1952

Impressed and Embossed Backstamps

The Ulster Ware tankards, produced from the early 1950s to the 1980s, all have a variety of impressed or embossed "Wade Ireland" marks. It is difficult to place an accurate date on the early Irish porcelain tankards, as no accurate records were kept. When moulds became worn they were replaced, and sometimes a new backstamp was added.

Impressed, c.1952-c.1962

Impressed, c.1952-c.1980

Some backstamps, especially the embossed types, were incorporated in the mould, and when worn moulds were replaced, the backstamps were not always changed. This resulted in old backstamps being used at the same time as the current one. Some backstamps are found with the letters A, B, C, E, F, G or P usually incorporated in the centre, under or beside a shamrock leaf. They are the potter's mark.

Transfer Prints

From 1953 to the present, most jugs and tankards, except for Ulster Ware, were given transfer-printed backstamps.

Transfer print, 1953-c.1968

Transfer print, 1956-1967

Commissioned pieces issued from the mid 1950s included the name Wade Regicor in the backstamp:

Transfer print, c.1953-c.1958

CHARACTER JUGS

FISHERMAN, c.1948-c.1953

A fish forms the handle of this jug.

Backstamp: **A.** Grey ink stamp "Wade England"
B. Red transfer print "Wade England"

No.	Description	Colourways	Size	U.S.$	Can.$	U.K.£
J-1a	Fisherman	Beige/pink	Miniature/75	50.00	70.00	25.00
J-1b	Fisherman	Green	Miniature/75	50.00	70.00	25.00

INDIAN CHIEF, c.1958-c.1962

The "Indian Chief" wears a feathered bonnet.

Photograph not available
at press time

Backstamp: Red transfer print "Wade England"

No.	Description	Colourways	Size	U.S.$	Can.$	U.K.£
J-2	Indian Chief	White/brown war bonnet; brown shoulders	Unknown	Unknown		

JIM, 1968

This character jug was modelled as the head and shoulders of a smiling man and based on the well-loved British radio and television comedian Jimmy Edwards, famous for his handlebar moustache.

Backstamp: Black ink stamp "Wade Regicor, Hand painted in Staffordshire England" with "Toby Jim Jug" impressed on the back of the collar

No.	Description	Colourways	Size	U.S.$	Can.$	U.K.£
J-3	Jim	Black hat; brown moustache; green coat	Large/110	120.00	165.00	60.00

McCALLUM, c.1952

See Liquor Section, page 314

R.C.M.P., c.1958-c.1962

This jug depicts the head and shoulders of an R.C.M.P. officer in uniform with a wide brimmed hat.

Photograph not available
at press time

Backstamp: Red transfer print "Wade England"

No.	Description	Colourways	Size	U.S.$	Can.$	U.K.£
J-4	R.C.M.P.	Brown hat; red jacket	Unknown	Unknown		

SAILOR, c.1948

This miniature character jug depicts the head of an 18th-century sailor. A plaited rope forms the handle.

Backstamp: Black ink stamp "Wade England"

No.	Description	Colourways	Size	U.S.$	Can.$	U.K.£
J-5a	Sailor	Green	Miniature/75	50.00	70.00	25.00
J-5b	Sailor	Honey	Miniature/75	50.00	70.00	25.00
J-5c	Sailor	Pink	Miniature/75	50.00	70.00	25.00

BEER STEINS

BEETHOVEN AND MOZART, 1991

These German-style beer steins are decorated with transfer prints of Beethoven or Mozart. The slightly larger size of style J-9 may be due to a new mould.

Backstamp: Gold transfer print "Royal Victoria Pottery Wade England"

No.	Description	Colourways	Size	U.S.$	Can.$	U.K.£
J-6a	Ludwig Van Beethoven	Royal blue; gold portrait, lettering	Small/127	60.00	80.00	30.00
J-6b	Wolfgang Amadeus Mozart	Royal blue; gold portrait, lettering	Small/127	60.00	80.00	30.00
J-7a	Ludwig Van Beethoven	Royal blue; gold portrait, lettering	Medium/153	60.00	80.00	30.00
J-7b	Wolfgang Amadeus Mozart	Royal blue; gold portrait, lettering	Medium/153	60.00	80.00	30.00
J-8a	Ludwig Van Beethoven	Royal blue; gold portrait, lettering	Large/177	70.00	95.00	35.00
J-8b	Wolfgang Amadeus Mozart	Royal blue; gold portrait, lettering	Large/177	70.00	95.00	35.00
J-9	Wolfgang Amadeus Mozart	Royal blue; gold portrait, lettering	Large/186	70.00	95.00	35.00

IRISH PORCELAIN STEINS, 1953-c.1980

These steins have two rows of impressed knurls around the rim and two rows of embossed knurls around the base. The print on the "Irish Harp Stein" is of a harp.

Photograph not available
at press time

Backstamp: Impressed "Irish Porcelain Made in Ireland" with "Wade" printed across a shamrock
Shape: I.P.3

No.	Description	Colourways	Size	U.S.$	Can.$	U.K.£
J-10a	Irish Harp Stein	Blue-grey; gold print	1/2 pint/160	20.00	30.00	10.00
J-10b	Stein	Grey/blue/brown	1/2 pint/160	20.00	30.00	10.00

THE QUEEN'S MEN, c.1962

The same transfer prints used on the *Queen's Men Tankards* were used on these tall, narrow beer steins, which were produced in a set of four. The transfer prints depict the regiments that guard the Queen's residences and parade through London on ceremonial occasions. Each stein has the legend of the regiment on the back

Life Guards

Backstamp: Black transfer print " By Wade of England"

No.	Description	Colourways	Size	U.S.$	Can.$	U.K.£
J-11a	The Drum Major	White; gold rim; multi-coloured print	146	25.00	35.00	12.00
J-11b	The Life Guards	White; gold rim; multi-coloured print	146	25.00	35.00	12.00
J-11c	Life Guards Trooper	White; gold rim; multi-coloured print	146	25.00	35.00	12.00
J-11d	The Scots Guards	White; gold rim; multi-coloured print	146	25.00	35.00	12.00

TOBY JUGS

HIGHWAY MAN, c.1948-c.1955

There were 1,000 "Highway Man Toby Jugs" issued.

Backstamp: **A.** Brown ink stamp "Wade England" inside an ornate crown
B. Black ink stamp "Wade England Highway Man"

No.	Description	Colourways	Size	U.S.$	Can.$	U.K.£
J-12a	Highway Man	Black/yellow hat; green coat; black cloak	150	200.00	275.00	100.00
J-12b	Highway Man	Black hat; green coat; red cloak	150	200.00	275.00	100.00
J-12c	Highway Man	Copper lustre	150	95.00	130.00	50.00
J-12d	Highway Man	Gold lustre	150	95.00	130.00	50.00

PIRATE, c.1948-c.1955

There were 750 pirate toby jugs produced.

Backstamp: A. Brown ink stamp "Wade England" inside an ornate crown, with the model name
B. Black ink stamp "Wade England Pirate"

No.	Description	Colourways	Size	U.S.$	Can.$	U.K.£
J-13a	Pirate	Black/yellow hat; green/yellow coat; purple trousers	150	200.00	275.00	100.00
J-13b	Pirate	Black hat; green coat; blue trousers	150	200.00	275.00	100.00
J-13c	Pirate	Copper lustre	150	95.00	130.00	50.00
J-13d	Pirate	Gold lustre	150	95.00	130.00	50.00

TOBY PHILPOT, c.1953-c.1958

The miniature toby depicts a seated Toby Philpot holding a pint of ale. It has a straight handle. The small and large Toby Philpots are sitting with glass of ale in one hand and a jug in the other.

Photograph not available
at press time

Backstamp: A. Red transfer print "Wade England"
B. Black transfer print "Wade Regicor, Hand painted in Staffordshire, England"

No.	Description	Colourways	Size	U.S.$	Can.$	U.K.£
J-14	Toby Philpot	Green coat; black hat, trousers, shoes	Miniature/75	50.00	70.00	25.00
J-15	Toby Philpot	Black hat, shoes; white/silver buckles; green coat; red trousers	Small/115	175.00	240.00	90.00
J-16	Toby Philpot	Black hat, shoes; white/silver buckles; green coat; red trousers	Large/180	175.00	240.00	90.00

TANKARDS

ANIMALS, c.1955

These traditional tankards all have transfer prints of African animals on them.

Photograph not available
at press time

Backstamp: **A.** Red transfer print "Wade England"
B. Red transfer print "Wade Ireland"

No.	Description	Colourways	Size	U.S.$	Can.$	U.K.£
J-17a	Eland	Amber; multi-coloured print	Miniature/49	10.00	15.00	5.00
J-17b	Elephant	Amber; multi-coloured print	Miniature/49	10.00	15.00	5.00
J-17c	Giraffe	Amber; multi-coloured print	Miniature/49	10.00	15.00	5.00
J-17d	Lion	Amber; multi-coloured print	Miniature/49	10.00	15.00	5.00
J-17e	Rhinoceros	Amber; multi-coloured print	Miniature/49	10.00	15.00	5.00
J-17f	Zebra	Amber; multi-coloured print	Miniature/49	10.00	15.00	5.00

BARBECUE, 1954

These tankards are in the form of a tree trunk with a gnarled-wood pattern. The pint size was produced by Wade England; the half-pint size by Wade Ireland. The original price for the pint tankard was 5/9d.

Backstamp: **A.** Black ink stamp "Wade England"
B. Black ink stamp "Made in Ireland"

No.	Description	Colourways	Size	U.S.$	Can.$	U.K.£
J-18a	Barbecue	Dark green	1/2 pint/91	15.00	20.00	8.00
J-18b	Barbecue	Honey brown	1/2 pint/91	15.00	20.00	8.00
J-19a	Barbecue	Dark green	Pint/111	25.00	35.00	12.00
J-19b	Barbecue	Beige brown	Pint/111	25.00	35.00	12.00
J-19c	Barbecue	Matt white	Pint/111	25.00	35.00	12.00

BARREL TANKARDS, c.1950–c.1962

BarrelTankards are commonly found in three sizes; however, a fourth—the four-pint size—is very rare. These barrel-shaped tankards were produced in Wade's amber glaze, with four wide silver cross bands and a silver twisted-rope handle.

A miniature tankard bearing a transfer print of the coat of arms of Windsor Castle was produced as a souvenir of England circa 1955. The copper lustre pint barrel tankard was produced circa 1961

Miniature, 1/2 pint, pint, 4-pint   Windsor Castle

Backstamp: A. Red transfer print "Wade England"
             B. Black transfer print "Wade England"

No.	Description	Colourways	Size	U.S.$	Can.$	U.K.£
J-20a	Barrel	Amber; silver bands, handle	Miniature/49	8.00	10.00	3.00
J-20b	Windsor Castle	Amber; silver bands, handle; multi-coloured print	Miniature/49	8.00	10.00	3.00
J-21	Barrel	Amber; silver bands, handle	1/2 pint/90	15.00	20.00	8.00
J-22a	Barrel	Amber; silver bands, handle	Pint/123	25.00	35.00	12.00
J-22b	Barrel	Amber; silver bands, handle	Pint/120	25.00	35.00	12.00
J-22c	Barrel	Copper luster	Pint/123	35.00	40.00	15.00
J-23	Barrel	Amber; silver bands, handle	4 pint/190	50.00	70.00	25.00

THE BEERSHIFTER'S TANKARD, c.1965

The poem, "The Beershifter's Dream of Paradise" is printed on one side of this traditional tankard, and a print of a hand holding a foaming tankard is on the other.

Backstamp: Gold transfer print "Royal Victoria Pottery Wade England"

No.	Description	Colourways	Size	U.S.$	Can.$	U.K.£
J-24	Beershifter's	Cream; brown print	Pint/115	10.00	15.00	5.00

COUNTRYMEN, c.1955-c.1962

The first set of these tankards, produced circa 1955, is glazed in amber; the second set, produced circa 1962, is in white. They were modelled in the traditional shape with a leaf-shaped thumb rest. The same decoration of country scenes, dogs and horses that was used on these tankards was also used on dishes and ashtrays.

Coaching Inn   Collie's Head

Backstamp: Red transfer print "Wade England"

No.	Description	Colourways	Size	U.S.$	Can.$	U.K.
J-25a	Coaching Inn	Amber; multi-coloured print (set 1)	Pint/115	25.00	35.00	12.00
J-25b	Collie's Head	Amber; multi-coloured print (set 1)	Pint/115	25.00	35.00	12.00
J-25c	Horse's Head	White; brown print (set 2)	Pint/115	25.00	35.00	12.00
J-25d	Horses' Heads (two)	Amber; dark brown/brown print (set 1)	Pint/115	25.00	35.00	12.00
J-25e	Horses' Heads (two)	White; grey/brown print (set 2)	Pint/115	25.00	35.00	12.00
J-25f	Huntsmen	Amber; multi-coloured print (set 1)	Pint/115	25.00	35.00	12.00
J-25g	Poodle's Head	White; black print (set 2)	Pint/115	25.00	35.00	12.00
J-25h	Poodle's Head	White; grey print (set 2)	Pint/115	25.00	35.00	12.00
J-25i	Spaniel's Head	White; black print (set 2)	Pint/115	25.00	35.00	12.00
J-25j	Spaniel's Head	White; brown print (set 2)	Pint/115	25.00	35.00	12.00

CRANKY, c.1938–c.1951

These half-pint and pint tankards are decorated with prints of cartoon animals on the front and a comic verse about the cartoon on the back. The *Cranky Tankards* produced in the late 1930s are shaped like a traditional tankard, which flares out at the base, except they do not have the leaf-shaped thumb rest typical of this type of tankard. The bulbous tankards, issued in the late 1940s and reissued in the early 1950s, do have the leaf-shaped thumb rest.

Traditional, c.1938

The Snoozle (front)

The Snoozle (back)

Backstamp: Black ink stamp "Wade Heath England" with "Cranky Tankard" and design number

No.	Description	Colourways	Size	U.S.$	Can.$	U.K.£
J-26a	The Drumbletum	Amber; black web-footed dog; design 3	1/2 pint/92	38.00	35.00	15.00
J-26b	The Floppity	Amber; black horse; design 4	1/2 pint/92	30.00	35.00	15.00
J-26c	The Hangovah	Amber; black spotted fly; design 2	1/2 pint/92	30.00	35.00	15.00
J-26d	The Hyperfloogie	Amber; black boar; design 5	1/2 pint/92	30.00	35.00	15.00
J-26e	The Miasma	Amber; black mule; design 1	1/2 pint/92	30.00	35.00	15.00
J-26f	The Snoozle	Amber; black anteater; design 6	1/2 pint/92	30.00	35.00	15.00
J-27a	The Drumbletum	Amber; black web-footed dog; design 3	Pint/118	40.00	55.00	20.00
J-27b	The Floppity	Amber; black horse; design 4	Pint/118	40.00	55.00	20.00
J-27c	The Hangovah	Amber; black spotted fly; design 2	Pint/118	40.00	55.00	20.00
J-27d	The Hyperfloogie	Amber; black boar; design 5	Pint/118	40.00	55.00	20.00
J-27e	The Miasma	Amber; black mule; design 1	Pint/118	40.00	55.00	20.00
J-27f	The Snoozle	Amber; black anteater; design 6	Pint/118	40.00	55.00	20.00

Bulbous, c.1948-c.1951

The Drumbletum

The Hangovah

Backstamp: **A.** Green ink stamp "Harvest Ware Wade England" with "Cranky Tankard" and design number in brown, green or maroon, c.1948

B. Green ink stamp "Wade England" with "Cranky Tankard" and the design number in brown, green or maroon, c.1951

No.	Description	Colourways	Size	U.S.$	Can.$	U.K.£
J-28a	The Drumbletum	Pinky cream; dark brown web-footed dog; design 3	123	70.00	90.00	35.00
J-28b	The Drumbletum	Pinky cream; green web-footed dog; design 3	123	70.00	90.00	35.00
J-28c	The Drumbletum	Pinky cream; maroon web-footed dog; design 3	123	70.00	90.00	35.00
J-28d	The Floppity	Pinky cream; dark brown horse; design 4	123	70.00	90.00	35.00
J-28e	The Floppity	Pinky cream; green horse; design 4	123	70.00	90.00	35.00
J-28f	The Floppity	Pinky cream; maroon horse; design 4	123	70.00	90.00	35.00
J-28g	The Hangovah	Pinky cream; dark brown spotted fly; design 2	123	70.00	90.00	35.00
J-28h	The Hangovah	Pinky cream; green spotted fly; design 2	123	70.00	90.00	35.00
J-28i	The Hangovah	Pinky cream; maroon spotted fly; design 2	123	70.00	90.00	35.00
J-28j	The Hyperfloogie	Pinky cream; dark brown boar; design 5	123	70.00	90.00	35.00
J-28k	The Hyperfloogie	Pinky cream; green boar; design 5	123	70.00	90.00	35.00
J-28l	The Hyperfloogie	Pinky cream; maroon boar; design 5	123	70.00	90.00	35.00
J-28m	The Miasma	Pinky cream; dark brown mule; design 1	123	70.00	90.00	35.00
J-28n	The Miasma	Pinky cream; green mule; design 1	123	70.00	90.00	35.00
J-28o	The Miasma	Pinky cream; maroon mule; design 1	123	70.00	90.00	35.00
J-28p	The Snoozle	Pinky cream; dark brown anteater; design 6	123	70.00	90.00	35.00
J-28q	The Snoozle	Pinky cream; green anteater; design 6	123	70.00	90.00	35.00
J-28r	The Snoozle	Pinky cream; maroon anteater; design 6	123	70.00	90.00	35.00

CRESTS, c.1955–c.1962

These tankards were modelled in the traditional shape with a leaf-shaped thumb rest.

| Royal Canadian Air Force | Rugby Football "Lets Have It Back" |

Backstamp: **A.** Red transfer print "Wade England"
B. Black transfer print "Royal Victoria Pottery Wade England"

No.	Description	Colourways	Size	U.S.$	Can.$	U.K.£
J-29a	Beer Drinkers, "The Same Again, Please"	Amber; red/black/white print	1/2 pint/91	25.00	35.00	12.00
J-29b	Golfers' Crest	Amber; multi-coloured print	1/2 pint/91	25.00	35.00	12.00
J-29c	Rugby Football, "Let's Have It Back"	Amber; pale blue/green/white print	1/2 pint/91	25.00	35.00	12.00
J-30a	Beer Drinkers, "The Same Again, Please"	Amber; red/black/white print	Pint/115	25.00	35.00	12.00
J-30b	Golfers' Crest	Amber; multi-coloured print	Pint/115	25.00	35.00	12.00
J-30c	Royal Canadian Air Force "Per Ardua Ad Astra"	White; multi-coloured print	Pint/115	25.00	35.00	12.00
J-30d	Rugby Football, "Let's Have It Back"	Amber; pale blue/green/white print	Pint/115	25.00	35.00	12.00
J-30e	St. George and the Dragon	White; multi-coloured print	Pint/115	25.00	35.00	12.00

THE GENT'S A GOURMET, c.1958

Backstamp: Red transfer print "Wade England"

No.	Description	Colourways	Size	U.S.$	Can.$	U.K.£
J-31	Gent's a Gourmet	White; gold rim; red/blue print	Pint/115	10.00	15.00	5.00

HUMPTY DUMPTY MUSICAL TANKARD, c.1940

This pint tankard has a music box contained in the base. The Swiss musical movement is dated August 26, 1940, and plays "Brahms Lullaby."

Backstamp: Green ink stamp "Wade Heath England"

No.	Description	Colourways	Size	U.S.$	Can.$	U.K.£
J-32	Humpty Dumpty	Cream; red line on rim; multi-coloured Humpty Dumpty	Pint/117	100.00	145.00	55.00

IN THE DOGHOUSE, c.1958-c.1962

The print on this tankard depicts a man lying in a doghouse on the front and a dog asleep in an armchair on the back.

Backstamp: Red transfer print "Wade England"

No.	Description	Colourways	Size	U.S.$	Can.$	U.K.£
J-33	Doghouse	Amber; dark brown; black print	Pint/116	25.00	35.00	12.00

MOURNE TANKARDS, 1976

These chunky tankards were produced by Wade Ireland in its *Mourne Series*. They have a flared base and are completely different in colour and style from previously produced Wade Ireland tankards.

Backstamp: Embossed "Made in Ireland Porcelain Wade eire tira dheanta"

No.	Description	Colourways	Size	U.S.$	Can.$	U.K.£
J-34a	C.351/Mourne	Mottled browny green; orange flower	1/2 pint/100	50.00	70.00	25.00
J-34b	C.351/Mourne	Mottled browny green; yellow flower	1/2 pint/100	50.00	70.00	25.00
J-35	C.352/Mourne	Mottled browny green; orange flower	Pint/124	65.00	85.00	30.00

OLDE WORLDE TAVERN, c.1955–c.1962

A souvenir tankard was issued with a transfer print of Tower Bridge on the front and a print of the coat of arms of the City of London on the back.

Japanese copies of this tankard exist and are slightly larger and lighter in weight. They have "Beer" printed on them, and the decoration on the top band and the moulded decoration are different than the Wade originals.

Tonic, Ale, Bilge

Tower Bridge

Backstamp: **A.** Red transfer print "Wade England"
B. Black transfer print "Wade England"

No.	Description	Colourways	Size	U.S.$	Can.$	U.K.£
J-36a	Ale	Amber; silver bands	118	25.00	35.00	12.00
J-36b	Bilge	Amber; silver bands	125	25.00	35.00	12.00
J-36c	Gin	Amber; silver bands	125	25.00	35.00	12.00
J-36d	Tonic	Amber; silver bands	125	25.00	35.00	12.00
J-36e	Tower Bridge	Amber; silver bands; black bridge; multi-coloured coat of arms	125	25.00	35.00	12.00

PLYMOUTH TANKARDS, C.1955

Plymouth Tankards are similar in design to the *Barrel Tankards*, but have straight sides tapering in at the top rim. Some of these tankards were issued as souvenirs, with transfer prints depicting various scenes from Canada's Maritime Provinces.

Nova Scotia Shield

Miniature, 1/2 pint, pint

Backstamp: A. Red transfer print "Wade England"
B. Red transfer print "Wade Ireland"

No.	Description	Colourways	Size	U.S.$	Can.$	U.K.£
J-37a	Plymouth	Amber; siver bands, handle	Miniature/49	8.00	10.00	3.00
J-37b	St. John	Amber; black lettering	Miniature/49	8.00	10.00	3.00
J-38a	Lobster From Canada's East Coast	Amber; multi-coloured print	1/2 pint/90	10.00	15.00	5.00
J-38b	Maritime Lobster Trap	Amber; multi-coloured print	1/2 pint/90	10.00	15.00	5.00
J-38c	New Brunswick Shield	Amber; multi-coloured print	1/2 pint/90	10.00	15.00	5.00
J-38d	Nova Scotia Shield	Amber; multi-coloured print	1/2 pint/90	10.00	15.00	5.00
J-38e	Plymouth	Amber; silver bands, handle	1/2 pint/90	15.00	20.00	8.00
J-39a	New Brunswick Shield	Amber; multi-coloured print	Pint/115	15.00	20.00	8.00
J-39b	Newfoundland Shield	Amber; multi-coloured print	Pint/115	15.00	20.00	8.00
J-39c	Plymouth	Amber; silver bands, handle	Pint/115	25.00	35.00	12.00
J-39d	Prince Edward Island Shield	Amber; multi-coloured print	Pint/115	15.00	20.00	8.00

PUNK PIG TANKARD, c.1958–c.1962

This slope-sided tankard has a cartoon pig on the front and the words "To commemorate the disappearing wonders of nature this tankard is dedicated to that noble beast—The Chauvinist Pig."

Photograph not available
at press time

Backstamp: Red transfer print "Wade England"

No.	Description	Colourways	Size	U.S.$	Can.$	U.K.£
J-40	Punk Pig	Honey-brown; multi-coloured print	Pint/112	25.00	35.00	12.00

THE QUEEN'S MEN TANKARDS, c.1955–c.1962

These traditional tankards are decorated with transfer prints depicting the regiments that guard the Queen's residences and parade through London on ceremonial occasions. Each tankard has the legend of the regiment on the back.

Photograph not available
at press time

Backstamp: **A.** Black transfer print "By Wade of England"
B. Red transfer print "Wade England"

No.	Description	Colourways	Size	U.S.$	Can.$	U.K.£
J-41a	The Drum Major	White; gold rim; multi-coloured print	Pint/117	25.00	35.00	12.00
J-41b	The Drum Major	Grey; gold rim; multi-coloured print	Pint/117	25.00	35.00	12.00
J-41c	Life Guard	Amber; black/red/white print	Pint/117	25.00	35.00	12.00
J-41d	The Life Guards	White; gold rim; silver breast plate, multi-coloured print	Pint/117	25.00	35.00	12.00
J-41e	Life Guards Trooper	White; gold rim; red cloak; multi-coloured print	Pint/117	25.00	35.00	12.00
J-41f	The Scots Guards	White; gold rim; multi-coloured print	Pint/117	25.00	35.00	12.00

ROLL OUT THE BARREL, c.1942

Two styles of *Roll Out the Barrel Tankards* were produced by Wade during World War II. One handle is made from a moulded British "tommy" (soldier) and the other is a moulded figure of Winston Churchill.

Tommy

Backstamp: Black ink stamp "Wade Heath England"

No.	Description	Colourways	Size	U.S.$	Can.$	U.K.£
J-42	Churchill	Amber; dark brown letters	145	70.00	90.00	35.00
J-43	Tommy	Amber; dark brown letters	145	70.00	90.00	35.00

SILVER LUSTRE TANKARD, c.1953

This all-over, one-colour tankard has no transfer print decoration.

Photograph not available
at press time

Backstamp: Red transfer print "Wade England"

No.	Description	Colourways	Size	U.S.$	Can.$	U.K.£
J-44	Silver Lustre	Silver; grey	1/2 pint/91	15.00	20.00	8.00

SOUVENIR TRADITIONAL TANKARDS

Souvenir of the Bahamas, c.1955-c.1962

Photograph not available
at press time

Backstamp: Red transfer print "Wade England"

No.	Description	Colourways	Size	U.S.$	Can.$	U.K.£
J-45	Island of New Providence, Nassau, Bahamas	Amber; multi-coloured print	1/2 pint/91	13.00	18.00	5.00
J-46a	Bahamian Constable	White; multi-coloured print	Pint/120	20.00	28.00	8.00
J-46b	Grand Bahama Map	Amber; multi-coloured print	Pint/117	20.00	28.00	8.00
J-46c	Nassau, Horse and Landau	Amber; multi-coloured print	Pint/117	20.00	28.00	8.00

Souvenir of Canada, c.1955-1973

Shaw Festival '73

Backstamp: Red transfer print "Wade England"

No.	Description	Colourways	Size	U.S.$	Can.$	U.K.£
J-47a	Nova Scotia Shield	Amber; multi-coloured print	Miniature/53	8.00	10.00	3.00
J-47b	Nova Scotia Shield	White; multi-coloured print	Miniature/53	8.00	10.00	3.00
J-48a	Maritime Lobster and Trap	Cream; red/brown print	1/2 pint/91	10.00	15.00	5.00
J-48b	New Brunswick Map	White; multi-coloured print	1/2 pint/91	10.00	15.00	5.00
J-48c	Nova Scotia Piper	White; blue/red kilt	1/2 pint/91	10.00	15.00	5.00
J-48d	Nova Scotia Shield	White; multi-coloured print	1/2 pint/91	10.00	15.00	5.00
J-49a	British Columbia, Arms	White; multi-coloured print	Pint/117	15.00	20.00	8.00
J-49b	Shaw Festival '73	White; gold print	Pint/115	10.00	15.00	5.00

Souvenir of England, c.1955–c.1962

The miniature traditional tankards were produced in the mid 1950s and the half-pint size from the mid 1950s to the early 1960s. The size variation is due to replaced moulds.

Windsor Castle

Backstamp: A. Red transfer print "Wade England"
B. Black transfer print "A Dee Cee Souvenir by Wade"
C. Black transfer print "Souvenirs of England by Wade England"

No.	Description	Colourways	Size	U.S.$	Can.$	U.K.£
J-50a	Big Ben	Amber; black/blue print	Miniature/49	8.00	10.00	3.00
J-50b	Guernsey	Amber; black print	Miniature/49	10.00	15.00	5.00
J-50c	Isle of Wight Pennant	Cream; red pennant	Miniature/55	8.00	10.00	3.00
J-50d	Shakespeare's Head	Amber; multi-coloured portrait	Miniature/49	10.00	15.00	5.00
J-50e	Southend	Silver/light grey; metal-coloured crest	Miniature/49	10.00	15.00	5.00
J-50f	Trafalgar Square	Cream; black/blue print	Miniature/49	8.00	10.00	3.00
J-50g	Tower Bridge	Cream; black/blue print	Miniature/49	8.00	10.00	3.00
J-50h	Windemere	Cream; black print	Miniature/49	10.00	15.00	5.00
J-50i	Windsor Castle	Pale yellow; multi-coloured print	Miniature/55	8.00	10.00	3.00
J-51a	Beefeater Yeoman of the Guard	Amber; multi-coloured print	1/2 pint/91	10.00	15.00	5.00
J-51b	Guernsey Shield	Yellow; red/green shield	1/2 pint/91	10.00	15.00	5.00
J-51c	Widdecombe Fair	Amber; black print, verse	1/2 pint/91	10.00	15.00	5.00

Souvenir of Kenya, c.1955

The print on this traditional tankard depicts the Treetops Hotel in the Nyeri Game Reserve.

Photograph not available
at press time

Backstamp: Red transfer print "Wade England"

No.	Description	Colourways	Size	U.S.$	Can.$	U.K.£
J-52	Kenya	White; black print	Pint/117	15.00	20.00	8.00

Souvenir of London, c.1955-c.1965

| Houses of Parliament and Big Ben | London | Trafalgar Square |

Backstamp: **A.** Red transfer print "Wade England"
B. Black transfer print "Souvenirs of London by Wade England"
C. Red transfer print "Wade Regicor England, Reginald Corfield, Redhill, Surrey"
D. Black transfer print "Souvenir by Wade"
E. Red transfer print "Wade Ireland"

No.	Description	Colourways	Size	U.S.$	Can.$	U.K.£
J-53a	Big Ben	Yellow; black print	Miniature/49	8.00	10.00	3.00
J-53b	Big Ben	Cream; black/blue print	Miniature/49	8.00	10.00	3.00
J-53c	Eros, Piccadilly Circus	Yellow; black print	Miniature/49	8.00	10.00	3.00
J-53d	Eros, Piccadilly Circus	Cream; black/blue print	Miniature/49	8.00	10.00	3.00
J-53e	Piccadilly Circus	White/yellow; black print	Miniature/55	8.00	10.00	3.00
J-53f	Piccadilly Circus	Amber; black print	Miniature/55	8.00	10.00	3.00
J-53g	Tower Bridge	White/yellow; black/blue print	Miniature/55	8.00	10.00	3.00
J-53h	Tower Bridge	Yellow; black print	Miniature/49	8.00	10.00	3.00
J-53i	Tower Bridge	Cream; black/blue print	Miniature/49	8.00	10.00	3.00
J-53j	Trafalgar Square	White/yellow tankard; black print	Miniature/55	8.00	10.00	3.00
J-54a	Big Ben	Amber; multi-coloured print	1/2 pint/91	10.00	15.00	5.00
J-54b	Big Ben	Amber; black print	1/2 pint/91	10.00	15.00	5.00
J-54c	Buckingham Palace	Amber; multi-coloured print	1/2 pint/91	10.00	15.00	5.00
J-54d	Buckingham Palace	White; multi-coloured print	1/2 pint/91	10.00	15.00	5.00
J-54e	Eros, Piccadilly Circus	White; multi-coloured print	1/2 pint/91	10.00	15.00	5.00
J-54f	Houses of Parliament	Amber; multi-coloured print	1/2 pint/91	10.00	15.00	5.00
J-54g	St. Pauls Cathedral	Amber; multi-coloured print	1/2 pint/91	10.00	15.00	5.00
J-54h	Tower Bridge	Amber; multi-coloured print	1/2 pint/91	10.00	15.00	5.00
J-54i	Trafalgar Square	Amber; multi-coloured print	1/2 pint/91	10.00	15.00	5.00
J-55a	Big Ben	Amber; multi-coloured print	Pint/117	25.00	30.00	12.00
J-55b	Buckingham Palace	White; multi-coloured print	Pint/117	25.00	30.00	12.00
J-55c	Buckingham Palace	Amber; multi-coloured print	Pint/117	25.00	30.00	12.00
J-55d	Eros, Piccadilly Circus	White; black print	Pint/117	15.00	20.00	8.00
J-55e	Eros, Piccadilly Circus	Black; white print	Pint/117	15.00	20.00	8.00
J-55f	Great Britain	White; multi-coloured flags	Pint/117	25.00	30.00	12.00
J-55g	Houses of Parliament	Amber; multi-coloured print	Pint/117	25.00	30.00	12.00
J-55h	London, Multiple Scenes	White; multi-coloured print	Pint/117	25.00	30.00	12.00
J-55i	Nelson's Column,	Amber; multi-coloured print	Pint/114	25.00	30.00	12.00
J-55j	St. Pauls Cathedral	Amber; multi-coloured print	Pint/117	25.00	30.00	12.00
J-55k	Tower Bridge	Amber; multi-coloured print	Pint/117	25.00	30.00	12.00
J-55l	Tower Bridge	White; multi-coloured print	Pint/117	25.00	30.00	12.00
J-55m	Trafalgar Square	Amber; black print	Pint/117	25.00	30.00	12.00

SPORTS, c.1955–c.1962

Man Playing Bowls

Backstamp: A. Red transfer print "Wade England"
B. Black transfer print "Wade England"

No.	Description	Colourways	Size	U.S.$	Can.$	U.K.£
J-56a	Man Playing Bowls	Cream; gold rim; black print	1/2 pint/91	13.00	18.00	5.00
J-56b	Man Playing Golf	Amber; multi-coloured print	1/2 pint/91	13.00	18.00	5.00

TOASTS, c.1958

Backstamp: Red transfer print "Wade England"

No.	Description	Colourways	Size	U.S.$	Can.$	U.K.£
J-57	Toasts	Amber; black prints	Pint/117	10.00	15.00	5.00

VETERAN CAR SERIES, 1956–1967

For over ten years Wade Heath produced an almost constant series of tankards, water jugs, dishes, plates, cigarette boxes, miniature oil jugs and miniature oil funnels with transfer prints of veteran cars on them. At the time this was the only series on veteran cars that was authenticated by the Veteran Car Club and by the Vintage Sports Car Club of Great Britain. Not only were the illustrations completely accurate, each piece was numbered in its set and series and had interesting information about the car on the back or base of the product. At the time of production, all the cars depicted were still in existence.

The *Veteran Car Series Tankards* were produced in miniature, half-pint and pint sizes. All are coloured in an amber glaze and have a leaf-shaped thumb rest on the handle, with a silver band around the rim.

At some time during the mid 1960s, the production of the tankards was moved from England to Wade Ireland. Due to the replacement of moulds, some of the Irish tankards are slightly larger and heavier than those from Wade England.

Series 1 to 4 are decorated with black transfer prints of cars; series 5 to 9 have coloured transfer prints.

Each tankard is marked on the back with the series number followed by the car number in parentheses. These are indicated in the colourways columns below.

Darracq

Backstamp: **A.** "A Moko Product by Wade England - Design authenticated by the Veteran Car Club of Great Britain"
B. "A Moko Line by Wade England - Design authenticated by the Vintage Sports Car Club of Great Britain"
C. "A Moko Product by Wade Made in Ireland"
D. "An RK Product by Wade of England"
E. "An RK Product by Wade of Ireland - Design authenticated by the Vintage Sports Car Club of Great Britain"
F. "Made by the Wolseley Sheep Shearing Machine Company" and a red transfer print "Wade England"

Series 1

No.	Description	Colourways	Size	U.S.$	Can.$	U.K.£
J-58a	Benz, 1899	Amber; silver rim; black print (1-1)	Miniature/49	8.00	10.00	3.00
J-58b	Darracq, 1904	Amber; silver rim; black print (1-3)	Miniature/49	8.00	10.00	3.00
J-58c	Ford, 1912	Amber; silver rim; black print (1-2)	Miniature/49	8.00	10.00	3.00
J-59a	Benz, 1899	Amber; silver rim; black print (1-1)	1/2 pint/91	15.00	20.00	8.00
J-59b	Darracq, 1904	Amber; silver rim; black print (1-3)	1/2 pint/91	15.00	20.00	8.00
J-59c	Ford, 1912	Amber; silver rim; black print (1-2)	1/2 pint/91	15.00	20.00	8.00
J-60a	Benz, 1899	Amber; silver rim; black print (1-1)	Pint/115	25.00	30.00	12.00
J-60b	Darracq, 1904	Amber; silver rim; black print (1-3)	Pint/115	25.00	30.00	12.00
J-60c	Ford, 1912	Amber; silver rim; black print (1-2)	Pint/115	25.00	30.00	12.00

Series 2

Baby Peugeot "Frae Aberdeen"

No.	Description	Colourways	Size	U.S.$	Can.$	U.K.£
J-61a	Baby Peugeot, 1902,	Amber; silver rim; black print (2-6)	Miniature/49	8.00	10.00	3.00
J-61b	Baby Peugeot, 1902, "Frae Aberdeen"	Amber; silver rim; black print; (2-6) black/gold label	Miniature/49	8.00	10.00	3.00
J-61c	Rolls-Royce, 1907	Amber; silver rim; black print (2-5)	Miniature/49	8.00	10.00	3.00
J-61d	Sunbeam, 1904	Amber; silver rim; black print (2-4)	Miniature/49	8.00	10.00	3.00
J-62a	Baby Peugeot, 1902	Amber; silver rim; black print (2-6)	1/2 pint/91	25.00	35.00	12.00
J-62b	Rolls-Royce, 1907	Amber; silver rim; black print (2-5)	1/2 pint/91	25.00	35.00	12.00
J-62c	Sunbeam, 1904	Amber; silver rim; black print (2-4)	1/2 pint/91	25.00	35.00	12.00
J-63a	Baby Peugeot, 1902	Amber; silver rim; black print (2-6)	Pint/115	25.00	35.00	12.00
J-63b	Rolls-Royce, 1907	Amber; silver rim; black print (2-5)	Pint/115	25.00	35.00	12.00
J-63c	Sunbeam, 1904	Amber; silver rim; black print (2-4)	Pint/115	25.00	35.00	12.00

Series 3

Photograph not available
at press time

No.	Description	Colourways	Size	U.S.$	Can.$	U.K.£
J-64a	De Dion Bouton, 1904	Amber; silver rim; black print (3-7)	Miniature/49	8.00	10.00	3.00
J-64b	Lanchester, 1903	Amber; silver rim; black print (3-9)	Miniature/49	8.00	10.00	3.00
J-64c	Spyker, 1905	Amber; silver rim; black print (3-8)	Miniature/49	8.00	10.00	3.00
J-65a	De Dion Bouton, 1904	Amber; silver rim; black print (3-7)	1/2 pint/91	15.00	20.00	8.00
J-65b	Lanchester, 1903	Amber; silver rim; black print (3-9)	1/2 pint/91	15.00	20.00	8.00
J-65c	Spyker, 1905	Amber; silver rim; black print (3-8)	1/2 pint/91	15.00	20.00	8.00
J-66a	De Dion Bouton, 1904	Amber; silver rim; black print (3-7)	Pint/115	25.00	30.00	12.00
J-66b	Lanchester, 1903	Amber; silver rim; black print (3-9)	Pint/115	25.00	30.00	12.00
J-66c	Spyker, 1905	Amber; silver rim; black print (3-8)	Pint/115	25.00	30.00	12.00

Series 4

White Steam Car   Itala

No.	Description	Colourways	Size	U.S.$	Can.$	U.K.£
J-67a	Cadillac, 1903	Amber; silver rim; black print (4-11)	Miniature/49	8.00	10.00	3.00
J-67b	Oldsmobile, 1904	Amber; silver rim; black print (4-10)	Miniature/49	8.00	10.00	3.00
J-67c	White Steam Car, 1903	Amber; silver rim; black print (4-12)	Miniature/49	8.00	10.00	3.00
J-68a	Cadillac, 1903	Amber; silver rim; black print (4-11)	1/2 pint/91	25.00	35.00	8.00
J-68b	Oldsmobile, 1904	Amber; silver rim; black print (4-10)	1/2 pint/91	25.00	35.00	8.00
J-68c	White Steam Car, 1903	Amber; silver rim; black print (4-12)	1/2 pint/91	25.00	35.00	8.00
J-69a	Cadillac, 1903	Amber; silver rim; black print (4-11)	Pint/115	25.00	35.00	12.00
J-69b	Oldsmobile, 1904	Amber; silver rim; black print (4-10)	Pint/115	25.00	35.00	12.00
J-69c	White Steam Car, 1903	Amber; silver rim; black print (4-12)	Pint/115	25.00	35.00	12.00

Series 5

No.	Description	Colourways	Size	U.S.$	Can.$	U.K.£
J-70a	Bugatti, 1913	Amber; silver rim; black/blue/ brown print (5-14)	Miniature/49	8.00	10.00	3.00
J-70b	Itala, 1908	Amber; silver rim; red/black/blue print (5-13)	Miniature/49	8.00	10.00	3.00
J-70c	Sunbeam, 1914	Amber; silver rim; green/black/brown/ blue print (5-15)	Miniature/49	8.00	10.00	3.00
J-71a	Bugatti, 1913	Amber; silver rim; black/blue/brown print (5-14)	1/2 pint/91	15.00	20.00	8.00
J-71b	Itala, 1908	Amber; silver rim; red/black/blue print (5-13)	1/2 pint/91	15.00	20.00	8.00
J-71c	Sunbeam, 1914	Amber; silver rim; green/black/brown/ blue print (5-15)	1/2 pint/91	15.00	20.00	8.00
J-72a	Bugatti, 1913	Amber; silver rim; black/blue/brown print (5-14)	Pint/115	25.00	30.00	12.00
J-72b	Itala, 1908	Amber; silver rim; red/black/blue print (5-13)	Pint/115	25.00	30.00	12.00
J-72c	Sunbeam, 1914	Amber; silver rim; green/black/brown print (5-15)	Pint/115	25.00	30.00	12.00

Series 6

Bugatti

No.	Description	Colourways	Size	U.S.$	Can.$	U.K.£
J-73a	Alfa Romeo, 1924	Amber; silver rim; red car (6-16)	Miniature/49	8.00	10.00	3.00
J-73b	Bentley, 1929	Amber; silver rim; green/black/blue car (6-18)	Miniature/49	8.00	10.00	3.00
J-73c	Bugatti, 1927	Amber; silver rim; blue car (6-17)	Miniature/49	8.00	10.00	3.00
J-74a	Alfa Romeo, 1924	Amber; silver rim; red/black/blue print (6-16)	1/2 pint/91	15.00	20.00	8.00
J-74b	Bentley, 1929	Amber; silver rim; green/black/blue print (6-18)	1/2 pint/91	15.00	20.00	8.00
J-74c	Bugatti, 1927	Amber; silver rim; blue/black/brown print (6-17)	1/2 pint/91	15.00	20.00	8.00
J-75a	Alfa Romeo, 1924	Amber; silver rim; red/black/blue print (6-16)	Pint/115	25.00	30.00	12.00
J-75b	Bentley, 1929	Amber; silver rim; green/black/blue print (6-18)	Pint/115	25.00	30.00	12.00
J-75c	Bugatti, 1927	Amber; silver rim; blue/black/brown print (6-17)	Pint/115	25.00	30.00	12.00

Series 7, Veteran, Vintage and Competition Cars

No.	Description	Colourways	Size	U.S.$	Can.$	U.K.£
J-76a	Fiat F2, 1907	Amber; silver rim; red/yellow print (7-21)	Pint/115-120	25.00	30.00	12.00
J-76b	MG, 1925	Amber; silver rim; green/black print (7-20)	Pint/115-120	25.00	30.00	12.00
J-76c	Vauxhall, 1913	Amber; silver rim; blue/black/cream print (7-19)	Pint/115	25.00	30.00	12.00

Series 8, Competition Cars

No.	Description	Colourways	Size	U.S.$	Can.$	U.K.£
J-77a	Dusenberg, 1933	Amber; silver rim; black/pale blue print (8-22)	Pint/115-120	25.00	30.00	12.00
J-77b	Hispano Suiza	Amber; green/grey print (8-24)	Pint/115-120	25.00	30.00	12.00
J-77c	Mercedes GP, 1908	Amber; silver rim; grey/black print (8-23)	Pint/120	25.00	30.00	12.00

Series 9, Competition Cars

No.	Description	Colourways	Size	U.S.$	Can.$	U.K.£
J-78a	Austin Seven, 1926	Amber; silver rim; red/black print (9-26)	Pint/120	25.00	30.00	12.00
J-78b	Model T Ford, 1915	Amber; silver rim; black car (9-27)	Pint/120	25.00	30.00	12.00
J-78c	Wolseley 6hp, 1904	Amber; silver rim; red/black/cream print (9-25)	Pint/120	25.00	30.00	12.00

VICTORY, 1942

The two handles of this tankard represent Winston Churchill (right) and President Roosevelt (left).

Backstamp: A. Black ink stamp "Wade Heath England"
           B. Black ink stamp "Wade England"

No.	Description	Colourways	Size	U.S.$	Can.$	U.K.£
J-79	Victory	Amber; dark brown/black coastlines, planes, ships	150	70.00	90.00	35.00

ULSTER WARE TANKARDS

KNURLED, c.1950–c.1980

The "Knurled Tankard" has four rows of impressed knurls, shamrock leaves, raised dots and raised knurls on it.

Backstamp: Impressed "Irish Porcelain" curved around a shamrock with "Made in Ireland" in a straight line underneath
  Shape: I.P.6

No.	Description	Colourways	Size	U.S.$	Can.$	U.K.£
J-80	Knurled	Blue/grey	105	25.00	30.00	12.00

TYRONE, c.1958–c.1980

These slender tankards can be easily recognized by their handles, which resemble one side of an Irish harp. The miniature tankard has three rows of knurls; the half-pint and pint sizes have two rows of knurls with a row of shamrocks in the centre.

Backstamp: **A.** Impressed "Irish Porcelain" curved around a shamrock and "Made in Ireland" in a straight line underneath
  B. Circular ink stamp "Seagoe Ceramics - Wade 91 Ireland"
  Shape: Miniature — I.P.9; 1/2 pint — I.P.8; Pint — I.P.10

No.	Description	Colourways	Size	U.S.$	Can.$	U.K.£
J-81	Tyrone	Blue/green	Miniature/75	8.00	10.00	3.00
J-82	Tyrone	Blue/green	1/2 pint/140	10.00	15.00	5.00
J-83a	Tyrone	Blue/green/brown	Pint/164	15.00	20.00	8.00
J-83b	Tyrone	Blue/green/brown	Pint/164	15.00	20.00	8.00

CHILDREN'S TANKARDS, c.1950-c.1980

Although they were described in an Irish Wade catalogue as children's tankards, the "Leprechauns and Toadstools Tankard" is the only one that has a child-like theme. They all have an embossed row of shamrock leaves around the base.

Irish Colleen Carrying Peat

Leprechauns and Toadstools

Backstamp: Embossed circular "Made in Ireland Eire tir a dheanta," "Irish Porcelain" curved over a shamrock crown and "Wade" underneath
Shape: I.P. 4

No.	Description	Colourways	Size	U.S.$	Can.$	U.K.£
J-84a	Bermuda Map	Blue/grey; black print	74	10.00	15.00	5.00
J-84b	Fisherman in River	Blue/grey; multi-coloured print	74	10.00	15.00	5.00
J-84c	Fisherman Walking	Blue/grey; multi-coloured print	74	10.00	15.00	5.00
J-84d	Flying Ducks	Blue/grey; multi-coloured print	74	10.00	15.00	5.00
J-84e	Flying Pheasants	Blue/grey; multi-coloured print	74	10.00	15.00	5.00
J-84f	The Giant Finn McCaul	Blue/grey; multi-coloured print	74	10.00	15.00	5.00
J-84g	Irish Colleen Carrying Peat	Blue/grey; multi-coloured print	74	10.00	15.00	5.00
J-84h	Leprechauns and Toadstools	Blue/grey; multi-coloured print	74	10.00	15.00	5.00
J-84i	Stag's Head	Blue/grey; brown print	74	10.00	15.00	5.00

MUSICAL TANKARDS, c.1950-c.1980

The lower quarter of these tankards is hollow and a Swiss musical movement is held in place inside the base by a wooden disc and metal rivets. There is a key for winding and a metal "brake" on the base, which allows the music to play when the tankard is lifted and switches it off when the tankard is put down. The music boxes play a variety of Irish tunes, the names of which are printed on paper labels glued onto the base.

Irish Coach

Backstamp: Black ink stamp "Made in Ireland" on the rim of the base
Shape: I.P.5

No.	Description	Colourways	Size	U.S.$	Can.$	U.K.£
J-85a	Air Force Crest ("My Wild Irish Rose")	Blue/grey; gold print	132	80.00	100.00	40.00
J-85b	Drinking Toasts ("Irish Lullaby")	Blue/grey; black prints	132	80.00	100.00	40.00
J-85c	Finn McCaul ("Rose of Tralee")	Blue/grey; multi-coloured print	132	80.00	100.00	40.00
J-85d	Flying Ducks (Tune Unknown)	Blue/grey; multi-coloured print	132	80.00	100.00	40.00
J-85e	Irish Coach ("My Wild Irish Rose")	Blue/grey; multi-coloured print	132	80.00	100.00	40.00
J-85f	Irish Colleen ("Irish Lullaby")	Blue/grey; multi-coloured print	132	80.00	100.00	40.00
J-85g	Irish Kitchen ("Galway Bay")	Blue/grey; multi-coloured print	132	80.00	100.00	40.00
J-85h	Jaunting Car (Tune Unknown)	Blue/grey; multi-coloured print	132	80.00	100.00	40.00

ULSTER WARE TANKARDS, c.1952-1977

The only decoration on the miniature tankards is the transfer prints; they do not have a knurled design on them like the larger sizes. They were produced from the 1950s to 1977.

The half-pint size, issued from the early 1950s to the 1970s, has one row of embossed knurls around the base. The "Paddy McGredy, Roses Tankard" has a print of roses on the front, and on the back is the inscription, "Paddy McGredy, Florabunda. Raised by Paddy McGredy From Spartan x Tzigane. Awarded Gold Medal National Rose Society, Award of Merit Royal Horticultural Society."

The pint tankards, produced from the early 1950s to the early 1960s, have a double row of impressed knurls around the rim and a double row of embossed knurls around the base. The "Drinkers' Toasts" version is covered with toasts from around the World-L'Chaim, Saludos, Prosit, Bottoms Up, Chin Chin, etc.

Flying Ducks

The Giant Finn MacCaul

Backstamp: **A.** Impressed "Irish Porcelain" curved over a shamrock with "Made in Ireland" in a straight line underneath
  B. Impressed "Irish Porcelain" curved over a shamrock
  C. Impressed "Irish Porcelain" slanted across a shamrock with "Wade Co. Armagh" in a straight line underneath
  D. Impressed "Irish Porcelain" curved around a shamrock with A, B, E, F or G in the centre, "Made in Ireland" in a straight line underneath (with and without C below shamrock)
  E. Impressed "Irish Porcelain" curved around shamrock with "Made in Ireland by Wade Co. Armagh" in a straight line underneath

Shape: Miniature — I.P.614; 1/2 pint — I.P.1; Pint — I.P.2

No.	Description	Colourways	Size	U.S.$	Can.$	U.K.£
J-86a	Flying Ducks	Blue/grey; multi-coloured print	Miniature/52	8.00	10.00	3.00
J-86b	The Giant Finn MacCaul	Blue/grey; multi-coloured print	Miniature/52	8.00	10.00	3.00
J-86c	Irish Colleen Carrying Peat	Blue/grey; multi-coloured print	Miniature/52	8.00	10.00	3.00
J-86d	Irish Jaunting Car	Blue/grey; multi-coloured print	Miniature/52	8.00	10.00	3.00
J-86e	Irish Kitchen	Blue/grey; multi-coloured print	Miniature/52	8.00	10.00	3.00
J-86f	My Fair Lady	Blue/grey; multi-coloured print	Miniature/52	8.00	10.00	3.00
J-86g	North Wales Mountain Cottage	Blue/grey; multi-coloured print	Miniature/52	8.00	10.00	3.00
J-86h	Red Dragon	Blue/grey; red print	Miniature/52	8.00	10.00	3.00
J-86i	Stagecoach	Blue/grey; multi-coloured print	Miniature/52	8.00	10.00	3.00

Fishermen on Riverbank   **Houses of Parliament and Big Ben**   **Royal Air Force Crest**

No.	Description	Colourways	Size	U.S.$	Can.$	U.K.£
J-87a	Cymru Am Byth	Blue/grey; multi-coloured print	1/2 pint/105	25.00	30.00	12.00
J-87b	Duck Hunter	Blue/grey; multi-coloured print	1/2 pint/105	25.00	30.00	12.00
J-87c	Fishermen on Riverbank	Blue/grey; multi-coloured print	1/2 pint/105	25.00	30.00	12.00
J-87d	Flying Pheasants	Blue/grey; multi-coloured print	1/2 pint/105	25.00	30.00	12.00
J-87e	Fox Hunter	Blue/grey; multi-coloured print	1/2 pint/105	25.00	30.00	12.00
J-87f	The Giant Finn MacCaul	Blue/grey; multi-coloured print	1/2 pint/105	25.00	30.00	12.00
J-87g	Irish Colleen Carrying Peat	Blue/grey; multi-coloured print	1/2 pint/105	25.00	30.00	12.00
J-87h	Irish Huntsman	Blue/grey; multi-coloured print	1/2 pint/105	25.00	30.00	12.00
J-87i	My Fair Lady	Blue/grey; multi-coloured print	1/2 pint/105	25.00	30.00	12.00
J-87j	Old Coach House, York	White; gold handle; multi-coloured print	1/2 pint/105	25.00	30.00	10.00
J-87k	Paddy McGredy Roses	Blue/grey; multi-coloured print	1/2 pint/105	25.00	30.00	12.00
J-87l	Stagecoach	Blue/grey; multi-coloured print	1/2 pint/105	25.00	30.00	12.00
J-87m	Stag's Head	Blue/grey; multi-coloured print	1/2 pint/105	25.00	30.00	12.00
J-88a	Drinkers' Toasts	Blue/grey; black prints	Pint/162	25.00	30.00	12.00
J-88b	Fishermen on Riverbank	Blue/grey; multi-coloured print	Pint/162	25.00	30.00	12.00
J-88c	The Giant Finn MacCaul	Blue/grey; multi-coloured print	Pint/162	25.00	30.00	12.00
J-88d	Houses of Parliament and Big Ben	Blue/grey; multi-coloured print	Pint/162	25.00	30.00	12.00
J-88e	Irish Colleen Carrying Peat	Blue/grey; multi-coloured print	Pint/162	25.00	30.00	12.00
J-88f	Irish Jaunting Car	Blue/grey; multi-coloured print	Pint/162	25.00	30.00	12.00
J-88g	Royal Air Force Crest	Blue/grey; gold print	Pint/162	25.00	30.00	12.00
J-88h	Stagecoach	Blue/grey; multi-coloured print	Pint/162	25.00	30.00	12.00

LIQUOR PRODUCTS

The items in this section were all commissioned by liquor companies to advertise their different brand names or alcohol products.

Drink Pourers:

Drink pourers can be either all porcelain or composed of a porcelain button only. The porcelain pourers come with either a metal venting tube and metal spout or have a plastic venting tube with a porcelain or plastic spout. When the tube composition is known, it has been listed. The all-porcelain pourers and the those with metal tubes and spouts are the early versions; plastic tubes and spouts came later. Since 1994 Wade PDM has manufactured a variety of plastic pourers.

Water Jugs:

The pub water jugs that advertise various alcoholic beverages were produced in a multitude of styles—tall rounded, short rounded, tall square sided, short square sided, oblong and the traditional harvest type, as well as the exclusive shapes of the Beefeater Gin castle-shaped jug and the Worthington E-shaped jug. They also have two types of spout—open and closed (ice check)—and two different handles—applied and recessed (moulded in with the jug).

Please note:

1. Some dates in this section are approximate only, as no information on production start or end dates is available.
2. When the liquor containers were originally sold, they were filled with liquor, but most containers bought at collector shows are empty; therefore, the prices listed here are for empty containers only. Decorative decanters with unbroken seals, in their original packaging and containing the original liquor, are worth considerably more.
3. The liquor companies are listed in alphabetical order, with their range of products listed under the company name, also in alphabetical order.

BACKSTAMPS

Wade Regicor and Wade PDM Backstamps

Wade Regicor and Wade PDM backstamps are found in black, blue, yellow, white, green, red and gold. The colour of the backstamps varied in order to contrast with the base colour of the models. The dating of a product is not determined by the colour of the backstamp, but by its style.

1955–1962: "Wade Regicor, London England" in between two upright rows of nine laurel-type leaves, large size (18 mm x 20 mm)

1962–1968: "Wade Regicor, London England" in between two upright rows of nine laurel-type leaves, small size (13 mm x 13 mm)

1968–1969: "Reginald Corfield Limited Redhill Surrey" printed in a circle, with "Wade Regicor England" printed through the circle

1969–1984: "Wade pdm England" printed in a circle (this was the first Wade PDM backstamp)

1984–1990: "Wade p d m England," with spaces between the letters *pdm*

1990–1996: "Wade P D M England" or "Wade P D M Made in England" within two red lines, one thick, the other thin

Private Backstamps

Some backstamps do not correspond to those listed above. They incorporate information about the liquor company and may not indicate that the item was produced by Wade.

Drink Pourers

A large number of drink pourers have been produced by Wade since 1955. Some of the first pourers issued are backstamped "Wade Regicor," but most are unmarked. From 1969 onwards, pourers were produced through Wade PDM. The backstamp (if any) is on the neck of the pourer, obscured by a cork which secures the pourer in the bottle. The cork is usually glued in place, making it difficult to see if there is a Wade backstamp underneath. Where a backstamp has been confirmed, it is noted in the text.

Transfer print, 1966-1969

ABBOT'S CHOICE SCOTCH WHISKY
(JOHN McEWAN & CO. LTD.)

ASHTRAYS, 1962–1969

The style-1 ashtray is decorated with a transfer print of an abbot.

Backstamp: A. "Wade Regicor London England," laurel leaves, small size
B. "Reginald Corfield Limited Redhill Surrey," "Wade Regicor England"

No.	Description	Colourways	Shape/Size	U.S.$	Can.$	U.K.£
L-1	Ashtray	Tan; black print, lettering "The Abbot's Choice Scotch Whisky"	Round/127	15.00	20.00	8.00
L-2	Ashtray	White; red/black lettering "Abbot Ale," "Harvest Ale"	Square/140	15.00	20.00	8.00

THE ABBOT'S CHOICE DECANTER, c.1980 AND 1987

This decanter was first produced c.1980 in a honey-amber glaze, with the volume of the contents listed on the label in fluid ounces. In 1987 a second bottle was issued, which was labeled in centilitres.

Backstamp: A. Embossed "Made Exclusively for the Abbots Choice Scotch Whisky John McEwan & Co. Ltd. Leith, Scotland"
B. Embossed "Made Exclusively for the Abbots Choice Scotch Whisky John McEwan & Co. Ltd. Leith, Scotland Liquor Bottle Scotland"

No.	Description	Colourways	Size	U.S.$	Can.$	U.K.£
L-3a	Decanter/Fluid ounces	Honey-amber	255	125.00	155.00	65.00
L-3b	Decanter/Centilitres	Burnt umber	253	120.00	150.00	60.00

AKITA SHOCHU

DRINK POURER

This pourer, intended for a sake bottle, has a straight base and is Wade PDM shape number C53.

Photograph not available
at press time

Backstamp: Unmarked

No.	Description	Colourways	Shape/Size	U.S.$	Can.$	U.K.£
L-4	Drink Pourer	Black porcelain tube; gold/red lettering "Akita Shochu"	Circular/41	30.00	35.00	15.00

ANSELLS BEER

ASHTRAYS, 1955–1990

Style L-6 of this ashtray is decorated with a transfer print of a squirrel.

Ansells The Better Beer

Backstamp: A. "Wade Regicor, London England," laurel leaves, large size
B. "Wade p d m England"

No.	Description	Colourways	Shape/Size	U.S.$	Can.$	U.K.£
L-5	Ashtray	Cream; black lettering "Ansells Beer"	Oval/171	15.00	20.00	8.00
L-6	Ashtray	Yellow; black/gold print; black/red lettering "Ansells"	Oval/190	15.00	20.00	8.00
L-7	Ashtray	Yellow; black lettering "Ansells The Better Beer"	Square/140	15.00	20.00	8.00

BACARDI RUM

ASHTRAY, 1984–1990

Photograph not available
at press time

Backstamp: "Wade p d m England"

No.	Description	Colourways	Size	U.S.$	Can.$	U.K.£
L-8	Rectangular	White; red lettering "Bacardi Rum"	210	13.00	18.00	5.00

BADGER BEER

ASHTRAYS AND WATER JUG, 1955–1990

Styles L-9 and L-10a of these ashtrays are decorated with a transfer print of a badger. The water jug was produced between 1955 and 1962. It has an open spout and also has a print of a badger on it.

Photograph not available
at press time

Backstamp: **A.** "Wade Regicor, London England," laurel leaves, large size
B. "Reginald Corfield Limited Redhill Surrey," "Wade Regicor England"
C. "Wade p d m England"

No.	Description	Colourways	Shape/Size	U.S.$	Can.$	U.K.£
L-9	Ashtray	Blue; yellow print, lettering "Badger Beer"	Oval/216	10.00	15.00	5.00
L-10a	Ashtray	Blue; yellow print, lettering "Badger Beer"	Square/135	15.00	20.00	8.00
L-10b	Ashtray	Blue; yellow lettering "Badger Beer"	Square/140	15.00	20.00	8.00
L-11	Water Jug	Blue; yellow print, lettering "Badger Beer"	Round/170	25.00	30.00	12.00

BALLANTINE'S SCOTCH WHISKY

ASHTRAY, SCOTCH WHISKY DECANTER AND WATER JUGS, 1969–1984

The ashtray and the style L-13b water jug are decorated with a transfer print of the company's crest. The whisky decanter, which has two handles on its neck, was originally produced by Wade Heath in 1969, later production was moved to Wade Ireland. The water jugs have ice-check spouts.

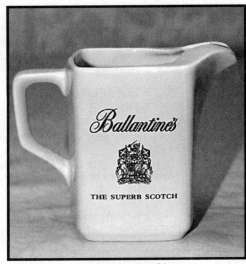

Water Jug (L-13b)

Backstamp: A. "Reginald Corfield Limited Redhill Surrey," "Wade Regicor England"
B. "Wade pdm England"

No.	Description	Colourways	Shape/Size	U.S.$	Can.$	U.K.£
L-12	Ashtray	Black; multi-coloured print; black lettering "Ballantines the Superb Scotch"	Square/108	10.00	15.00	5.00
L-13a	Water Jug	Yellow; red/black lettering "Ballantines Whisky"	Rectangular/150	30.00	35.00	15.00
L-13b	Water Jug	White; multi-coloured print; black lettering "Ballantine's The Superb Scotch"	Rectangular/153	30.00	35.00	15.00
L-14	Whisky Decanter	Black; gold lettering "Ballantines Very Old Scotch Whisky"	Round/75	40.00	45.00	20.00

BANK'S BEER

ASHTRAY, c.1967–1969

Backstamp: A. "Reginald Corfield Limited Redhill Surrey," "Wade Regicor England"
B. "Wade pdm England"

No.	Description	Colourways	Shape/Size	U.S.$	Can.$	U.K.£
L-15	Ashtray	White; black print; red/black lettering "Bank's Beer is Best"	Round/120	15.00	20.00	8.00

BASS BEER

ASHTRAYS, 1955–1984

"Bass For Men" (L-22)

Backstamp: **A.** "Wade Regicor, London England," laurel leaves, large size
B. "Wade pdm England"
C. "Wade p d m England"
D. "Wade P D M Made in England"

No.	Description	Colourways	Shape/Size	U.S.$	Can.$	U.K.£
L-16a	Ashtray	Black; red lettering "Bass Cask Ale"	Oval /171	15.00	20.00	8.00
L-16b	Ashtray	Black; red/gold lettering "Bass Our Finest Ale"	Oval /171	15.00	20.00	8.00
L-17	Ashtray	Mottled black/light brown; brown lettering "Bass"	Rectangular/153	10.00	15.00	5.00
L-18a	Ashtray	White/red; red print, lettering "Bass"	Round/133	25.00	30.00	12.00
L-18b	Ashtray	White/red; red lettering "Bass For Men"	Round/133	25.00	30.00	12.00
L-19	Ashtray	White; gold rim; red/black lettering "Bass Export"	Round/228	10.00	15.00	5.00
L-20	Ashtray	Black; red/gold lettering "Bass"	Square/159	10.00	15.00	5.00
L-21	Ashtray	Mustard yellow; black/red lettering "Great Stuff This Bass"	Square/177	10.00	15.00	5.00
L-22	Ashtray	White; red lettering "Bass For Men"	Square/140 clipped corners	10.00	15.00	5.00

CRUETS, 1968–1969

The mustard cruet in this set is the same square shape as the salt and pepper cruets, with the addition of a lift-off lid.

Salt Cruet

Backstamp: "Reginald Corfield Limited Redhill Surrey," "Wade Regicor England"

No.	Name	Colourways	Size	U.S.$	Can.$	U.K.£
L-23a	Pepper Cruet	White; blue/red lettering "Bass Naturally"	80	8.00	10.00	3.00
L-23b	Salt Cruet	White; blue/red lettering "Bass Naturally"	80	8.00	10.00	3.00
L-24	Mustard Cruet	White; blue/red lettering "Bass Naturally"	76	8.00	10.00	3.00

WATER JUG, 1969–1984

This water jug is round with an open spout and is decorated with a print of hops.

Photograph not available
at press time

Backstamp: "Wade pdm England"

No.	Description	Colourways	Size	U.S.$	Can.$	U.K.£
L-25	Water Jug	White; green/yellow print; multi-coloured lettering "Bass Label"	177	30.00	35.00	15.00

BEAUFORD PLC

BOTTLE OVEN DECANTER, 1994

One hundred of these decanters were produced for the staff of Beauford PLC (the owners of Wade Ceramics) for Christmas 1994. Another 400 decanters were produced for Christmas 1995, 350 for the George Wade staff and 50 for Beauford Engineering. The decanter is shaped like a bottle oven (an old pottery kiln) and has the names of the six Staffordshire pottery towns embossed around the bottom edge: "Burslem—Stoke—Hanley—Fenton—Longton— Tunstall."

Backstamp: A. Embossed "Potteries Decanter by Wade for Beauford PLC"
B. Embossed "Potteries Decanter by Wade"

No.	Description	Colourways	Size	U.S.$	Can.$	U.K.£
L-26a	Christmas 1994	Grey	200	80.00	100.00	40.00
L-26b	Christmas 1995	Dark green	200	80.00	100.00	40.00

BEEFEATER GIN
(BURROUGHS)

ASHTRAYS, 1955–1984

Styles L-28, L-29 and L-30 of these ashtrays are decorated with prints of the Yeomen of the Guard, better known as Beefeaters.

Square ashtray

Ashtray with clipped corners

Backstamp: A. "Wade Regicor, London England," laurel leaves, large size
B. "Reginald Corfield Limited Redhill Surrey," "Wade Regicor England"
C. "Wade pdm England"

No.	Description	Colourways	Shape/Size	U.S.$	Can.$	U.K.£
L-27	Ashtray	White; red lettering "Beefeater London Gin"	Round/205	15.00	20.00	8.00
L-28	Ashtray	Yellow; multi-coloured print; red lettering "Beefeater Dry Gin"	Square/120	15.00	20.00	8.00
L-29	Ashtray	White; multi-coloured print; red lettering "Beefeater The Gin of England"	Square/140	10.00	15.00	5.00
L-30	Ashtray	Yellow; multi-coloured print; red lettering "Beefeater Dry Gin"	Square/120 clipped corners	15.00	20.00	8.00

DRINK POURERS, 1966–1969

These hand-painted Beefeater Gin pourers were first produced in 1966 for Burroughs Beefeater Gin. Style L-31 has a large hat and a porcelain neck below the cork, with the backstamp on the neck; style L-32 has a large hat, with the backstamp on the ruff; style L-33 has a small hat, with the backstamp also on the ruff.

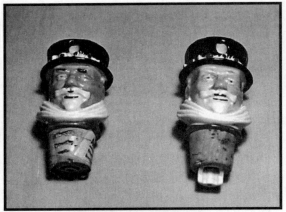

L-33b, left; L-31 right

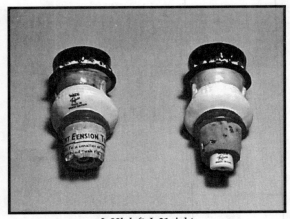

L-33b left, L-31 right

Backstamp: A. "Wade Regicor Made in U.K." on back of collar
B. "Wade Regicor Made in Great Britain" on back of ruff

No.	Description	Colourways	Size	U.S.$	Can.$	U.K.£
L-31	Large Hat/neck	Black hat; pale pink face; light grey hair, eyebrows	82	80.00	100.00	40.00
L-32	Large Hat/ruff	Black hat; pale pink face; light grey hair, eyebrows	77	70.00	90.00	35.00
L-33a	Small Hat/ruff	Black hat; light pink face; dark grey hair, eyebrows	74	63.00	80.00	30.00
L-33b	Small Hat/ruff	Black hat; dark pink face; dark grey hair, eyebrows	74	63.00	80.00	30.00

WATER JUGS

Style L-34 water jugs are round with recessed handles and ice-check spouts. Version L-34-a is decorated with a print of a Beefeater; version L-34b has a print of a Beefeater and Tower Bridge.

Style L-35 water jugs are in the shape of a castle tower and have open spouts. The words "Beefeater The Gin of England" appear on the embossed Beefeater panel of version L-35a, and version L-35b has a print of a Beefeater on the embossed panel with the words "Beefeater Gin" underneath.

Beefeater

Beefeater/Tower Bridge

Backstamp: A. "Reginald Corfield Limited Redhill Surrey," "Wade Regicor England"
B. "Wade pdm England"

No.	Description	Colourways	Size	U.S.$	Can.$	U.K.£
L-34a	Beefeater	White; multi-coloured print; red lettering "Beefeater London Distilled Dry Gin"	153	25.00	30.00	12.00
L-34b	Beefeater/ Tower Bridge	White; multi-coloured print; red lettering "Beefeater London Distilled Dry Gin"	153	25.00	30.00	12.00
L-35a	Gin of England	White; multi-coloured print; red/black lettering "Beefeater The Gin of England"	146	30.00	35.00	15.00
L-35b	Beefeater Gin	White; multi-coloured print; red lettering "Beefeater Gin"	146	30.00	35.00	15.00

ARTHUR BELL AND SONS LTD
(UNITED DISTILLERS UK PLC)

BELL'S WHISKY

ASHTRAYS, 1965–1996

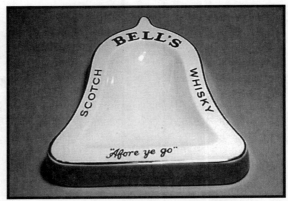

Bell's Scotch Whisky "Afore ye go" (L-36b)

Backstamp: A. "Wade Regicor, London England," laurel leaves, small size
B. "Wade pdm England"
C. "Wade p d m England"

No.	Description	Colourways	Shape\Size	U.S.$	Can.$	U.K.£
L-36a	Ashtray	White; gold lines; red lettering "Bell's Scotch Whisky 'Afore Ye Go'"	Bell\195	30.00	35.00	15.00
L-36b	Ashtray	Cream; black/red lettering "Bell's Scotch Whisky 'Afore Ye Go'"	Bell\195	30.00	35.00	15.00
L-37	Ashtray	Cream; brown/red/cream lettering "Bell's Extra Special"	Bell\228	30.00	35.00	15.00
L-38	Ashtray	Cream; brown/red/cream lettering "Bell's Old Scotch Whisky Extra Special"	Round\177	10.00	15.00	5.00

DECANTERS

For over thirty years, George Wade and Son, now Wade Ceramics, has collaborated with Arthur Bell & Sons Ltd. in producing the bell-shaped decanters with which collectors are so familiar. Bell's is now owned by United Distillers.

Church-Bell Decanters, 1988–1996

In 1988 Bell's changed its decanter design from that resembling a hand bell to what can best be described as a church bell. The new bell shape has a shorter neck, a three-tiered shoulder and a banded skirt. The first decanter issued in the new shape was for the birth of Princess Beatrice on August 8, 1988 (see section on commemoratives). From this date on, all Bell's decanters were produced in the new shape.

Bell's 12-year-old Scotch whisky came in style L-41a and L-41b decanters. They have a recessed shield on the centre of the top shoulder, in which there is a gold label with the words "12 years old" in black lettering.

75 cl

12-Yr.-Old Whisky, black cap

Backstamp: "Genuine Wade Porcelain"

No.	Description	Colourways	Size	U.S.$	Can.$	U.K.£
L-39	Bell, 5 Cl	Gold cap; tan/cream bottle	Miniature/85	30.00	35.00	15.00
L-40	Bell, 75 Cl	Gold cap; tan/cream bottle	200	20.00	30.00	10.00
L-41a	12-Yr.-Old Whisky	Black cap; dark brown/brown bottle	200	50.00	70.00	25.00
L-41b	12-Yr.-Old Whisky	Gold cap; dark blue bottle	200	50.00	70.00	25.00

Church-Bell Chinese New Year, 1990–1996

In 1990 Bell's introduced a series of decanters filled with 12-year-old whisky and decorated with a print of the animal that represents each year. Although Chinese New Year is in February, these decanters were sold during the Christmas season. They have a recessed shield on the centre of the top shoulder, in which there is a gold label with the words "12 years old" in black lettering.

Photograph not available
at press time

Backstamp: "Genuine Wade Porcelain"

No.	Description	Colourways	Size	U.S.$	Can.$	U.K.£
L-42a	1990 Horse	Gold cap; black bottle; gold print	200	60.00	80.00	30.00
L-42b	1991 Sheep	Gold cap; black bottle; gold print	200	60.00	80.00	30.00
L-42c	1992 Monkey	Gold cap; black bottle; gold print	200	60.00	80.00	30.00
L-42d	1993 Rooster	Gold cap; black bottle; gold print	200	60.00	80.00	30.00
L-42e	1994 Dog	Gold cap; black bottle; gold print	200	60.00	80.00	30.00
L-42f	1995 Pig	Gold cap; black bottle; gold print	200	60.00	80.00	30.00
L-42g	1996 Rat	Gold cap; black bottle; gold print	200	30.00	35.00	15.00

Church-Bell Christmas Decanters, 1988–1996

Bell's issued its first Christmas decanter in 1988. The print on the 1988 decanter is of Christmas carollers; a winter scene is on the 1989 decanter. In 1990 the first Christmas-bell decanter with a series theme was introduced. Each year a decanter was issued with a transfer decoration depicting the process of distilling whisky. The 1994 decanter was the first decanter filled with Bell's new 8-year-old blended whisky. It can be distinguished from the other Christmas decanters by a gold band around the rim with "8 yr old" printed on it.

All decanters are green and cream with a multi-coloured scene within a holly wreath.

Christmas 1989

Christmas 1991

Backstamp: "Genuine Wade Porcelain"

No.	Description	Colourways	Size	U.S.$	Can.$	U.K.£
L-43a	Christmas 1988	"We Wish You a Merry Christmas"	200	60.00	80.00	30.00
L-43b	Christmas 1989	"Perth Scotland Winter 1895"	200	60.00	80.00	30.00
L-43c	Christmas 1990	"The Art of Distilling," brewery print	200	60.00	80.00	30.00
L-43d	Christmas 1991	"The Art of Distilling," Oast House print	200	60.00	80.00	30.00
L-43e	Christmas 1992	"The Cooper's Art"	200	60.00	80.00	30.00
L-43f	Christmas 1993	"The Maltman's Art"	200	60.00	80.00	30.00
L-43g	Christmas 1994	"The Blender's Art"	200	60.00	80.00	30.00
L-43h	Christmas 1995	Design unknown	200	60.00	80.00	30.00

Church-Bell Christmas Decanter, Sportsmanship, 1992-1995

In 1992 a series of Bell's Christmas decanters was issued for the export market. They are green and cream and are decorated with transfer prints relating to sportsmanship, framed by a red and green holly wreath.

Christmas 1994

Christmas 1995

Backstamp: "Genuine Wade Porcelain"

No.	Description	Colourways	Size	U.S.$	Can.$	U.K.£
L-44a	Christmas 1992	Sport unknown	200	60.00	80.00	30.00
L-44b	Christmas 1993	"The Royal and Ancient Sport of Golf"	200	60.00	80.00	30.00
L-44c	Christmas 1994	"The Art of Salmon Fishing"	200	60.00	80.00	30.00
L-44d	Christmas 1995	"The Tradition of Highland Games"	200	40.00	45.00	20.00

Church-Bell Decanter, Hawaii, 12-Year-Old Whisky, 1996

Photograph not available
at press time

Backstamp: "Genuine Wade Porcelain"

No.	Description	Colourways	Size	U.S.$	Can.$	U.K.£
L-45	Decanter	Gold cap; red/white/blue flag	200	60.00	80.00	30.00

Church-Bell Decanter, South Africa, 1988-1996

Since 1988 Wade has produced decanters for export to South Africa. They contained Bell's Extra Special and 12-year-old Blend. Versions L-46a and L-46b were produced from 1988 to 1991; versions L-46c and L-46d were produced from 1992 to 1996.

Photograph not available
at press time

Backstamp: "Genuine Wade Porcelain"

No.	Description	Colourways	Size	U.S.$	Can.$	U.K.£
L-46a	12-Year-Old Blend	Green/cream	200	30.00	35.00	15.00
L-46b	Extra Special	Green/cream	200	30.00	35.00	15.00
L-46c	12-Year-Old Blend	Green	200	30.00	35.00	15.00
L-46d	Extra Special	Green	200	30.00	35.00	15.00

Church-Bell Decanter, 20-Year-Old Royal Preserve Whisky, 1994

No.	Description	Colourways	Size	U.S.$	Can.$	U.K.£
L-47	Decanter	Blue bottle; white embossed lettering "Royal Reserve Years 20 Old"	210	40.00	45.00	20.00

Church-Bell Wedding Day Decanter, 1988

This brightly decorated decanter, which contained 12-year-old blended whisky, has the same print of a bridal couple on it that was used on the "Hand-Bell Wedding Day Decanter" of the early 1980s.

Photograph not available
at press time

Backstamp: "Wade Porcelain Decanter from Bell's Scotch Whisky Perth Scotland, 75cl Product of Scotland 40% vol"

No.	Description	Colourways	Size	U.S.$	Can.$	U.K.£
L-48	Decanter	Gold cap; white bottle; multi-coloured print	200	50.00	70.00	25.00

Hand-Bell Decanters, 1965–1988

From 1965 to the late 1970s, the caps on the bells were ceramic; at some time in the late 1970s, they were replaced by plastic ones. The wording on the gold whisky labels varied over the years, as the metric system of weights and measures was introduced. For Bell's commemorative decanters, see the section on commemorative ware.

Hand-Bell Decanters, 750ml, 375ml, 125ml, 50ml

Backstamp: **A.** "Wade Bell's Scotch Whisky, Perth Scotland"
B. "Wade"

No.	Description	Colourways	Size	U.S.$	Can.$	U.K.£
L-49a	Decanter	Brown ceramic cap; red-brown/honey bottle	26 fl. oz./250	30.00	35.00	15.00
L-49b	Decanter	Brown plastic cap; red-brown/honey bottle	750 ml/250	20.00	30.00	10.00
L-50a	Decanter	Brown ceramic cap; red-brown/honey bottle	13 fl. oz./200	20.00	30.00	10.00
L-50b	Decanter	Brown plastic cap; red-brown/honey bottle	375 ml/200	15.00	20.00	8.00
L-51a	Decanter	Brown ceramic cap; red-brown/honey bottle	6 2/3 fl. oz./160	15.00	20.00	8.00
L-51b	Decanter	Brown plastic cap; red-brown/honey bottle	125 ml/160	10.00	15.00	5.00

Miniature Hand-Bell Decanters, 1979–Date Unknown

Backstamp: "Wade Bell's Scotch Whisky, Perth Scotland"

No.	Item	Colourways	Size	U.S.$	Can.$	U.K.£
L-52a	Decanter	Brown ceramic cap; red-brown/honey bottle;	40% vol./103	20.00	30.00	10.00
L-52b	Decanter	Brown plastic cap; red-brown/honey bottle;	50 ml/103	20.00	30.00	10.00

Hand-Bell Decanter, Wedding Day, c.1980

The design for this hand bell is the same as on the 1988 church-bell decanter.

Backstamp: "Wade Porcelain Decanter from Bell's Scotch Whisky Perth Scotland, 75cl Product of Scotland 40% vol"

No.	Description	Colourways	Size	U.S.$	Can.$	U.K.£
L-53	Decanter	Gold cap; white bottle; multi-coloured bridal print "To Celebrate a Joyous Wedding Day"	250	60.00	80.00	30.00

DRINK POURERS, c.1965–1995

These drink pourers are circular with straight bases and can be found with either metal or plastic tubes. The shape number is C53.

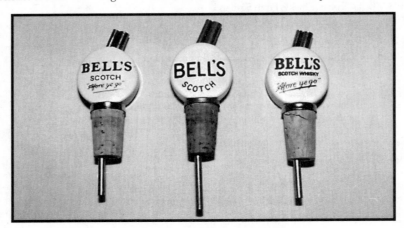

Backstamp: "Wade Regicor Made in UK" on neck

No.	Description	Colourways	Size	U.S.$	Can.$	U.K.£
L-54a	Drink Pourer	White; metal tube, spout; red/black lettering "Bell's Scotch 'Afore Ye Go'"	41 x 44	30.00	35.00	15.00
L-54b	Drink Pourer	White; metal tube, spout; dark blue lettering "Bell's Scotch"	41 x 44	30.00	35.00	15.00
L-54c	Drink Pourer	White; metal tube, spout; red/black lettering "Bell's Scotch Whisky 'Afore Ye Go'"	41 x 44	30.00	35.00	15.00
L-54d	Drink Pourer	White; metal tube, spout; red lettering "Bell's Scotch"	41 x 44	30.00	35.00	15.00
L-54e	Drink Pourer	Yellow; plastic tube; brown/red lettering "Bell's Extra Special"	41 x 44	30.00	35.00	15.00

WATER JUGS, 1968-1996

The style-L-56 jug is decorated with a print of a 19th-century publican holding a bottle of whisky, with a dog beside him.

Backstamp: A. "Reginald Corfield Limited Redhill Surrey," "Wade Regicor England"
B. "Wade p d m England"

No.	Description	Colourways	Shape/Size	U.S.$	Can.$	U.K.£
L-55	Ice-check spout	Cream; brown/red crest, lettering "Bell's Old Scotch Whisky"	Round/205	15.00	20.00	8.00
L-56	Ice-check spout	White; light/dark brown print	Square/127	30.00	35.00	15.00
L-57	Open spout	White; red/black lettering "Bell's Scotch Whisky 'Afore Ye Go'"	Square/140	30.00	35.00	15.00

BIG BEN SCOTCH WHISKY

WATER JUG, 1969–1984

Backstamp: "Wade pdm England"

No.	Description	Colourways	Shape/Size	U.S.$	Can.$	U.K.£
L-58	Open spout	Black; gold print, lettering "Big Ben Very Old Scotch Whisky"	Square/120	25.00	30.00	12.00

BLACK AND WHITE SCOTCH WHISKY
(JAMES BUCHANAN & CO LTD)

ASHTRAYS, c.1969–1990

Backstamp: **A.** "Wade pdm England"
 B. Reginald Corfield Limited Redhill Surrey," "Wade Regicor England"

No.	Description	Colourways	Shape/Size	U.S.$	Can.$	U.K.£
L-59	Ashtray	Black; white lettering "Black & White Scotch Whisky"	Round/127	10.00	15.00	5.00
L-60	Ashtray	White; black lettering "Black & White Scotch Whisky"	Square/127	15.00	20.00	8.00

SCOTTISH TERRIERS WHISKY DECANTER, 1986–1988

The black-and-white "Scottish Terriers Whisky Decanter," which was made for export only, is considered one of Wade's most attractive. There is no Wade backstamp on the decanter; the only reference to Wade is on a gold-and-black oval leaflet which hangs from the neck of one of the dogs. Part of the inscription on the leaflet reads, "This gift decanter has been specially commissioned by James Buchanan and Co. Ltd. from George Wade and Son Ltd."

Backstamp: "Scotch Black & White Whisky Premium, Distilled, Blended and Bottled in Scotland by James Buchanan and Co. Ltd."

No.	Description	Colourways	Size	U.S.$	Can.$	U.K.£
L-61	Decanter	White dog; pink mouth, dark brown eyes; grey nose Black dog; brown eyes	190-200	120.00	150.00	60.00

DRINK POURERS, c.1968

The circular drink pourers have straight bases and are shape number C53. The octagonal pourers are shape number 5455/1.

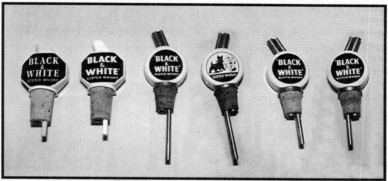

L-63a, L-63b, L-62a, L62a (back), L-62b, L-62b (back)

Backstamp: "Wade Regicor Made in UK" on neck

No.	Description	Colourways	Shape/Size	U.S.$	Can.$	U.K.£
L-62a	Drink Pourer	White; metal tube, spout; black/white dogs, lettering "Black & White Scotch Whisky"	Circular/41	30.00	35.00	15.00
L-62b	Drink Pourer	White; metal tube, spout; black/white lettering "Black & White Scotch Whisky"	Circular/41	30.00	35.00	15.00
L-63a	Drink Pourer	White/black; plastic tube; small white lettering "Black & White Scotch Whisky"	Octagonal/40	30.00	35.00	15.00
L-63b	Drink Pourer	White/black; plastic tube; large white lettering "Black & White Scotch Whisky"	Octagonal/40	30.00	35.00	15.00

WATER JUGS, 1969–1984

Black & White Scotch Whisky

Backstamp: **A.** "Reginald Corfield Limited Redhill Surrey," "Wade Regicor England"
   B. "Wade pdm England"

No.	Description	Colourways	Shape/Size	U.S.$	Can.$	U.K.£
L-64	Ice-check spout	Black; gold rim; black/white print; white lettering "Black & White Scotch Whisky"	Round/155	25.00	30.00	12.00
L-65	Open spout	Black; white lettering "Black & White Scotch Whisky Buchanan's"	Round/127	30.00	35.00	15.00

BLACK BOTTLE SCOTCH WHISKY
(GORDON GRAHAM)

ASHTRAY AND WATER JUGS, 1984–1990

The style L-67 jug has an ice-check spout and is decorated with a print of a bottle. Style L-68 has an open spout.

Ashtray   Jug, open spout

Backstamp: "Wade p d m England"

No.	Description	Colourways	Shape/Size	U.S.$	Can.$	U.K.£
L-66	Ashtray	Black; black/white lettering "Black Bottle Scotch Whisky"	Square/133	10.00	15.00	5.00
L-67	Water Jug ice-check spout	Black; white print, lettering "Black Bottle Scotch Whisky"	Rectangular/140	25.00	30.00	12.00
L-68	Water Jug open spout	Black; gold/white lettering "Black Bottle Scotch Whisky"	Rectangular/140	15.00	20.00	8.00

BLACK VELVET RYE

DRINK POURERS, c.1980

The Wade shape number for the octagonal drink pourer is 5455/1. The square pourer has a notched base and shoulders and came with a plastic tube. It is Wade shape number C52A.

Photograph not available
at press time

Backstamp: Unmarked

No.	Description	Colourways	Shape/Size	U.S.$	Can.$	U.K.£
L-69	Drink Pourer	Black; gold lettering "Black Velvet Rye"	Octagonal/40	30.00	35.00	15.00
L-70	Drink Pourer	Black; gold lettering "Black Velvet Rye"	Square/38	30.00	35.00	15.00

BOMBAY GIN
(BOMBAY SPIRITS COMPANY)

ASHTRAY, ICE BUCKET AND WATER JUG, 1969–1990

The print on these items is of Queen Victoria. The ashtray was produced between 1969 and 1984, the ice bucket in 1971 and the water jug between 1984 and 1990.

Photograph not available
at press time

Backstamp: A. "Wade pdm England"
B. "Wade p d m England"

No.	Description	Colourways	Shape/Size	U.S.$	Can.$	U.K.£
L-71	Ashtray	White; black print, lettering "Bombay London Dry Gin"	Round/153	15.00	20.00	8.00
L-72	Ice Bucket with lid	White; green/gold print, lettering "Bombay Gin"	165	80.00	100.00	40.00
L-73	Water Jug open spout	White; black print, lettering "Bombay London Dry Gin"	Round/165	15.00	20.00	8.00

BOOTH'S GIN

ASHTRAYS, 1955–1984

"Booth's & Orange"

Backstamp: A. "Wade Regicor, London England," laurel leaves, large size
B. "Reginald Corfield Limited Redhill Surrey," "Wade Regicor England"
C. "Wade pdm England"

No.	Description	Colourways	Shape\Size	U.S.$	Can.$	U.K.£
L-74a	Ashtray	White/orange; red print; black lettering "Booth's & Orange"	Round\140	10.00	15.00	5.00
L-74b	Ashtray	White/black; red print; white lettering "Booth's Gin"	Round\146	10.00	15.00	5.00
L-75	Ashtray	Black; red print, white lettering "Booth's Ltd"	Square\140	15.00	20.00	8.00
L-76	Ashtray	Black; red print, white lettering "Booth's Gins"	Square\159	15.00	20.00	8.00

BORZOI VODKA

ASHTRAY AND WATER JUG, 1968–1984

The ashtray was produced between 1968 and 1969, and the water jug between 1969 and 1984. The jug has an ice-check spout and a print on it of the vodka label.

Backstamp: "Reginald Corfield Limited Redhill Surrey," "Wade Regicor England"

No.	Description	Colourways	Shape/Size	U.S.$	Can.$	U.K.£
L-77	Ashtray	White; red/black/white lettering "Borzoi Vodka"	Square/153	15.00	20.00	8.00
L-78	Water Jug	White; multi-coloured print	Rectangular/159	25.00	30.00	12.00

BOWMORE MALT WHISKY

ASHTRAY, 1969–1984

Backstamp: "Wade pdm England"

No.	Description	Colourways	Shape/Size	U.S.$	Can.$	U.K.£
L-79	Ashtray	Dark brown; gold print/lettering "Bowmore Pure Malt Whisky"	Round/146	15.00	20.00	8.00

BRAKSPEAR'S HENLEY ALES

WATER JUG, 1968–1969

Backstamp: "Reginald Corfield Limited Redhill Surrey," "Wade Regicor England"

No.	Description	Colourways	Shape/Size	U.S.$	Can.$	U.K.£
L-80	Water Jug/ open spout	White; red/black print; black lettering "Brakspear's Henley Ales"	Rectangular/145	30.00	35.00	15.00

BREAKER REAL MALT LIQUOR

ASHTRAY, 1969–1984

Backstamp: "Wade pdm England"

No.	Description	Colourways	Shape/Size	U.S.$	Can.$	U.K.£
L-81	Ashtray	Peach; blue and white print; white lettering "Breaker Real Malt Liquor"	Round/205	10.00	15.00	5.00

BRONTE LIQUEUR

LIQUEUR JUGS, 1991-1993

Jugs style L-83 and L-84 have a cameo portrait of Emily Bronte as part of the label, while jug L-85 has an embossed portrait of Emily Bronte on the front of the jug.

Amber jug with spout	**White and amber jug without spout**	**White and amber jug with spout**

Backstamp: **A.** Raised "Created for the James B Beam Import Corp by Bronte Liqueur Co. Ltd"
B. Embossed "Created for the James Beam Import Corp by Bronte Liqueur York Yorkshire England Made by Wade Ireland"
C. Unmarked

No.	Name	Colourways	Shape/Size	U.S.$	Can.$	U.K.£
L-82a	Jug	White/amber; yellow/brown label	Miniature/74	15.00	20.00	8.00
L-82b	Jug	Amber; brown/yellow label	Miniature/76	15.00	20.00	8.00
L-83	Jug with spout	Amber; cream/brown label	3/4 pint/150	40.00	45.00	20.00
L-84	Jug without spout	White/amber; yellow/brown label	35 cl/175	40.00	45.00	20.00
L-85	Jug with spout	White/amber; embossed cameo	35 cl/175	50.00	70.00	25.00

BUCHANAN'S SCOTCH WHISKY

ASHTRAY AND WATER JUGS, 1968-1990

The ashtray was produced between 1968 and 1969, the style L-87 jug between 1969 and 1984 and style L-88 between 1969 and 1990. The style L-87 jug has an ice-check spout and no handle; style L-88 has an open spout. The print on L-88b is a portrait of a man.

"Buchanan's de luxe Scotch Whisky" Ashtray

"Buchanan's de luxe Scotch Whisky" Jug (L-87)

Backstamp: **A.** "Reginald Corfield Limited Redhill Surrey," "Wade Regicor England"
B. "Wade pdm England"
C. "Wade p d m England"

No.	Description	Colourways	Shape/Size	U.S.$	Can.$	U.K.£
L-86	Ashtray	Royal blue; gold lettering "Buchanan's de luxe Scotch Whisky"	Square/205	15.00	20.00	8.00
L-87	Jug	Royal blue; gold lettering "Buchanan's de luxe Scotch Whisky"	Round/177	25.00	30.00	12.00
L-88a	Jug	Yellow; black lettering "Buchanan's Scotch"	Round/155	25.00	30.00	12.00
L-88b	Jug	White; multi-coloured print; black lettering "The Buchanan The Scotch of a Lifetime"	Round/153	30.00	35.00	15.00

BULMERS CIDER

ASHTRAY, 1969-1984

The print on this ashtray is of a woodpecker.

Photograph not available
at press time

Backstamp: "Wade pdm England"

No.	Description	Colourways	Shape/Size	U.S.$	Can.$	U.K.£
L-89	Ashtray	Yellow; multi-coloured print; red/white lettering "Bulmers Woodpecker Cider"	Oval/171	10.00	15.00	5.00

BUSHMILL'S IRISH WHISKEY

WATER JUG, 1984-1990

This jug has an ice-check spout.

Photograph not available
at press time

Backstamp: "Wade p d m England"

No.	Description	Colourways	Shape/Size	U.S.$	Can.$	U.K.£
L-90	Water Jug	Black; gold/black/red label, lettering, "Special Old Irish Whiskey Black Bush"	Rectangular/133	25.00	30.00	12.00

CAIN'S BEER

ASHTRAY, 1993-1996

The print on this ashtray is of a building.

Photograph not available
at press time

Backstamp: "Wade P D M Made in England"

No.	Description	Colourways	Shape/Size	U.S.$	Can.$	U.K.£
L-91	Ashtray	Yellow; gold/black print; red/gold/black lettering "Cain's Traditional English Beer"	Arch/171	15.00	20.00	8.00

CANADIAN CLUB WHISKY

ASHTRAY AND WATER JUGS, 1968-1984

Both water jugs have ice-check spouts.

Photograph not available
at press time

Backstamp: A. "Wade p d m England"
B. "Reginald Corfield Limited Redhill Surrey," "Wade Regicor England"

No.	Description	Colourways	Shape/Size	U.S.$	Can.$	U.K.£
L-92	Ashtray	White; red/black lettering "Canadian Club"	101	15.00	20.00	8.00
L-93	Water Jug	White; black lettering "Canadian Club"	Oval/171	30.00	35.00	15.00
L-94	Water Jug	White; red/black lettering "Canadian Club"	Square/140	30.00	35.00	15.00

CAPTAIN MORGAN RUM

ASHTRAY AND DRINK POURER, c.1958-1962

The ashtrays were produced between 1960 and 1962, and the drink pourer circa 1958 to circa 1962. The drink pourer is all porcelain and has a round base. These items are decorated with a print of Captain Morgan.

Rowboat Ashtray (L-95b)

Drink Pourer

Backstamp: A. "Wade Regicor, London England," laurel leaves, large size
B. "Wade Regicor Made in UK"

No.	Description	Colourways	Shape/Size	U.S.$	Can.$	U.K.£
L-95a	Ashtray	Black/white boat; multi-coloured print; black/white lettering on stern, sides and inside boat "Captain Morgan Rum"	Boat/235	40.00	45.00	20.00
L-95b	Ashtray	Black/white boat; multi-coloured print; black/white lettering inside boat "Captain Morgan Rum"	Boat/235	40.00	45.00	20.00
L-96	Drink Pourer	White; porcelain spout, tube; multi-coloured print	Circular/41	30.00	35.00	15.00

CARLING BLACK LABEL

ASHTRAYS AND WATER JUGS, 1968-1990

The ashtrays were produced between 1968 and 1990 and the water jugs between 1969 and 1990. The style L-99 jug has an ice-check spout; the spout on style L-100 is open.

Photograph not available
at press time

Backstamp: A. "Reginald Corfield Limited Redhill Surrey," "Wade Regicor England"
B. "Wade pdm England"
C. "Wade p d m England"

No.	Description	Colourways	Shape/Size	U.S.$	Can.$	U.K.£
L-97	Ashtray	Black/gold; red/white/black lettering "Carling Black Label Lager Beer"	Rectangular/210	15.00	20.00	8.00
L-98	Ashtray	Black; red/white/black lettering "Black Label"	Square/140	10.00	15.00	5.00
L-99	Water Jug	Black; red/white/gold lettering " Carling Black Label Lager"	Triangular/165	25.00	30.00	12.00
L-100	Water Jug	White; black/red/white "Carling Black Label Lager"	Triangular/165	25.00	30.00	12.00

CARLSBERG LAGER

ASHTRAYS, 1969-1984

The print on version L-101a is of a scene of Copenhagen.

Photograph not available
at press time

Backstamp: "Wade pdm England"

No.	Description	Colourways	Shape/Size	U.S.$	Can.$	U.K.£
L-101a	Ashtray	White; black print; red lettering "Carlsberg"	Square/140	15.00	20.00	8.00
L-101b	Ashtray	White; black lettering "Carlsberg Export HOF"	Square/140	15.00	20.00	8.00

CATTO'S SCOTCH WHISKY

ASHTRAY AND WATER JUG, 1955-1990

The jug has an ice-check spout.

Ashtray "Catto's Scotch Whisky"

Backstamp: A. "Wade Regicor, London England" laurel leaves, large size
B. "Wade p d m England"

No.	Description	Colourways	Shape/Size	U.S.$	Can.$	U.K.£
L-102	Ashtray	Black; gold lettering "Catto's Scotch Whisky"	Square/171	10.00	15.00	5.00
L-103	Water Jug	Black; gold lettering "Catto's Scotch Whisky"	Round/165	25.00	30.00	12.00

CELEBRATION CREAM

ASHTRAY, 1962-1968

Backstamp: "Wade Regicor, London England" laurel leaves, small size

No.	Description	Colourways	Shape/Size	U.S.$	Can.$	U.K.£
L-104	Ashtray	White; gold/black logo; black lettering "Celebration Cream Sherry by Domecq"	Round/120	15.00	20.00	8.00

CHARRINGTON

ASHTRAYS AND TOBY JUGS, c.1958-1990

The ashtrays were produced between 1969 and 1990 and the toby jugs were issued circa 1958.

Oval Ashtray (L-105)

"Charrington" Toby Jug (L-107a)

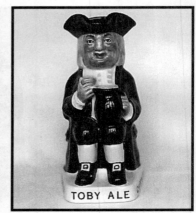

"Toby Ale" Jug (L-107b)

Backstamp: **A.** "Wade Regicor, London England, Hand Painted"
B. "Wade pdm England"
C. "Wade p d m England"

No.	Description	Colourways	Shape/Size	U.S.$	Can.$	U.K.£
L-105	Ashtray	Mottled grey; green/yellow print; yellow lettering "Charrington Established 1757"	Oval/216	20.00	30.00	10.00
L-106	Ashtray	Cream; black lettering "Charrington IP"	Square/140	10.00	15.00	5.00
L-107a	Toby Jug	Maroon trousers; dark green coat; lettering "Charrington"	180	165.00	230.00	85.00
L-107b	Toby Jug	Maroon trousers; dark green coat; lettering "Toby Ale"	180	165.00	230.00	85.00

Derivative

CHARRINGTON TOBY ALE LAMP, c.1958-1984

Advertising lamps were not sold to the public but were commissioned by breweries to advertise and decorate the public houses and hotel bars that sold their beers. This "Charrington Toby Ale Lamp" is from the same mould as that used for the toby jugs. A hole was drilled in the base for the wiring and lamp fittings were added. The lettering is around the sides of the base. This lamp was originally produced c.1958, then reissued between 1969 and 1984.

Photograph not available
at press time

Backstamp: **A.** "Wade Regicor, London England, Hand Painted"
B. "Wade pdm England"

No.	Description	Colourways	Size	U.S.$	Can.$	U.K.£
L-107c1	Lamp	Maroon trousers; dark green coat	180	125.00	155.00	65.00

CHEQUERS SCOTCH WHISKY

WATER JUG, 1969-1984

This jug has an ice-check spout.

Photograph not available
at press time

Backstamp: "Wade pdm England"

No.	Description	Colourways	Shape/Size	U.S.$	Can.$	U.K.£
L-108	Water Jug	Green; white lettering "Chequers Scotch Whisky"	Round/153	25.00	30.00	12.00

CHIVAS SCOTCH WHISKY

ASHTRAY, 1984-1995

Photograph not available
at press time

Backstamp: "Wade P D M England"

No.	Description	Colourways	Shape/Size	U.S.$	Can.$	U.K.£
L-109	Round	Black; white lettering "Chivas Scotch"	Round/140	15.00	20.00	8.00

HIP FLASKS AND WATER JUG, 1974-1996

These flat-sided flasks were issued between 1974 and 1995 and the water jug was issued between 1984 and 1996.

Photograph not available
at press time

Backstamp: A. "Chivas Brothers Limited, Aberdeen Scotland, Wade England, Liquor Bottle"
B. Wade p d m England"

No.	Description	Colourways	Size	U.S.$	Can.$	U.K.£
L-110a	Hip Flask	Brown	200ml/153	25.00	30.00	12.00
L-110b	Hip Flask	Indigo blue	200ml/153	25.00	30.00	12.00
L-110c	Hip Flask	Light green	200ml/153	25.00	30.00	12.00
L-110d	Hip Flask	Pink	200ml/153	25.00	30.00	12.00
L-110e	Hip Flask	Sea green	200ml/153	25.00	30.00	12.00
L-111	Water Jug/ open spout	Maroon; gold lettering "Chivas Regal 12 yr old Whisky"	205	25.00	30.00	12.00

ROYAL SALUTE WHISKY BOTTLES, 1974-1996

Backstamp: "Chivas Brothers Limited, Aberdeen Scotland, Wade England, Liquor Bottle"

No.	Description	Colourways	Size	U.S.$	Can.$	U.K.£
L-112a	Whisky Bottle	Brown; gold labels	750ml/215	40.00	45.00	20.00
L-112b	Whisky Bottle	Indigo blue; gold labels	750ml/215	40.00	45.00	20.00
L-112c	Whisky Bottle	Light green; gold labels	750ml/215	40.00	45.00	20.00
L-112d	Whisky Bottle	Pink; gold labels	750ml/215	40.00	45.00	20.00
L-112e	Whisky Bottle	Sea green; gold labels	750ml/215	40.00	45.00	20.00
L-113a	Whisky Bottle	Brown; gold labels	375ml/185	30.00	35.00	15.00
L-113b	Whisky Bottle	Indigo blue; gold labels	375ml/185	30.00	35.00	15.00
L-113c	Whisky Bottle	Light green; gold labels	375ml/185	30.00	35.00	15.00
L-113d	Whisky Bottle	Pink; gold labels	375ml/185	30.00	35.00	15.00
L-113e	Whisky Bottle	Sea green; gold labels	375ml/185	30.00	35.00	15.00
L-114a	Whisky Bottle	Brown; gold labels	200ml/153	20.00	30.00	10.00
L-114b	Whisky Bottle	Indigo blue; gold labels	200ml/153	20.00	30.00	10.00
L-114c	Whisky Bottle	Light green; gold labels	200ml/153	20.00	30.00	10.00
L-114d	Whisky Bottle	Pink; gold labels	200ml/153	20.00	30.00	10.00
L-114e	Whisky Bottle	Sea green	200ml/153	20.00	30.00	10.00
L-115a	Whisky Bottle	Indigo blue; gold labels	50ml/101	26.00	36.00	8.00
L-115b	Whisky Bottle	Pink; gold labels	50ml/101	26.00	36.00	8.00
L-115c	Whisky Bottle	Sea green; gold labels	50ml/101	26.00	36.00	8.00

CINZANO

ASHTRAY, 1969-1984

Photograph not available
at press time

Backstamp: "Wade pdm England"

No.	Description	Colourways	Shape/Size	U.S.$	Can.$	U.K.£
L-116	Ashtray	White; black lettering "Cinzano Secco"	Square/140	10.00	15.00	5.00

CLUNY SCOTCH WHISKY

ASHTRAYS, 1955-1969

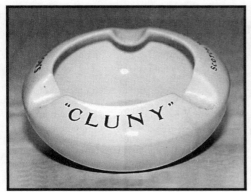

Round Ashtray (L-117)

Square Ashtray (L-118)

Backstamp: **A.** "Wade Regicor, London England," laurel leaves, large size
B. "Reginald Corfield Limited Redhill Surrey," "Wade Regicor England"

No.	Description	Colourways	Shape/Size	U.S.$	Can.$	U.K.£
L-117	Ashtray	White; red/black lettering "Cluny Scotch Whisky"	Round/159	15.00	20.00	8.00
L-118	Ashtray	Black; gold lettering "Cluny Scotch Whisky"	Square/114	15.00	20.00	8.00

COSSACK VODKA

WATER JUG, 1984-1990

This jug has an ice-check spout and no handle.

Photograph not available
at press time

Backstamp: "Wade p d m England"

No.	Description	Colourways	Shape/Size	U.S.$	Can.$	U.K.£
L-119	Water Jug	Royal blue; white lettering "Cossack Vodka"	Round/177	15.00	20.00	8.00

COURVOISIER COGNAC

ASHTRAY AND DRINK POURER, 1969-1984

The drink pourer was produced circa 1970. It is shape number 5455/1.

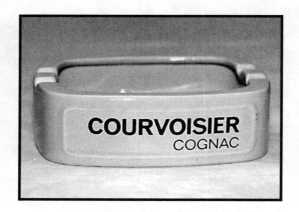

Backstamp: "Wade pdm England"

No.	Description	Colourways	Shape/Size	U.S.$	Can.$	U.K.£
L-120	Ashtray	Grey; red lettering "Courvoisier Cognac"	Rectangular /147	10.00	15.00	5.00
L-121	Drink Pourer	Black; plastic tube; gold lettering "Courvoisier Cognac"	Octagonal/40	30.00	35.00	15.00

CRAWFORD'S SCOTCH WHISKY

WATER JUGS, 1955-1984

The spouts on both these jugs are open.

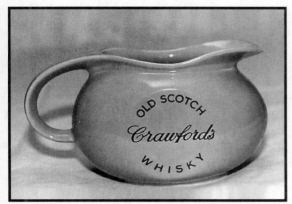

Round Jug "Old Scotch Crawford's Whisky"

Square Jug "Crawford's Scotch Whisky"

Backstamp: A. "Wade Regicor, London England," laurel leaves, large size
B. "Wade pdm England"

No.	Description	Colourways	Shape/Size	U.S.$	Can.$	U.K.£
L-122	Water Jug	Salmon pink; red/black lettering " Old Scotch Crawford's Whisky"	Round/102	30.00	35.00	15.00
L-123	Water Jug	Maroon; white lettering "Crawford's Scotch Whisky"	Square/101	25.00	30.00	12.00

CREAM OF THE BARLEY

ASHTRAY, 1955-1962

The print on this ashtray is of a whisky bottle.

Photograph not available
at press time

Backstamp: "Wade Regicor, London England," laurel leaves, large size

No.	Description	Colourways	Shape/Size	U.S.$	Can.$	U.K.£
L-124	Ashtray	White; honey print; black/red lettering "Cream of the Barley Quality Scotch"	Square/133	15.00	20.00	8.00

CROFT WHISKY

DRINK POURER

This pourer, shape number 52A, is square with a notched base and shoulders.

Photograph not available
at press time

Backstamp: Unmarked

No.	Description	Colourways	Shape/Size	U.S.$	Can.$	U.K.£
L-125	Drink Pourer	Black; plastic tube; gold/white lettering "Croft Original"	Square/38	30.00	35.00	15.00

CUTTY SARK SCOTCH WHISKY
(BERRY BROS. & RUDD LTD.)

ASHTRAY AND WATER JUGS, 1968-1990

The ashtray was produced between 1968 and 1969, the water jugs between 1969 and 1990. The round jug has an ice-check spout and is decorated with a print of the bottle label. Jug L-128 has an open spout and no handle. The print on it depicts a sailing ship.

Water Jug "Bottle Label"

Water Jug "Scotch Whisky"

Backstamp: A. "Reginald Corfield Limited Redhill Surrey," "Wade Regicor England"
B. "Wade p d m England"
C. "Wade pdm England Imported by the Buckingham Corporation New York NY. Distilled Blended and Bottled in Scotland 86 proof"

No.	Description	Colourways	Shape/Size	U.S.$	Can.$	U.K.£
L-126	Ashtray	Black; yellow lettering "Cutty Sark Scotch Whisky"	Round/127	10.00	15.00	5.00
L-127	Water Jug	Dark green; yellow bottle label print; black lettering "Cutty Sark"	Round/165	20.00	30.00	10.00
L-128	Water Jug	Yellow; white print; black lettering "Cutty Sark Scotch Whisky"	Rectangular/170	40.00	45.00	20.00

DEWAR'S WHISKY

ASHTRAYS AND DRINK POURERS, 1955-1990

The ashtrays were produced between 1955 and 1990 and the drink pourers were issued circa 1960. These circular pourers, shape number C53, have a straight base. Version L-135a is an older pourer, with a flap on the top of the metal spout to prevent dust getting in.

Oval Ashtray "Dewar's Special Scotch Whisky"

Drink Pourer (L-135a)

Backstamp: **A.** "Wade Regicor, London England," laurel leaves, large size
B. "Wade Regicor, London England," laurel leaves, small size
C. "Wade pdm England"
D. "Wade p d m England"
E. "Wade Regicor Made in UK" on neck

No.	Description	Colourways	Shape/Size	U.S.$	Can.$	U.K.£
L-129	Ashtray	White; red/black lettering "Dewar's"	D-shaped/190	30.00	35.00	15.00
L-130	Ashtray	Yellow; red/black lettering "Dewar's Special Scotch Whisky"	Oval/152	10.00	15.00	5.00
L-131	Ashtray	Yellow; red/black lettering "Dewar's Scotch Whisky"	Oval/165	10.00	15.00	5.00
L-132a	Ashtray	White; red/black lettering "Dewar's White Label"	Round/120	15.00	20.00	8.00
L-132b	Ashtray	Yellow; red/black lettering "Dewar's White Label"	Round/120	15.00	20.00	8.00
L-133	Ashtray	Black; maroon/white lettering "Dewar's De Luxe Ancestor Scotch Whisky"	Square/101	25.00	30.00	12.00
L-134	Ashtray	Black/maroon; white lettering "Dewar's De Luxe Ancestor Scotch Whisky"	Square/140	10.00	15.00	5.00
L-135a	Drink Pourer	White/yellow; metal tube, spout, flap; red/black lettering "Dewar's Special Scotch Whisky"	Circular/41	30.00	35.00	15.00
L-135b	Drink Pourer	White; plastic tube; black/red lettering "Dewar's White Label"	Circular/41	30.00	35.00	15.00
L-135c	Drink Pourer	White; metal tube, spout; red/black lettering "White Label Dewar's"	Circular/41	30.00	35.00	15.00

WATER JUGS, 1955-1990

These jugs all have ice-check spouts and are decorated with a print of the Dewar's "Highlander." Style L-137 has a recessed handle.

Round Jug, short spout (L-136)

Round Jug, long spout (L-138)

Backstamp:
- **A.** "Wade Regicor, London England," laurel leaves, large size
- **B.** "Reginald Corfield Limited Redhill Surrey," "Wade Regicor England"
- **C.** "Wade pdm England"

No.	Description	Colourways	Shape/Size	U.S.$	Can.$	U.K.£
L-136	Water Jug, short spout	Yellow; black print, lettering "Dewar's Special Scotch Whisky"	Round/159	30.00	35.00	15.00
L-137	Water Jug, flat sides	Yellow; red/black print, lettering "Dewar's Fine Scotch Whisky"	Round/146	25.00	30.00	12.00
L-138	Water Jug, long spout	White; black print, black/red lettering "Dewars White Label Scotch Whisky"	Round/153	25.00	30.00	12.00
L-139a	Water Jug, long spount	Yellow; black print, black/red lettering "Dewars is the Scotch"	Round/165	25.00	30.00	12.00
L-139b	Water Jug, long spout	Yellow; black/red print, lettering "White Label Dewar's Scotch Whisky"	Round/165	25.00	30.00	12.00

DIMPLE SCOTCH WHISKY

ASHTRAY, 1994-1996

Photograph not available
at press time

Backstamp: "Wade P D M Made in England"

No.	Description	Colourways	Shape/Size	U.S.$	Can.$	U.K.£
L-140	Ashtray	Maroon; gold crest, lettering "The Original Dimple"	Triangular/177	10.00	15.00	5.00

DECANTERS

Souvenir Decanters, 1984-1990

Dimple Superior de luxe Scotch Whisky

Backstamp: "John Haig & Co Ltd. Edinburgh, Scotland"

No.	Description	Colourways	Size	U.S.$	Can.$	U.K.£
L-141a	Superior de luxe Scotch Whisky	White; gold laurel leaves; multi-coloured print, lettering "Dimple"	215	40.00	45.00	20.00
L-141b	Dimple Export, Hawaii	White; gold laurel leaves; multi-coloured print	216	40.00	45.00	20.00
L-141c	Dimple Export, Hong Kong	Unknown	216	40.00	45.00	20.00

Sports Decanters, 1984-1986

1984 Los Angeles

1985 Tsukuba

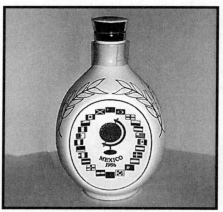

1986 Mexico

1986 Scotland

Backstamp: " John Haig & Co. Ltd 75cl 43GL Markinch Scotland"

No.	Description	Colourways	Size	U.S.$	Can.$	U.K.£
L-142a	1984 Los Angeles	White/gold laurel leaves; blue/red wreath "In Commemoration of the Summer Games Los Angeles 1984"	216	40.00	45.00	20.00
L-142b	1985 Tsukuba	White/gold laurel leaves; blue/yellow birds "In Commemoration of Tsukuba Expo '85"	216	40.00	45.00	20.00
L-142c	1986 Mexico	White/gold laurel leaves; flags of the world "Mexico 1986"	216	40.00	45.00	20.00
L-142d	1986 Scotland	White/gold laurel leaves; emblems of Scotland and the Games "XIII Commonwealth Games Scotland 1986"	216	40.00	45.00	20.00

Chinese New Year Decanters, 1986-1990

These decanters are decorated with prints of the animals that represent each year.

1989 Year of the Snake

1990 Year of the Horse

Backstamp: Circular gold print "John Haig 75cl 43 GL Edinburgh Scotland"

No.	Description	Colourways	Size	U.S.$	Can.$	U.K.£
L-143a	1986 Year of the Tiger	Unknown colours	216	40.00	45.00	20.00
L-143b	1987 Year of the Rabbit	Unknown colours	216	40.00	45.00	20.00
L-143c	1988 Year of the Dragon	Unknown colours	216	40.00	45.00	20.00
L-143d	1989 Year of the Snake	White; gold laurel leaves; gold snake	216	40.00	45.00	20.00
L-143e	1990 Year of the Horse	Black; gold archer	216	40.00	45.00	20.00

DRINK POURER, 1990-1995

This drink pourer, shape C53, has a straight base.

Photograph not available
at press time

No.	Description	Colourways	Shape/Size	U.S.$	Can.$	U.K.£
L-144	Drink Pourer	White/red; black lettering "Haig"	Circular/41	30.00	35.00	15.00

DON CORTEZ

ASHTRAY, 1968-1969

Backstamp: "Reginald Corfield Limited Redhill Surrey," "Wade Regicor England"

No.	Description	Colourways	Shape/Size	U.S.$	Can.$	U.K.£
L-145	Ashtray	White; black/orange lettering "Don Cortez Spanish Wines by Grants of St. James's"	Square/146	15.00	20.00	8.00

DON JON ALE

ASHTRAY, 1955-1962

Backstamp: "Wade Regicor, London England," laurel leaves, large size

No.	Description	Colourways	Shape/Size	U.S.$	Can.$	U.K.£
L-146	Ashtray	White; yellow print; red/yellow lettering "You're on the Spot for Don Jon The Gold Medal Ale"	Square/140	15.00	20.00	8.00

DOUBLE CENTURY SHERRY

ASHTRAY, 1955-1962

Photograph not available
at press time

Backstamp: "Wade Regicor, London England," laurel leaves, large size

No.	Description	Colourways	Shape/Size	U.S.$	Can.$	U.K.£
L-147	Ashtray	White; black lettering "Double Century Sherry"	Round/140	15.00	20.00	8.00

DOUBLE DIAMOND

ASHTRAYS, 1968-1990

Photograph not available
at press time

Backstamp: A. "Reginald Corfield Limited Redhill Surrey," "Wade Regicor England"
B. "Wade p d m England"

No.	Description	Colourways	Shape/Size	U.S.$	Can.$	U.K.£
L-148	Ashtray	White; green lettering "Double Diamond"	Round/114	15.00	20.00	8.00
L-149	Ashtray	Black; multi-coloured label, print "Double Diamond"	Square/101	10.00	15.00	5.00

DRAMBUIE

DRINK POURERS

The style L-150 pourer, shape number C52A, has a notched base and shoulders. Style L-151 is shape C57, which has a rounded top and base and straight sides.

Photograph not available
at press time

Backstamp: Unmarked

No.	Description	Colourways	Shape/Size	U.S.$	Can.$	U.K.£
L-150	Drink Pourer	White; plastic tube; red lettering "Drambuie"	Square/38	30.00	35.00	15.00
L-151	Drink Pourer	White; metal tube; red lettering "Drambuie"	Oval/41	30.00	35.00	15.00

DRYBROUGHS

LOVING CUP, 1981

This loving cup has a print of the brewery with the words, "The Location of Drybroughs' First Brewery 1750-1981" on the front.

Photograph not available
at press time

Backstamp: Unknown

No.	Description	Colourways	Shape/Size	U.S.$	Can.$	U.K.£
L-152	Loving Cup	Brown; black/brown label, lettering	Pint/120	50.00	70.00	25.00

DUNCAN MACGREGOR SCOTCH WHISKY

WATER JUG, 1969-1984

This jug has an ice-check spout.

Photograph not available
at press time

Backstamp: "Wade pdm England"

No.	Description	Colourways	Shape/Size	U.S.$	Can.$	U.K.£
L-153	Water Jug	Cream; brown lettering "Duncan MacGregor Scotch Whisky"	Triangular/146	25.00	30.00	12.00

THE FAMOUS GROUSE SCOTCH WHISKY
(MATTHEW CLOAG)

ASHTRAYS, DECANTER, DRINK POURERS AND WATER JUGS, 1969-1996

The ashtrays were produced between 1969 and 1996, the decanter from 1993 to 1996, the drink pourers circa 1970 and the water jugs between 1984 and 1996. The octagonal pourer is shape number 5455/1. The square pourers, shape C52A, have a notched base and shoulders. The water jugs have open spouts. All items are decorated with the Grouse Scotch logo.

Ashtray (L-155)

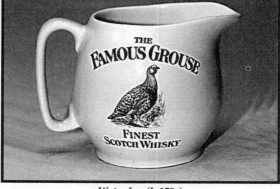

Water Jug (L-159a)

Backstamp: **A.** "Wade pdm England"
     B. "Wade P D M England"
     C. "Genuine Wade Porcelain"

No.	Description	Colourways	Shape/Size	U.S.$	Can.$	U.K.£
L-154	Ashtray	Yellow; red lettering, "The Famous Grouse"	Round/140	15.00	20.00	5.00
L-155	Ashtray	White; brown print; red/black lettering "The Famous Grouse Finest Scotch Whisky"	Round/185	15.00	20.00	5.00
L-156	Decanter	Pale yellow; multi-coloured print, lettering "Famous Grouse Decanter"	248	70.00	90.00	35.00
L-157	Pourer	Cream/white; plastic tube; brown/black lettering "The Famous Grouse"	Octagonal/40	30.00	35.00	15.00
L-158a	Pourer	White/cream; plastic tube; brown lettering "The Famous Grouse"	Square/38	30.00	35.00	15.00
L-158b	Pourer	White/cream; red/black lettering "The Famous Grouse"	Square/38	30.00	35.00	15.00
L-159a	Water Jug	White; brown print; red/brown lettering "The Famous Grouse Finest Scotch Whisky"	Round/114	30.00	35.00	15.00
L-159b	Water Jug	Cream; brown print; red/brown lettering "The Famous Grouse"	Round/114	30.00	35.00	15.00

FINDLATERS SCOTCH WHISKY LTD.

DECANTERS, 1986-1990

These decanters are shaped like footballs and rugby balls. The lettering on the rugby balls includes, "Findlaters First XV 43% Vol. Blended Scotch Whisky."

"1889 Centenary 1989"

Backstamp: Black transfer print "Designed for Findlaters Scotch Whisky—hand crafted porcelain by Wade Ceramics"

No.	Decsription	Colourways	Size	U.S.$	Can.$	U.K.£
L-160a	Football	White/black; black lettering	130	80.00	100.00	40.00
L-160b	Football	White/black; black lettering "1889 Centenary 1989"	130	80.00	100.00	40.00
L-160c	Football	White/black; black lettering "World Cup Italy 1990"	130	90.00	135.00	50.00
L-161a	Rugby Ball	Beige; black lettering	200	80.00	100.00	40.00
L-161b	Rugby Ball	White; black lettering	200	80.00	100.00	40.00

FLOWERS BEER

THE FLOWERS BREWMASTER, c.1958-c1962

The Flowers brewmaster was the logo for the Flowers Brewery before it was taken over by Whitbread, and he serves as the model for this figure. This extremely rare figure was produced as an advertising model, meant to stand on the bar of a public house.

Backstamp: "Wade Regicor, London England" laurel leaves, large size

No.	Description	Colourways	Size	U.S.$	Can.$	U.K.£
L-162	Bar Figure	Red hat, leggings; white shirt, apron; black shoes; gold medallion, red/gold tankard, gold lettering "Brewmaster Brewed by Flowers"	140	290.00	325.00	150.00

FULLER SMITH & TURNER P.L.C.

WATER JUGS, 1984-1995

The spouts on these water jugs are open.

Backstamp: A. "Wade p d m England"
B. "Wade p d m Made in England"

No.	Description	Colourways	Shape/Size	U.S.$	Can.$	U.K.£
L-163	Water Jug	Brown; off-white print; embossed lettering "Fuller Smith & Turner P.L.C. Established 1845 Griffin Brewery Chiswick Fullers"	Rectangular/155	25.00	30.00	12.00
L-164	Water Jug	Dark brown; light brown lettering "Fullers-Griffin Brewery Chiswick"	Rectangular/165	25.00	30.00	12.00

GEORGE SANDEMAN AND CO. LTD.

DECANTERS, 1958-1960

Backstamp: Embossed "Wade England," white transfer print "Wade England"

No.	Description	Colourways	Size	U.S.$	Can.$	U.K.£
L-165a	Sandeman Port	Black; ruby red glass	215	60.00	80.00	30.00
L-165b	Sandeman Sherry	Black; golden yellow glass	215	60.00	80.00	30.00

GILBEY'S GIN
(W & A GILBEYS LIMITED)

ASHTRAYS, 1955-1984

Ashtray "Gilbey's London Dry Gin"

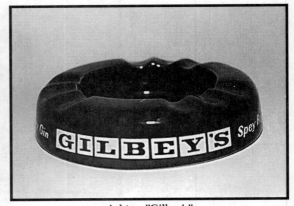

Ashtray "Gilbey's"

Backstamp: "Wade Regicor, London England" laurel leaves, large size
"Wade pdm England"

No.	Description	Colourways	Shape/Size	U.S.$	Can.$	U.K.£
L-166	Ashtray	Dark green; white lettering "Gilbey's London Dry Gin"	Round/127	15.00	20.00	8.00
L-167	Ashtray	Green; white lettering, "Gilbey's"	Round/127	10.00	15.00	5.00

WINE BARRELS, 1958-1961

Backstamp: "Royal Victoria Pottery, Wade England"

No.	Description	Colourways	Size	U.S.$	Can.$	U.K.£
L-168a	Brandy	White; gold/purple bands; black lettering	1/2 bottle/115	25.00	30.00	12.00
L-168b	Cognac	White; gold bands; black lettering	1/2 bottle/115	25.00	30.00	12.00
L-168c	Gin	White; gold/blue bands; black lettering	1/2 bottle/115	25.00	30.00	12.00
L-168d	Irish	White; gold/yellow bands; black lettering	1/2 bottle/115	25.00	30.00	12.00
L-168e	Port	White; gold/maroon bands; black lettering	1/2 bottle/115	25.00	30.00	12.00
L-168f	Rye	White; gold/red bands; black lettering	1/2 bottle/115	25.00	30.00	12.00
L-168g	Rum	White; gold/orange bands; black lettering	1/2 bottle/115	25.00	30.00	12.00
L-168h	Scotch	White; gold/red bands; black lettering	1/2 bottle/115	25.00	30.00	12.00
L-168i	Sherry	White; gold/green bands; black lettering	1/2 bottle/115	25.00	30.00	12.00
L-168j	Whisky	White; gold/red bands; black lettering	1/2 bottle/115	25.00	30.00	12.00
L-169a	Cognac	White; gold bands; black lettering	Quart/133	25.00	30.00	12.00
L-169b	Cognac	Black; gold bands; black lettering	Quart/133	25.00	30.00	12.00
L-169c	Gin	White; gold/blue bands; black lettering	Quart/133	25.00	30.00	12.00
L-169d	Port	White; gold/maroon bands; black lettering	Quart/133	25.00	30.00	12.00
L-169e	Scotch	White; gold/red bands; black lettering	Quart/133	25.00	30.00	12.00
L-169f	Sherry	White; gold/red/green bands; black lettering	Quart/133	25.00	30.00	12.00

GILLESPIE'S STOUT

ASHTRAY, 1994-1996

Photograph not available
at press time

Backstamp: "Wade P D M Made in England"

No.	Description	Colourways	Shape/Size	U.S.$	Can.$	U.K.£
L-170	Ashtray	Dark blue; multi-coloured lettering "Gillespie's Malt Stout"	Oval/171	15.00	20.00	8.00

GLENLIVET WHISKY

DRINK POURER, c.1990

This pourer was modelled in the shape of a golf ball.

Photograph not available
at press time

No.	Description	Colourways	Shape/Size	U.S.$	Can.$	U.K.£
L-171	Drink Pourer	White; black lettering "The Glenlivet"	Round/40	40.00	45.00	20.00

GLENTURRET WHISKY
(THE HIGHLAND DISTILLERIES CO. PLC)

DECANTERS, 1991-1996

The 75-centilitre, circular "Globe Decanter" was filled with 25-year-old Glenturret Whisky. It has an embossed map of the world around it. The "Copper Lustre Flagon," also 75 centilitres, contained Glenturret's 21-year-old blend of whisky.

Photograph not available
at press time

Backstamp: "Genuine Wade Porcelain"

No.	Item	Colourways	Size	U.S.$	Can.$	U.K.£
L-172	Globe Decanter	Blue/green; gold/white lettering "75cl The Glenturret Rare Single Highland Malt Scotch Whisky"	195	80.00	100.00	40.00
L-173	Copper Lustre Flagon	Copper; gold/white lettering "The Glenturret"	195	80.00	100.00	40.00

GORDON HIGHLANDER LTD

FOX HUNTING DECANTER , 1991

Backstamp: "The Fox hunting Decanter is made by The Royal Victoria Pottery, Staffordshire, England—
Designed by Gordon Highlander Ltd.—Collectors series"

No.	Description	Colourways	Shape/Size	U.S.$	Can.$	U.K.£
L-174	Decanter	White; multi-coloured prints; black lettering	Hexagonal/255	80.00	100.00	40.00

GORDON'S GIN

ASHTRAY, DRINK POURERS AND WATER JUGS, 1968-1990

The octagonal pourers are shape number 5455/1. The square pourers, shape C52A, have a notched base and shoulders. The circular pourer is shape C53 and has a straight base. Water jugs were produced between 1968 and 1990. Both have ice-check spouts.

Drink Pourer "Gordon's"

Water Jug "Gordon's Gin"

Backstamp: A. "Reginald Corfield Limited Redhill Surrey," "Wade Regicor England"
B. "Wade p d m England"
C. "Wade Regicor Made in UK" on neck of pourer

No.	Description	Colourways	Shape/Size	U.S.$	Can.$	U.K.£
L-175	Ashtray	Yellow; red/black lettering "Gordon's Special Dry Gin"	Square/155	15.00	20.00	8.00
L-176	Drink Pourer	White; plastic tube; green lettering "Gordon's"	Circular/41	30.00	35.00	15.00
L-177a	Drink Pourer	Cream; plastic tube; white/gold lettering "Gordon's Gin"	Octagonal/40	30.00	35.00	15.00
L-177b	Drink Pourer	White; plastic tube; yellow/red lettering "Gordon's Gin"	Octagonal/40	30.00	35.00	15.00
L-178a	Drink Pourer	White; metal tube; dark green lettering "Gordon's"	Square/48	30.00	35.00	15.00
L-178b	Drink Pourer	White; metal tube; red lettering "Gordon's Gin"	Square/48	30.00	35.00	15.00
L-179	Water Jug	Yellow; red lettering "Gordon's Gin"	Rectangular/127	25.00	30.00	12.00
L-180	Water Jug	Yellow; red print, lettering "Gordon's Special London Dry Gin"	Square/130	25.00	30.00	12.00

GRAND MACNISH SCOTCH WHISKY
(MACNISH SCOTCH WHISKY)

ASHTRAYS AND WATER JUG, 1955-1990

The ashtrays were produced between 1955 and 1984. The water jug, produced between 1984 and 1990, has an ice-check spout.

Ashtray "Grand MacNish Scotch Whisky"

Backstamp: A. "Wade Regicor, London England," laurel leaves, large size
        B. "Wade Regicor, London England," laurel leaves, small size
        C. "Wade p d m England"
        D. "Wade pdm England, 86 Proof Blended Scotch Whisky Maidstone Importers Los Angeles California"

No.	Description	Colourways	Shape/Size	U.S.$	Can.$	U.K.£
L-181a	Ashtray	Primrose yellow; black/red lettering "MacNish"	Round/140	15.00	20.00	8.00
L-181b	Ashtray	White; black lettering "MacNish is Grand Scotch Whisky"	Round/140	15.00	20.00	8.00
L-182	Ashtray	Yellow; black/red lettering "Grand MacNish"	Round/165	10.00	15.00	5.00
L-183	Water Jug	Yellow; red/black lettering "Grand MacNish Scotch Whisky"	Round/140	15.00	20.00	8.00

GRANT'S SCOTCH WHISKY
(WILLIAM GRANT AND SONS LTD)

ASHTRAYS, 1955-1962

Ashtray, square with clipped corners

Ashtray, triangular

Backstamp: "Wade Regicor, London England," laurel leaves, large size

No.	Description	Colourways	Shape/Size	U.S.$	Can.$	U.K.£
L-184	Ashtray	Black; gold lettering "Grant's Scotch Whisky"	Square/140 clipped corners	20.00	20.00	8.00
L-185	Ashtray	White; red/white lettering "Grant's Scotch Whisky"	Triangular/115	15.00	20.00	8.00
L-186	Ashtray	White; red/white lettering "Grant's Scotch Whisky"	Triangular/140	15.00	20.00	8.00

DECANTERS AND WATER JUG, 1955-1962, 1991-1992

The bulbous, 700-millilitre decanters were issued between 1991 and 1992. They resemble 18th-century brandy bottles, with gold coloured caps and gold leaf decoration. They contained 18-year-old Glenfiddich Whisky. The water jug, which has an ice-check spout, was produced between 1955 and 1962.

Photograph not available
at press time

Backstamp: A. "Wade Regicor, London England," laurel leaves, large size
B. "Specially Commissioned by William Grant and Sons Ltd"

No.	Description	Colourways	Shape/Size	U.S.$	Can.$	U.K.£
L-187a	Decanter	Black; gold decoration, lettering "Glenfiddich"	220	50.00	70.00	25.00
L-187b	Decanter	Dark green; gold decoration, lettering "Glenfiddich"	220	50.00	70.00	25.00
L-187c	Decanter	Royal blue; gold decoration, lettering "Glenfiddich"	220	50.00	70.00	25.00
L-188	Water Jug	White; red/white lettering "Grant's Scotch Whisky"	Triangular/165	25.00	30.00	12.00

GREENALL WHITLEY

ASHTRAYS, 1969-1996

The print on the style L-189 ashtray is of a woman.

Photograph not available
at press time

Backstamp: A. "Wade pdm England"
B. "Wade P D M Made in England"

No.	Description	Colourways	Shape/Size	U.S.$	Can.$	U.K.£
L-189	Ashtray	Dark green; yellow/grey/red print; yellow lettering "Greenall Whitley"	Round/205	10.00	15.00	5.00
L-190	Ashtray	Dark green; yellow lettering "Greenall's Original"	Square/101	10.00	15.00	5.00

GREENE KING

ASHTRAY AND WATER JUG, 1968-1984

The jug has an open spout and a print on it of a king's head.

Photograph not available
at press time

Backstamp: A. "Reginald Corfield Limited Redhill Surrey," "Wade Regicor England"
B. "Wade pdm England"

No.	Description	Colourways	Shape/Size	U.S.$	Can.$	U.K.£
L-191	Ashtray	Olive green; yellow lettering "Greene King"	Round/127	15.00	20.00	8.00
L-192	Ashtray	Dark green; yellow lettering "Greene King"	Round/195	15.00	20.00	8.00
L-193	Ashtray	White; red/black lettering "Greene King Abbot Ale"	Square/146	15.00	20.00	8.00
L-194	Water Jug	Dark green; gold print, lettering "Greene King"	Round/101	25.00	30.00	12.00

GUINNESS

ASHTRAY, c.1990-1996

Photograph not available
at press time

Backstamp: "Wade P D M Made in England"

No.	Description	Colourways	Size	U.S.$	Can.$	U.K.£
L-195	Round	Black; gold lettering "Guinness"	216	20.00	28.00	8.00

CIGARETTE BOXES, c.1958-c.1960

Style L-196 was produced by Wade Ireland in the late 1950s. On the sides and lid it is decorated with an embossed design of whales in a frame of knurls. In the centre of the lid is a transfer print of the *Mayflower*, from the 1956-1957 *Snippets* series. On the inside of the box is an embossed poem to drink Guinness.

The "Guinness Cigarette Box" was issued in the 1960s. It has a print of a horse-drawn bus on the lid with the words, "Guinness one of the Best Cordials not in the Pharmacopoeia—the lancet 1837."

Wade Ireland Cigarette Box

Backstamp: A. "Irish Porcelain," "Made in Ireland by Wade Co. Armagh"
B. "Wade England"

No.	Description	Colourways	Size	U.S.$	Can.$	U.K.£
L-196	Wade Ireland	Grey/blue; multi-coloured print	45 x 125	70.00	90.00	35.00
L-197	Guinness	Black; white lid; multi-coloured print; black lettering	55 x 140	70.00	90.00	35.00

PEANUT BOWLS, c.1962

Kangaroo Peanut Dish

Pelican Peanut Dish

Sea Lion Peanut Dish

Toucan Peanut Dish

Backstamp: "Wade Regicor, London England," laurel leaves, small size

No.	Description	Colourways	Shape/Size	U.S.$	Can.$	U.K.£
L-198a	Kangaroo	Pale green; multi-coloured kangaroo	Round/35	30.00	35.00	15.00
L-198b	Pelican	Pale blue; multi-coloured pelican	Round/35	30.00	35.00	15.00
L-198c	Sea Lion	Yellow; multi-coloured sea lion	Round/35	30.00	35.00	15.00
L-198d	Toucan	Light grey; multi-coloured toucan	Round/35	30.00	35.00	15.00

HAIG SCOTCH WHISKY

DRINK POURER AND WATER JUG, 1984-1990

This drink pourer, shape C53, has a straight base. This water jug, which was produced between 1984 and 1990, has an open spout.

Backstamp: "Wade p d m England"

No.	Description	Colourways	Shape/Size	U.S.$	Can.$	U.K.£
L-199	Drink Pourer	White/red button; black lettering "Haig"	Circular/41	30.00	35.00	15.00
L-200	Water Jug	White; gold lettering "Haig The Oldest Name in Scotch Whisky"	Rectangular/169	25.00	20.00	12.00

HAMM'S BEER

Santa's Helper Decanter, 1995

Commissioned by Silver State Specialties of California, this decanter was issued in a limited edition of 2,000. The original price was $25.95 US.

Backstamp: "1995 Wade England S.S.S."

No.	Description	Colourways	Size	U.S.$	Can.$	U.K.£
L-201	Decanter	Red/white hat; black/white bear	120	30.00	35.00	30.00

HARP LAGER

ASHTRAYS, 1955-1990

The print on styles L-203 and L-205 is of a harp.

Ashtray "Harp Lager"

Backstamp: **A.** "Wade Regicor, London England," laurel leaves, large size
B. "Wade Regicor, London England," laurel leaves, small size
C. "Reginald Corfield Limited Redhill Surrey," "Wade Regicor England"
D. "Wade p d m England"

No.	Description	Colourways	Shape/Size	U.S.$	Can.$	U.K.£
L-202a	Ashtray	White/royal blue; white/blue/yellow lettering "Harp"	Round/177	15.00	20.00	8.00
L-202b	Ashtray	White/blue; white/blue/yellow lettering "Keg Harp Lager"	Round/177	15.00	20.00	8.00
L-203	Ashtray	Blue/white; white print; black/yellow lettering "Keg Harp Lager"	Hexagonal/146	15.00	20.00	8.00
L-204	Ashtray	Cream; white/black lettering "Harp Golden Lager"	Triangular/177	25.00	30.00	12.00
L-205	Ashtray	Dark blue; white and white print; white lettering "Harp Lager"	Triangular/185	25.00	30.00	12.00

HEBRIDES SCOTCH WHISKY

DECANTERS

My Fair Ladies Whisky Miniatures, 1992

In 1992 surplus stock of Wade's *My Fair Ladies* figurines were sold to Hebrides Scotch Whisky, a small Scottish distillery which filled the models with whisky and exported them to the U.S.A. as whisky miniatures. The label on the figures reads "Hebrides Scotch Whisky from Glasgow." A plastic seal over the whisky cork in the base prevents some models from standing upright. The *Miniature Bottle Collector Magazine* of California offered two of the filled figures, "Lisa" and "Kate" for sale at $50 U.S. per pair or $25 U.S. each. For original *My Fair Ladies* models, see Figures section.

Photograph not available
at press time

Backstamp: "My Fair Ladies, fine porcelain, Wade Made in England"; model name

No.	Name	Colourways	Size	U.S.$	Can.$	U.K.£
F-124	Marie	Dark green hat; dark green/grey-green dress	92	20.00	30.00	12.00
F-125	Sarah	Greenish grey hat; greenish grey/white dress; pink flowers	92	20.00	30.00	12.00
F-126	Hannah	Brown hair; green/grey/white dress	94	20.00	30.00	12.00
F-127	Lisa	Brown hair; pastel blue/white dress	94	20.00	30.00	12.00
F-128	Caroline	Dark blue hat; yellow flower; dark blue bodice grey-blue skirt; yellow bow	94	20.00	30.00	12.00
F-129	Rebecca	Yellow/beige hat; pink flower; grey bodice; white skirt; pink bow	94	20.00	30.00	12.00
F-130	Rachel	White/grey-blue dress; grey-blue hat	96	20.00	30.00	12.00
F-131	Kate	Grey hat; off-white/grey dress; red roses	96	20.00	30.00	12.00
F-132	Melissa	Light brown hat; dark blue jacket; pale blue skirt; white petticoat	95	20.00	30.00	12.00
F-133	Amanda	Dark brown jacket; pink skirt; white petticoat	95	20.00	30.00	12.00
F-134	Belinda	Pearl/white/yellow dress	90	20.00	30.00	12.00
F-135	Anita	Shell pink dress	90	20.00	35.00	12.00
F-136	Emma	White dress; creamy yellow shawl, ribbons, bows	90	20.00	30.00	12.00
F-137	Natalie	Pale pink dress; light grey shawl, ribbons, bows	90	20.00	30.00	12.00
F-138	Lucy	Grey hat, skirt; dark brown jacket, handbag	90	20.00	30.00	12.00
F-139	Diane	Pale blue/white hat, jacket, handbag; off-white skirt	90	20.00	30.00	12.00

HEINEKEN LAGER

ASHTRAY, 1969-1984

The print on this ashtray depicts a tower and mountains.

Photograph not available
at press time

Backstamp: "Wade pdm England"

No.	Description	Colourways	Shape/Size	U.S.$	Can.$	U.K.£
L-206	Ashtray	Green; multi-coloured print; white lettering "Heineken Lager"	Oval/229	15.00	20.00	8.00

HENRY STRATTON AND CO. LTD.

Bird Liqueur and Spirit Containers, 1961

The George Wade Pottery was commissioned to produce a set of five liqueur and spirit containers for a small British distillery, Henry Stratton and Co. Ltd. of Bolton. Before Wade finished the production run and Henry Stratton and Co. Ltd. had taken delivery of all models, the distillery was destroyed by fire. The remaining containers were sold for 1/- each to Boots The Chemist, which retailed them in its giftware departments. A few of the remaining "Chick Containers" may have been sold off to other liqueur distributers, as one has been found with a Rawlings and Son Advocaat label. The original Henry Stratton containers (of which there are a limited number) are found with white paper labels bearing the name of the liqueur inside and "Henry Stratton & Co. Ltd., Bolton." The original stoppers were plastic topped corks, although some have been found with plain corks. To date the "Cockatoo Container" has not been reported with a liqueur label.

Penguins

Chick

Cockatoo

Backstamp: **A.** Chick — Paper label "Contains Egg Nog Produce of Holland Henry Stratton & Co. Ltd., Bolton"
B. Penguin, small — Paper label "Contains Finest Creme De Menthe Produce of France (44% proof) Henry Stratton & Co. Ltd., Bolton"
C. Penguin, medium — Paper label "Contains Choice Old Port Produce of Portugal Henry Stratton & Co. Ltd., Bolton"
D. Penguin, large — Paper label "Finest Cherry Brandy 42% proof Henry Stratton & Co. Ltd., Bolton"
E. Chick — Paper label "Guernsey Cream, Advocaat, Channel Islands Fine Distillers Ltd, Guernsey. Sole Concessionaire Rawlings & Son (London) Ltd."

No.	Name	Colourways	Size	U.S.$	Can.$	U.K.£
L-207	Chick	Yellow; black eyes, brown beak, toes, green/yellow base	87	50.00	70.00	25.00
L-208	Cockatoo	White; yellow crest; green mottled base	130	135.00	175.00	70.00
L-209	Penguin, small	Blue-grey/white; blue/green base	95	50.00	70.00	25.00
L-210	Penguin, medium	Blue-grey/white; blue/green base	115	60.00	80.00	30.00
L-211	Penguin, large	Blue-grey/white; blue/green base	118	70.00	90.00	35.00

HIGH AND DRY GIN

ASHTRAY, 1955-1962

Photograph not available
at press time

Backstamp: "Wade Regicor, London England," laurel leaves, large size

No.	Description	Colourways	Shape/Size	U.S.$	Can.$	U.K.£
L-212	Ashtray	White; black lettering "High & Dry Gin"	Square/140	15.00	20.00	8.00

HIGHLAND QUEEN SCOTCH WHISKY

ASHTRAY, 1955-1962

Photograph not available
at press time

Backstamp: "Wade Regicor, London England," laurel leaves, large size

No.	Description	Colourways	Shape/Size	U.S.$	Can.$	U.K.£
L-213	Ashtray	Black; red lettering "Highland Queen"	Round/140	15.00	20.00	8.00

HOOK NORTON ALES

ASHTRAY, 1955-1962

Backstamp: "Wade Regicor, London England," laurel leaves, large size

No.	Description	Colourways	Shape/Size	U.S.$	Can.$	U.K.£
L-214	Ashtray	Pale green; yellow print, green lettering "Hook Norton Ales"	Round/133	15.00	20.00	8.00

HUDSONS BAY SCOTCH WHISKY

ASHTRAY, 1968-1969

Photograph not available
at press time

Backstamp: "Reginald Corfield, London England," "Wade Regicor England"

No.	Description	Colourways	Shape/Size	U.S.$	Can.$	U.K.£
L-215	Ashtray	White; black lettering "Hudsons Bay Scotch Whisky"	Round/159	15.00	20.00	8.00

IMPERIAL VODKA

WATER JUG, 1962-1968

This water jug, which has an open spout, is decorated with a print of a large double-headed eagle.

Photograph not available
at press time

Backstamp: "Wade Regicor, London England," laurel leaves, small size

No.	Description	Colourways	Shape/Size	U.S.$	Can.$	U.K.£
L-216	Water Jug	Royal blue; black print; yellow/white/blue lettering "Imperial Vodka Taplow's Ltd London"	Round/165	38.00	50.00	15.00

IRISH MIST LIQUEUR COMPANY LTD.

DECANTER, 1970-1975

Backstamp: Embossed "This is a fine piece of Irish Porcelain made by Wade—Liqueur Bottle Tullamore, Ireland"

No.	Description	Colourways	Size	U.S.$	Can.$	U.K.£
L-217	Decanter	Blue; multi-coloured label, lettering "Irish Mist Liqueur"	225	50.00	70.00	25.00

J & B SCOTCH WHISKY

ASHTRAYS, DRINK POURERS AND WATER JUGS, 1955-1984

The ashtrays were produced between 1955 and 1984. The drink pourers are shape C53 and they have a straight base. The water jugs were produced between 1968 and 1984. They both have ice-check spouts.

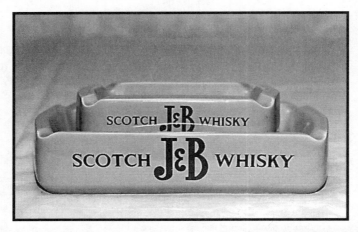

Backstamp: **A.** "Wade Regicor, London England," laurel leaves, large size
          B. "Wade pdm England"
          C. "Reginald Corfield Limited Redhill Surrey," "Wade Regicor England"

No.	Description	Colourways	Shape/Size	U.S.$	Can.$	U.K.£
L-218	Ashtray	Cream; black/red lettering "Scotch J & B Whisky"	Rectangular/153	10.00	15.00	5.00
L-219	Ashtray	Cream; black/red lettering "Scotch J & B Whisky"	Rectangular/216	15.00	20.00	8.00
L-220a	Drink Pourer	Cream; metal tube, spout; red lettering "J & B"	Circular/41	30.00	35.00	15.00
L-220b	Drink Pourer	Green; plastic tube; red lettering "J & B"	Circular/41	30.00	35.00	15.00
L-221	Water Jug	Dull yellow; red/black lettering "J & B Scotch Whisky"	Rectangular/153	25.00	30.00	12.00

JACK DANIEL'S WHISKY

DRINK POURERS, 1990-1996

The octagonal pourer is shape number 5455/1. The square pourer, shape number C52A, has a notched base and shoulders.

Photograph not available
at press time

Backstamp: Unmarked

No.	Description	Colourways	Shape/Size	U.S.$	Can.$	U.K.£
L-222	Drink Pourer	Black; plastic tube; white lettering "Jack Daniel's"	Octagonal/40	30.00	35.00	15.00
L-223	Drink Pourer	Black; plastic tube; white lettering "Jack Daniel's Old No 7"	Square/38	30.00	35.00	15.00

JAMESON IRISH WHISKEY
(JOHN JAMESON & SON)

ASHTRAY AND DECANTER, 1982-1990

The ashtray was produced between 1984 and 1990, the decanter between 1982 and 1986.

Backstamp: A. "Wade p d m England"
B. "Made in Ireland—Porcelain—Wade—eire tire a dheanta"

No.	Description	Colourways	Shape/Size	U.S.$	Can.$	U.K.£
L-224	Ashtray	Cream; black/red/yellow lettering "Jameson Irish Whiskey"	Round/216	10.00	15.00	5.00
L-225	Decanter	White; green shamrocks, gold lettering "Jameson Irish Whiskey"	235	50.00	70.00	25.00

JIM BEAM

In 1993 Wade PDM was asked by the International Association of Jim Beam Bottle and Specialties Club to produce items for its members due to the closure of Regal China, the previous producer. Decorative bottles, decanters and other ceramic items are produced exclusively for the membership.

JOHN PAUL JONES SHIP'S DECANTER, 1993

This one-litre decanter was produced for the 1993 convention of the International Association of Jim Beam Bottle and Specialties Club in Charlotte, North Carolina. It is from the same mould as the "Admiral Lord Nelson Decanter (page 329)," but the decorations have been changed to show scenes honouring John Paul Jones and the United States Navy and Marine Corps. Nine hundred decanters were produced, 450 with cobalt blue stoppers and 450 with white stoppers.

Backstamp: "1993 Convention of the International Association of Jim Beam Bottle & Specialties Club, Charlotte, North Carolina, Wade"

No.	Description	Colourways	Size	U.S.$	Can.$	U.K.£
L-226a	Decanter	Blue decanter, stopper; multi-coloured prints	220	100.00	140.00	55.00
L-226b	Decanter	Blue decanter; white stopper; multi-coloured prints	220	100.00	140.00	55.00

"DRAKE'S VOYAGE 1585" JUG, 1995

Two thousand of these one-litre jugs were produced, 900 blue, 750 white and 350 green, for the district meetings of the International Association of Jim Beam Bottle and Specialties Club.

No.	Description	Colourways	Size	U.S.$	Can.$	U.K.£
L-227a	Jug	Blue jug, stopper; multi-coloured prints	200	40.00	55.00	20.00
L-227b	Jug	Green jug, stopper; multi-coloured prints	200	40.00	55.00	20.00
L-227c	Jug	White jug, stopper; multi-coloured prints	200	40.00	55.00	20.00

200TH ANNIVERSARY BARREL, 1995

This ceramic barrel was produced for the 1995 convention of the International Association of Jim Beam Bottle and Specialties Club held in Louisville, Kentucky. There were 1,750 barrels produced, 700 in cobalt blue, 700 in black and 350 in dark green.

| 200th Anniversary Barrel (front) | 200th Anniversary Barrel (back) |

Backstamp: "Produced under licensing agreement with Jim Beam's Brands, Wade Porcelain"

No.	Description	Colourways	Size	U.S.$	Can.$	U.K.£
L-228a	Barrel	Cobalt blue; gold bands; multi-coloured print	224	100.00	140.00	55.00
L-228b	Barrel	Black; gold bands; multi-coloured print	224	100.00	140.00	55.00
L-228c	Barrel	Dark green; gold bands; multi-coloured print	224	125.00	170.00	60.00

JOHN BEGG SCOTCH WHISKY

ASHTRAYS AND WATER JUGS, 1955-1984

The water jugs have open spouts.

Water Jug "Take a Peg of John Begg!"

Backstamp: **A.** "Wade Regicor, London England," laurel leaves, large size
B. "Reginald Corfield Limited Redhill Surrey," "Wade Regicor England"
C. "Wade pdm England"

No.	Description	Colourways	Shape/Size	U.S.$	Can.$	U.K.£
L-229	Ashtray	Blue; white lettering "John Begg Scotch Whisky"	Triangular/153	15.00	20.00	8.00
L-230a	Water Jug	Dark blue; white lettering "John Begg Scotch Whisky"	Square/127	30.00	35.00	15.00
L-230b	Water Jug	White; dark blue lettering "Take a Peg of John Begg!"	Square/127	30.00	35.00	15.00

JOHN BULL BITTER

ASHTRAYS, 1969-1990

The print on style L-231 is of the brewery gates. A print of John Bull is on style L-232.

Photograph not available
at press time

Backstamp: **A.** "Wade pdm England"
B. "Wade P D M England"

No.	Description	Colourways	Shape/Size	U.S.$	Can.$	U.K.£
L-231	Ashtray	Cream; black print; black/red lettering "John Bull Bitter"	Round/165	10.00	15.00	5.00
L-232a	Ashtray	Cream; black/red print, lettering "John Bull Bitter"	Triangular/177	25.00	30.00	12.00
L-232b	Ashtray	Yellow; black/red print, lettering "John Bull Bitter"	Triangular/177	25.00	30.00	12.00

JOHN COURAGE

ASHTRAY, 1969-1984

The print on this ashtray is a silhouette of the head of John Courage.

Backstamp: "Wade pdm England"

No.	Description	Colourways	Shape/Size	U.S.$	Can.$	U.K.£
L-233	Ashtray	Black; black print; yellow/white lettering "John Courage IPA"	Round/230	10.00	15.00	5.00

JOHN SMITH BREWERY

PUMP HANDLE, c.1980

Backstamp: Unmarked

No.	Description	Colourways	Size	U.S.$	Can.$	U.K.£
L-234	Pump Handle	Off white; green print, lettering "Registered Trade Mark Estd. 1758. The John Smith Brewery Tadcaster"	225	30.00	35.00	15.00

JOHNNIE WALKER SCOTCH WHISKY

ASHTRAYS, 1955-1996

Ashtray (L-235)   **Ashtray (L-236)**

Backstamp: A. "Wade Regicor, London England," laurel leaves, large size
B. "Wade pdm England"
C. "Wade p d m England"
D. "Wade P D M Made in England"

No.	Description	Colourways	Shape/Size	U.S.$	Can.$	U.K.£
L-235	Ashtray	Pale blue; multi-coloured print; black lettering "Born 1820 - Still Going Strong"	Oval/260	15.00	20.00	8.00
L-236	Ashtray	Pale blue; multi-coloured print; black lettering "Born 1820 - Still Going Strong"	Rectangular/225	15.00	20.00	8.00
L-237	Ashtray	White; multi-coloured print, red lettering "Johnnie Walker Scotch Whisky"	Square/120	25.00	30.00	12.00
L-238a	Ashtray	White; multi-coloured print, red lettering "Johnnie Walker"	Square/127	25.00	30.00	12.00
L-238b	Ashtray	Cream; red/black lettering "Johnnie Walker"	Square/127	15.00	20.00	8.00
L-239	Ashtray	Light blue; multi-coloured print; black lettering "Johnnie Walker"	Square/159	10.00	15.00	5.00
L-240	Ashtray	Light blue; multi-coloured print, black lettering "Johnnie Walker"	Square/165	10.00	15.00	5.00
L-241	Ashtray	White/red; gold lettering "Johnnie Walker England Old Scotch Whisky"	Square/171	10.00	15.00	5.00
L-242	Ashtray	Black; red/gold lettering "Johnnie Walker Black Label"	Square/159	10.00	15.00	5.00

DRINK POURERS AND WATER JUGS, 1955-1996

The drink pourers were issued between 1960 and 1970. The style L-243 drink pourer is shape number C53, with a straight base and a dust flap at the end of the metal tube. Style L-244 is shape number 5455/4.

The water jugs were issued from 1955 to 1996. The style L-245 jug has an ice-check spout. The neck on style L-246 is short and tapered, and it has an open spout. Style L-247 has a recessed handle and an ice-check spout. The style L-248 jug has an open spout.

| Drink Pourer (L-243) | Water Jug (L-245) | Water Jug (L-246) |

Backstamp: **A.** "Wade Regicor, London England," laurel leaves, large size
B. "Wade Regicor, London England," laurel leaves, small size
C. "Reginald Corfield Limited Redhill Surrey," "Wade Regicor England"
D. "Fine Staffordshire Pottery Duncan Fox & Co, Inc, New York - Regicor, Wade England"

No.	Description	Colourways	Shape/Size	U.S.$	Can.$	U.K.£
L-243	Drink Pourer	White; metal tube, spout, flap; red/black lettering "Johnnie Walker Scotch Whisky Born 1820 - Still Going Strong"	Circular/41	30.00	35.00	15.00
L-244a	Drink Pourer	Black; metal tube; gold lettering "Johnnie Walker Black Label"	Rectangular/46	30.00	35.00	15.00
L-244b	Drink Pourer	White; metal tube; red/gold lettering "Johnnie Walker"	Rectangular/46	30.00	35.00	15.00
L-245	Water Jug	Pale blue; multi-coloured print, black lettering "Johnnie Walker Born 1820 - Still Going Strong"	Round/133	30.00	35.00	15.00
L-246	Water Jug	Grey; multi-coloured print; red lettering "Johnnie Walker Red Label"	Round base/190	50.00	70.00	25.00
L-247	Water Jug	White; red/black print, lettering "Johnnie Walker Scotch Whisky"	Square/146	40.00	45.00	20.00
L-248	Water Jug	Red/white/black print, lettering "Johnnie Walker"	Square/160	25.00	30.00	12.00

JUBILEE STOUT

ASHTRAY, CRUETS AND WATER JUG, 1955-1984

The ashtray and cruets were produced between 1955 and 1962, the water jug between 1969 and 1984. The mustard cruet is the same shape as the salt and pepper cruets, with the addition of a lid. The water jug has an open spout.

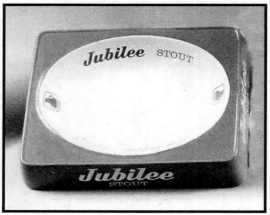

Ashtray

Backstamp: A. "Wade Regicor, London England," laurel leaves, large size
B. "Wade pdm England"

No.	Description	Colourways	Shape/Size	U.S.$	Can.$	U.K.£
L-249	Ashtray	Dark blue/white; blue lettering "Jubilee Stout"	Rectangular/210	10.00	15.00	5.00
L-250	Mustard Pot	White; blue/red lettering "Jubilee Stout Mustard"	Square/76	8.00	10.00	3.00
L-251a	Pepper Pot	White; blue/red lettering "Jubilee Stout Pepper"	Square/80	8.00	10.00	3.00
L-251b	Salt Cellar	White; blue/red lettering "Jubilee Stout Salt"	Square/80	8.00	10.00	3.00
L-252	Water Jug	White; red/blue label, lettering "Jubilee Stout"	Square/120	25.00	30.00	12.00

KENTUCKY TAVERN BOURBON

WATER JUG, 1968-1969

This jug has a recessed handle and an open spout.

Backstamp: "Reginald Corfield Limited Redhill Surrey," "Wade Regicor England,
"KY. Straight Bourbon Whisky 86 and 100 Bottled in Bond Glenmore Distilleries Co. Louisville, Owensbord K.Y."

No.	Description	Colourways	Shape/Size	U.S.$	Can.$	U.K.£
L-253	Water Jug	White; black/red lettering "8 Year Old Kentucky Tavern The Vintage Bourbon"	Round/190	30.00	35.00	15.00

KING GEORGE SCOTCH WHISKY

ASHTRAY AND WATER JUGS, 1955-1968

The ashtray was produced between 1955 and 1962, the water jugs between 1955 and 1968. Each item is decorated with a print of King George IV. The style L-255 jug has a recessed handle and an open spout. Style L-256 has an ice-check spout, and style L-257 has an open spout.

Photograph not available
at press time

Backstamp: **A.** "Wade Regicor, London England," laurel leaves, large size
B. "Wade Regicor, London England," laurel leaves, small size

No.	Description	Colourways	Shape/Size	U.S.$	Can.$	U.K.£
L-254	Ashtray	Creamy yellow; multi-coloured print; red/black lettering "King George IV Scotch Whisky"	Square/108	10.00	15.00	5.00
L-255	Water Jug	Black; gold print, lettering "King George Old Scotch Whisky"	Round/120	30.00	35.00	15.00
L-256	Water Jug	Yellow; multi-coloured print; red/black lettering "King George Old Scotch Whisky"	Round/114	30.00	35.00	15.00
L-257	Water Jug	Yellow; multi-coloured print; black/red lettering "King George Old Scotch Whisky"	Square/114	30.00	35.00	15.00

KINGSFORD'S WHISKY LTD

DECANTER, c.1988

On the front of this Irish Wade decanter is a transfer print of mounted fox hunters.

Photograph not available
at press time

Backstamp: "Wade Ireland"

No.	Description	Colourways	Size	U.S.$	Can.$	U.K.£
L-258	Decanter	White; multi-coloured print; black lettering "Kingsford's Decanter"	175	50.00	70.00	25.00

KISKADEE

DRINK POURER, 1970s

This semi-circular pourer, shape 5455/2, has a straight top and base and is decorated with a print of a bird.

Photograph not available
at press time

Backstamp: Unmarked

No.	Description	Colourways	Size	U.S.$	Can.$	U.K.£
L-259	Drink Pourer	White; plastic tube; dark green/yellow print; green lettering "Kiskadee"	35 x 40	30.00	35.00	15.00

KRONENBOURG LAGER

ASHTRAY AND BEER STEIN, 1969-1990

The ashtrays were issued between 1969 and 1990, the beer steins between 1969 and 1984. The beer stein came with a pewter lid.

Ashtray (L-260)

Beer Stein (L-263)

Backstamp: **A.** "Wade pdm England"
B. "Wade P D M England"

No.	Description	Colourways	Shape/Size	U.S.$	Can.$	U.K.£
L-260	Ashtray	Grey; red/white shield, embossed letters "Kronenbourg"	Castle/90	25.00	30.00	12.00
L-261	Ashtray	Grey; gold/red/white lions, shield; white lettering "Kronenbourg"	Square/127	10.00	15.00	5.00
L-262	Beer Stein	Grey; red/white crest; pewter lid; gold lettering "Kronenbourg"	Pint/175	60.00	80.00	30.00
L-263	Beer Stein	Grey; red/white crest; pewter lid; gold lettering "Kronenbourg"	1 1/2 pint/215	80.00	100.00	40.00

LABATT'S BEER, 1967-1995

ASHTRAY AND TANKARDS, 1967-1996

The ashtray was produced from 1993 to 1996, the "Labatts Million Barrels Tankard" in 1967 and the "Labatts Traditional Tankards" between 1967 and the mid 1980s.

Million Barrels Tankard (L-265)

"Labatt's" (L-266a)

"Labatt's Blue" (L-266b)

"Labatt's 50" (L-266c)

Backstamp: **A.** "Wade P D M Made in England"
B. "Wade England"

No.	Description	Colourways	Shape/Size	U.S.$	Can.$	U.K.£
L-264	Ashtray	Blue; red/white/gold lettering "Labatt's"	Square/210	10.00	15.00	5.00
L-265	Million Barrels Tankard	Gold; black lettering "Labatt's"	Pint/125	70.00	90.00	35.00
L-266a	Traditional Tankard	Amber; black lettering "Labatt's"	Pint/120	25.00	30.00	12.00
L-266b	Traditional Tankard	Royal blue; gold lettering "Labatt's Blue"	Pint/120	25.00	30.00	12.00
L-266c	Traditional Tankard	Royal blue; gold lettering, "Labatt's 50"	Pint/120	25.00	30.00	12.00
L-266d	Traditional Tankard	White; gold lettering "Labatt's"	Pint/120	25.00	30.00	12.00

LANG BROTHERS LTD

CHINESE NEW YEAR DECANTERS, 1993-1995

These 750-millimetre decanters were filled with 12-year-old whisky and produced in a limited edition of 4,000. As well as an ornate 24-karat gold leaf decoration, they have a gold coloured chain with a Lang Brothers medallion around the neck. These are the first in a series that celebrates the Chinese New Year. The decanters were available by post direct from Lang Brothers in November 1993 and 1994 at a cost of £95.00 each, including the whisky.

1994 Year of the Dog

1995 Year of the Pig

Backstamp: "Langs ® select 1861 Founders Reserve Scotch Whisky—Genuine Wade Porcelain"

No.	Description	Colourways	Size	U.S.$	Can.$	U.K.£
L-267a	1994 Year of the Dog	White; gold/dark blue/pale blue decoration, lettering "Year of the Dog"	235	95.00	135.00	50.00
L-267b	1995 Year of the Pig	White; gold/dark blue/turquoise/red decoration, lettering "Year of the Pig"	235	95.00	135.00	50.00

LONG JOHN SCOTCH WHISKY

ASHTRAYS AND WATER JUG, 1955-1984

The ashtrays were produced between 1955 and 1962, the water jug between 1969 and 1984. The jug has an open spout.

Ashtray "Long John Scotch Whisky"

Backstamp: A. "Wade Regicor, London England," laurel leaves, large size
B. "Wade pdm England"

No.	Description	Colourways	Shape/Size	U.S.$	Can.$	U.K.£
L-268	Ashtray	Amber/white; black lettering "Long John Scotch Whisky"	Round/140	15.00	20.00	8.00
L-269	Ashtray	Amber/white; black lettering "Long John Scotch Whisky"	Round/153	15.00	20.00	8.00
L-270	Water Jug	Black; gold/white lettering "Long John"	Oval/175	25.00	30.00	12.00

LYLE & KINAHAN LTD

WATER JUG, c.1958-1966

This water jug has an open spout.

Backstamp: "Porcelain by Wade (Ulster) Ltd Co Armagh N.I."

No.	Description	Colourways	Shape/Size	U.S.$	Can.$	U.K.£
L-271	Water Jug	Black; gold lettering "Old Friends are Best Lyle & Kinahan Ltd"	Round/120	40.00	45.00	20.00

MCCALLUM'S SCOTCH WHISKY

ASHTRAY AND DRINK POURER, c.1960-1984

The ashtray was produced between 1969 and 1984. The drink pourer, produced circa 1960, is shape number C53, with a straight base.

Backstamp: **A.** "Wade pdm England"
 B. "Wade Regicor Made in UK"

No.	Description	Colourways	Shape/Size	U.S.$	Can.$	U.K.£
L-272	Ashtray	Maroon; white print, lettering "McCallum's Perfection Scotch Whisky"	Triangular/159	20.00	30.00	10.00
L-273	Drink Pourer	White; multi-coloured print	Circular/41	30.00	35.00	15.00

CHARACTER JUGS, c.1950-c.1959

These character jugs are in the form of a bearded Scotsman wearing a glengarry, with the ribbons forming the handle. They were first issued by Wade in the early 1950s, then reissued in collaboration with Regicor in the late 1950s.

Backstamp: **A.** "Wade Regicor, London, England"
B. "Wade England"
C. "Wade Made in England Hand Painted"

No.	Description	Colourways	Size	U.S.$	Can.$	U.K.£
L-274a	Character Jug	Treacle	Miniature/70	50.00	70.00	25.00
L-274b	Character Jug	Dark brown/red/black hat; amber face	Miniature/70	50.00	70.00	25.00
L-275a	Character Jug	Treacle	Small/115	70.00	95.00	35.00
L-275b	Character Jug	Dark brown/red/black hat; amber face	Small/115	70.00	95.00	35.00
L-276a	Character Jug	Treacle	Large/160	90.00	130.00	45.00
L-276b	Character Jug	Dark brown/red/black hat; amber	Large/160	90.00	130.00	45.00

WATER JUGS, 1969-1984

These jugs have recessed handles and open spouts. Version L-277b has a print of a Scotsman on it.

Photograph not available
at press time

Backstamp: "Wade pdm England"

No.	Description	Colourways	Shape/Size	U.S.$	Can.$	U.K.£
L-277a	Water Jug	Black; white lettering "McCallum's Perfected Scotch Whisky"	Round/127	25.00	30.00	12.00
L-277b	Water Jug	Maroon; white print, lettering "McCallum's Perfected Scotch Whisky "	Round/127	25.00	30.00	12.00

MACKENZIE SCOTCH WHISKY

WATER JUG, 1969-1984

This water jug has an open spout.

Photograph not available at press time

Backstamp: "Wade pdm England"

No.	Description	Colourways	Shape/Size	U.S.$	Can.$	U.K.£
L-278	Water Jug	White; black/gold lettering "MacKenzie Whisky"	Square/110	25.00	30.00	12.00

MACKINLEY'S SCOTCH WHISKY

ASHTRAY AND DRINK POURER, 1955-1962

The ashtray was produced between 1955 and 1962. The pourer, produced circa 1960, is shape C53, which has a straight base.

Photograph not available at press time

Backstamp: "Wade Regicor Made in UK" on the neck

No.	Description	Colourways	Shape/Size	U.S.$	Can.$	U.K.£
L-279	Ashtray	Creamy yellow; red lettering "MacKinley's Scotch"	Shield/184	30.00	35.00	15.00
L-280	Pourer	White; red/black lettering "MacKinley's Scotch Whisky"	Circular/41	30.00	35.00	15.00

MACLEAY DUFF SCOTCH WHISKY

ASHTRAY, 1955-1962

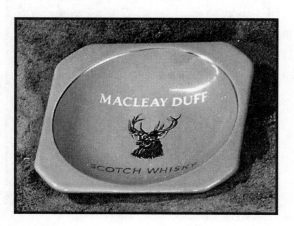

Backstamp: "Wade Regicor, London England," laurel leaves, large size

No.	Description	Colourways	Shape/Size	U.S.$	Can.$	U.K.£
L-281	Ashtray	Grey; black print; white/black lettering "Macleay Duff Scotch Whisky"	Square/140 clipped corners	15.00	20.00	8.00

MACLEOD'S SCOTCH WHISKY

WATER JUG, 1984-1990

This water jug has an ice-check spout.

Photograph not available at press time

Backstamp: "Wade p d m England"

No.	Description	Colourways	Shape/Size	U.S.$	Can.$	U.K.£
L-282	Water Jug	Yellow; brown lettering "Macleod's Isle of Skye 8 yr old Blend"	Rectangular/133	25.00	30.00	12.00

MCMULLEN'S ALES

ASHTRAYS, 1955-1968

Photograph not available at press time

Backstamp: **A.** "Wade Regicor, London England," laurel leaves, large size
B. "Wade Regicor, London England," laurel leaves, small size

No.	Description	Colourways	Shape/Size	U.S.$	Can.$	U.K.£
L-283	Ashtray	White; red horse, wagon, lettering "McMullen's Ales"	Round/133	15.00	20.00	8.00
L-284	Ashtray	White; red lettering "McMullen's Ales"	Round/140	15.00	20.00	8.00

MANSFIELD ALES

ASHTRAYS, 1955-1984

Ashtray (L-285)

Backstamp: **A.** "Wade Regicor, London England," laurel leaves, large size
B. "Wade pdm England"

No.	Description	Colourways	Shape/Size	U.S.$	Can.$	U.K.£
L-285	Ashtray	Pale green; black/green lettering "Mansfield Ales"	Round/140	15.00	20.00	8.00
L-286	Ashtray	Green; yellow logo, lettering "Mansfield Ales"	Square/205	10.00	15.00	5.00

MARKSMAN

ASHTRAY, 1984-1990

The print on this ashtray is of a hand holding an empty glass.

Backstamp: "Wade P D M England"

No.	Description	Colourways	Shape/Size	U.S.$	Can.$	U.K.£
L-287	Ashtray	Blue/pink; white/yellow print white lettering "Down With Marksman"	Round/216	10.00	15.00	5.00

MARSTON'S

ASHTRAY, 1991-1996

Photograph not available
at press time

Backstamp: "Wade P D M Made in England"

No.	Description	Colourways	Size	U.S.$	Can.$	U.K.£
L-288	Oval	Dark blue; gold lettering "Marston's Head Brewers Choice"	171	15.00	20.00	8.00

MARTELL

DRINK POURERS, c.1970

The style L-289 pourers are shape C53, which has a straight base. The style L-290 pourer is shape 5455/1. Style L-291, which is shape number C52A, has a notched base and shoulders.

Backstamp: Unmarked

No.	Description	Colourways	Shape/Size	U.S.$	Can.$	U.K.£
L-289a	Drink Pourer	White; red/black lettering "Martell Brandy"	Circular/40	30.00	35.00	15.00
L-289b	Drink Pourer	White; blue lettering "Martell Brandy"	Circular/41	30.00	35.00	15.00
L-290	Drink Pourer	Cream; plastic tube; black/gold lettering "Martell Cognac"	Octagonal/40	30.00	35.00	15.00
L-291	Drink Pourer	Cream; plastic tube; black/gold lettering "Martell Cognac"	Square/38	30.00	35.00	15.00

MARTINI VERMOUTH

ASHTRAY, 1968-1969

Backstamp: "Reginald Corfield Limited Redhill Surrey," "Wade Regicor England"

No.	Description	Colourways	Shape/Size	U.S.$	Can.$	U.K.£
L-292	Ashtray	White; red/black; white lettering "Martini"	Round/210	15.00	20.00	8.00

MITCHELL & BUTLER BEER

WATER JUG, 1979

A special-edition water jug was produced for Mitchell & Butler to mark its centenary. It is in the shape of a Dutch jug, which is round and squat with an open spout. The jug bears the dates "1879-1979" and is highly decorated with ears of barley and bunches of hops.

Photograph not available
at press time

Backstamp: Black transfer print "This Jug has been produced in a limited edition to mark the 100 yrs that have passed since beer was first brewed at the Cope Hill Brewery of Mitchell and Butler. Supplied by Wade PDM Ltd"

No.	Description	Colourways	Shape/Size	U.S.$	Can.$	U.K.£
L-293	Water Jug	White; blue/green/honey brown decoration, lettering "M & B Centenary Jug"	Round/140	120.00	150.00	60.00

MORLAND BEER

ASHTRAY AND DRINK POURER, c.1970, 1984–1990

The ashtray was produced between 1984 and 1990 and bears a print of a man with a beer barrel. The pourer, which is shape number 5455/1, was produced circa 1970.

Photograph not available
at press time

Backstamp: **A.** "Wade P D M England"
B. Unmarked

No.	Description	Colourways	Shape/Size	U.S.$	Can.$	U.K.£
L-294	Ashtray	Black; red/white print; white lettering "Morland Brewers since 1711"	Square/140	10.00	15.00	5.00
L-295	Pourer	Black; plastic tube; white lettering "Morland Brewers since 1711"	Octagonal/40	30.00	35.00	15.00

MOUNT GAY BARBADOS RUM

ASHTRAY, 1969-1984

The print on this ashtray is of a map of Barbados.

Photograph not available
at press time

Backstamp: "Wade pdm England"

No.	Description	Colourways	Shape/Size	U.S.$	Can.$	U.K.£
L-296	Ashtray	White; yellow print; red/black lettering "Mount Gay Barbados Rum"	Square/133	10.00	15.00	5.00

NICHOLSON'S GIN

ASHTRAY AND WATER JUG, 1955-1969

The ashtray was produced between 1955 and 1962 and bears a print of a lamp lighter. The jug, which has an ice-check spout, was produced between 1968 and 1969.

Backstamp: A. "Wade Regicor, London England," laurel leaves, large size
B. "Reginald Corfield Limited Redhill Surrey," "Wade Regicor England"

No.	Description	Colourways	Shape/Size	U.S.$	Can.$	U.K.£
L-297	Ashtray	White; black print; black/red lettering "Nicholson's Lamplighter Gin"	Round/133	20.00	30.00	10.00
L-298	Water Jug	Dark grey; red/white lettering "Nicholson's Lamplighter English Dry Gin"	Rectangular/153	30.00	35.00	15.00

OLD CHARTER BOURBON

WATER JUG, 1968-1969

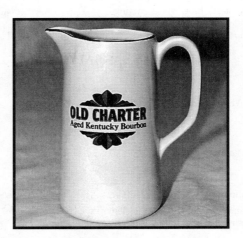

Backstamp: A. "Reginald Corfield Limited Redhill Surrey," "Wade Regicor England- 86 proof Kentucky Straight Bourbon Whisky - Old Charter Distillery Co. Louisville, K.Y."

No.	Description	Colourways	Shape/Size	U.S.$	Can.$	U.K.£
L-299	Water Jug/ open spout	White; multi-coloured design; red/black lettering "Old Charter Aged Kentucky Bourbon"	Round/165	25.00	30.00	15.00

OLD PARR SCOTCH WHISKY
(MACDONALD GREENLEES LTD.)

ASHTRAY AND WATER JUG, 1969-1984

The jug has an ice-check spout.

Backstamp: "Wade pdm England"

No.	Description	Colourways	Shape/Size	U.S.$	Can.$	U.K.£
L-300	Ashtray	Maroon; white lettering "Old Parr Real Antique & Rare Scotch Whisky"	Round/153	15.00	20.00	8.00
L-301	Water Jug	Maroon; white lettering "Old Parr Real Antique & Rare Old Scotch Whisky"	Round/133	30.00	35.00	15.00

OLD RARITY SCOTCH WHISKY

WATER JUG, 1984-1990

The spout on this jug is open.

Photograph not available
at press time

Backstamp: "Wade p d m England"

No.	Description	Colourways	Shape/Size	U.S.$	Can.$	U.K.£
L-302	Water Jug	White; red lettering "Old Rarity De Luxe Scotch Whisky"	Square/127	25.00	30.00	12.00

ORANJEBOOM LAGER

ASHTRAYS, 1969-1990

The print on these ashtrays is of a tree.

Photograph not available
at press time

Backstamp: A. "Wade pdm England"
B. "Wade p d m England"

No.	Description	Colourways	Shape/Size	U.S.$	Can.$	U.K.£
L-303a	Ashtray	Black; orange print; white lettering "Oranjeboom Lager Beer"	Oval/210	15.00	20.00	8.00
L-303b	Ashtray	Black; red print; white/green lettering "Oranjeboom"	Oval/210	10.00	15.00	5.00

PADDY IRISH WHISKEY

DRINK POURER AND WATER JUG, 1969–1984

This pourer has a notched base and shoulders, with a metal tube. It is shape number C52A. The water jug has an ice-check spout.

Backstamp: A. "Wade pdm England"
B. Unmarked

No.	Description	Colourways	Shape/Size	U.S.$	Can.$	U.K.£
L-304	Drink Pourer	White; yellow/black lettering "Paddy Old Irish Whiskey"	Square/38	30.00	35.00	15.00
L-305	Water Jug	Brown; multi-coloured lettering "Paddy Old Irish Whiskey"	Round/165	30.00	35.00	15.00

PERNOD

ASHTRAYS, 1995–1996

Photograph not available
at press time

Backstamp: "Wade P D M Made in England"

No.	Description	Colourways	Shape/Size	U.S.$	Can.$	U.K.£
L-306	Ashtray	Dark blue; red/white lettering "Pernod Cafe des pres"	Square/159	10.00	15.00	5.00
L-307	Ashtray	Dark blue; red/white lettering "Pernod Cafe des pres"	Square/184	10.00	15.00	5.00

PETER THOMPSON (PERTH) LTD.

CURLING-STONE CONTAINERS, 1975–1981

The circular *Curling Stone Containers* were first produced for Peter Thompson in 1975 for Air Canada's duty free shops. Printed on top of version L-308a is, "World Curling Championship, Air Canada Silver Broom, Perth Scotland 1975."

Curling Stone (L-308a)

Backstamp: A. Embossed "Beneagles Scotch Whisky, Wade 74"
B. Embossed "Beneagles Scotch Whisky, Wade Ireland"

No.	Name	Colourways	Size	U.S.$	Can.$	U.K.£
L-308a	Air Canada Curling Stone	Light grey/dark grey flecks; black handle; tartan ribbon; black lettering	65	70.00	90.00	35.00
L-308b	Curling Stone	Light grey/dark grey flecks; black handle; tartan ribbon	65	50.00	70.00	25.00

THE THISTLE AND THE ROSE HISTORICAL CHESS SET, 1979-c.1982

The matt biscuit-porcelain chess set was produced exclusively for Peter Thompson Ltd. The models were designed by Ann Whittet and modelled by Frederick Mellor (indicated on the backstamps by WFM). The master pieces represent the royal house of Scotland (the thistle) and the royal house of England (the rose). The pawns resemble a ship's decanter and have no backstamps. They were originally issued as a boxed set, complete with a copper and brass chess board, which pulled out from the bottom of the box like a drawer. Included in the box was a bottle of Beneagles Scotch Whisky; the chess pieces were unfilled. The principal pieces could be purchased individually as whisky miniatures filled with 1 2/3 ounces (50 millilitres) of Beneagles Scotch Whisky. The pawns were too small to fill, so were not issued individually.

At the end of 1980, the remainder of the chess pieces were exported to North America, a large number to the Las Vegas Distributing Company. They were sold as a boxed pair, a chessman and a pawn in a gold-and-black chequered box; only the master pieces were filled with whisky. The boxed pair was also sold in Ontario, Canada, for $5.00 a pair, with a Liquor Control Board of Ontario label.

In the early 1980s the black chess pieces were produced in a gloss glaze. They were given as complimentary gifts to first-class passengers on British Caledonian Airways or could be purchased from the airlines by mail order.

The Rose Chess Pieces

The Thistle Chess Pieces

Backstamp: Embossed "Beneagles Scotch Whisky"

The Rose Chess Pieces, White

No.	Name	Finish	Size	U.S.$	Can.$	U.K.£
L-309	King Henry VIII	Matt	134	25.00	30.00	12.00
L-310	Queen Elizabeth I	Matt	133	25.00	30.00	12.00
L-311	Bishop Thomas áBecket	Matt	135	25.00	30.00	12.00
L-312	Knight—Sir Francis Drake	Matt	130	25.00	30.00	12.00
L-313	Castle—Norman English Tower	Matt	100	25.00	30.00	12.00
L-314	Pawn	Matt	95	30.00	35.00	15.00

The Thistle Chess Pieces, Black

No.	Name	Finish	Size	U.S.$	Can.$	U.K.£
L-315a	Mary, Queen of Scots	Matt	125	25.00	30.00	12.00
L-315b	Mary, Queen of Scots	Gloss	125	25.00	30.00	12.00
L-316a	King Robert the Bruce	Matt	130	25.00	30.00	12.00
L-316b	King Robert the Bruce	Gloss	130	25.00	30.00	12.00
L-317a	Bishop John Knox	Matt	128	25.00	30.00	12.00
L-317b	Bishop John Knox	Gloss	128	25.00	30.00	12.00
L-318a	Knight—Sir William Wallace	Matt	135	25.00	30.00	12.00
L-318b	Knight—Sir William Wallace	Gloss	135	25.00	30.00	12.00
L-319a	Castle—Scottish Tower House	Matt	102	25.00	30.00	12.00
L-319b	Castle—Scottish Tower House	Gloss	102	25.00	30.00	12.00
L-320a	Pawn	Matt	100	30.00	35.00	15.00
L-320b	Pawn	Gloss	100	30.00	35.00	15.00

GOLDEN EAGLE AND GRIZZLY BEAR WHISKY MINIATURES, 1981

The golden eagle, which sits on a rock, is very similar to the more commonly found Beswick "Golden Eagle Whisky Miniature."

Grizzly Bear

Backstamp: "Beneagles Scotch Whisky - Peter Thompson, (Perth) Ltd Scotland"

No.	Name	Colourways	Size	U.S.$	Can.$	U.K.£
L-321	Golden Eagle	Dark brown; grey/brown rock	110	70.00	90.00	35.00
L-322	Grizzly Bear	Dark brown	120	80.00	100.00	40.00

GOLF BALL WHISKY MINIATURE, c.1985

Backstamp: Unmarked

No.	Description	Colourways	Shape/Size	U.S.$	Can.$	U.K.£
L-323	Golf Ball	White; red lettering "3 Peter Thomson's"	Round/50	10.00	15.00	5.00

PIMM'S NO. 1

DRINK POURER

This pourer, shape number C62, was produced with either a plastic or metal tube.

Photograph not available
at press time

Backstamp: Unmarked

No.	Description	Colourways	Shape/Size	U.S.$	Can.$	U.K.£
L-324	Drink Pourer	White; red/black/gold lettering "Pimm's"	Rectangular/48	30.00	35.00	15.00

PIPER

ASHTRAYS, 1962–1968

Ashtray (L-325)

Backstamp: "Wade Regicor, London England," laurel leaves, large size

No.	Description	Colourways	Shape/Size	U.S.$	Can.$	U.K.£
L-325	Ashtray	White; black print; black/red lettering "Piper Extra Export Ale"	Square/140	20.00	28.00	8.00

PLYMOUTH GIN

WATER JUG, 1968–1969

This water jug has an ice-check spout and is decorated with a print of the bottle label.

Photograph not available
at press time

Backstamp: "Reginald Corfield Limited Redhill Surrey," "Wade Regicor England"

No.	Description	Colourways	Shape/Size	U.S.$	Can.$	U.K.£
L-326	Water Jug	White; red/blue print, lettering "Plymouth Dry Gin Distilled in England Since 1783"	Square/153	30.00	35.00	15.00

PRESIDENT SPECIAL

ASHTRAY, 1969–1984

This ashtray is decorated with a print of a shield.

*Photograph not available
at press time*

Backstamp: "Wade pdm England"

No.	Description	Colourways	Shape/Size	U.S.$	Can.$	U.K.£
L-327	Ashtray	Cream; gold print; black/white lettering "President Special Reserve"	Rectangular/177	10.00	15.00	5.00

PUSSER'S RUM

Pusser's Rum has been part of the Royal Navy tradition for centuries, with the Royal Navy Sailors Fund receiving a substantial donation from its worldwide sales.

ROYAL NAVY RUM JUGS, 1981

These rum jugs, with a handle and spout, were made of heavy earthenware in a squat shape, for stability in rough seas. Produced in royal blue and white glaze, they have a red wax seal and are often decorated with different types of transfer prints.

Miniature Rum Jug, 1981

Miniature Jug (front)

Miniature Jug (back)

Backstamp: Unmarked

No.	Description	Colourways	Size	U.S.$	Can.$	U.K.£
L-328	Rum Jug	Blue/white; blue cap	Miniature/63	25.00	30.00	12.00

Jolly Jack Pusser Rum Jug, 1981

Jolly Jack Pusser Rum Jug (front)   Jolly Jack Pusser Rum Jug (back)

Backstamp: "Wade Made in England"

No.	Name	Colourways	Size	U.S.$	Can.$	U.K.£
L-329	Jolly Jack Pusser Rum Jug	Blue/white; blue cap; multi-coloured prints	200	40.00	45.00	20.00

HIP FLASKS, 1981-1996

The date of production for the "Royal Navy Rum Terminology Hip Flask" is unknown.

Royal Navy Rum Terminology (front)   Royal Navy Rum Terminology (back)

Backstamp: **A.** Embossed "Made in England"
B. Embossed "Hand Cast Porcelain Made in England"

No.	Name	Colourways	Size	U.S.$	Can.$	U.K.£
L-330a	Royal Navy Toasts	Blue/white; multi-coloured label	146	60.00	80.00	30.00
L-330b	West Indies	Blue/white; multi-coloured label	150	60.00	80.00	30.00
L-330c	Royal Navy Rum Terminology	Blue/white; multi-coloured prints	146	70.00	90.00	35.00
L-330d	Victory America's Cup Challenge	Blue/white; multicoloured print	146	70.00	90.00	35.00

SHIP'S DECANTERS

Ship's decanters are heavy and very wide at the bottom, giving them stability in rough seas. All Pusser's Rum decanters are sealed with red wax, and ceramic-capped corks are attached by a cord to the handles.

Admiral Lord Nelson, 1983-1996

One-Litre Decanter (front)

One-Litre Decanter (back)

Backstamp: "Nelson Finest English Porcelain Wade Staffordshire England"

No.	Description	Colourways	Size	U.S.$	Can.$	U.K.£
L-331	Decanter	White: blue cap/neck; multi-coloured prints	Miniature/90	40.00	45.00	20.00
L-332	Decanter	Blue/white; multi-coloured prints	One Litre/240	95.00	135.00	50.00

John Paul Jones, 1992

Backstamp: "Pusser's Ltd. British Virgin Islands, West Indies, The John Paul Jones - U.S. Navy and Marine Corps Decanter"

No.	Description	Colourways	Size	U.S.$	Can.$	U.K.£
L-333	Decanter	Blue/white; multi-coloured prints	220	60.00	80.00	30.00

WATER JUG, 1996

This water jug has a recessed handle and open spout. It has a print of the Pusser's Rum label on the front and the traditional toasts of the Royal Navy on the back.

Water Jug (front)

Water Jug (back)

Backstamp: "Royal Victoria Pottery Staffordshire England"

No.	Description	Colourways	Shape/Size	U.S.$	Can.$	U.K.£
L-334	Water Jug	White; blue rim; multi-coloured prints	Round/146	30.00	35.00	12.00

QUEEN ANNE SCOTCH WHISKY

ASHTRAYS AND WATER JUGS, 1955–1990

The ashtrays were produced between 1955 and 1962, the water jugs between 1955 and 1990. The style L-338 jug has an ice-check spout, and style L-339 has an open spout with a recessed handle. Style L-339 is decorated with a transfer print of Queen Anne.

Ashtray (L-335)

Backstamp: **A.** "Wade Regicor, London England," laurel leaves, large size
B. "Wade p d m England"

No.	Description	Colourways	Shape/Size	U.S.$	Can.$	U.K.£
L-335	Ashtray	Black; grey/gold crest; white lettering "Queen Anne Rare Scotch Whisky"	Round/153	15.00	20.00	8.00
L-336	Ashtray	Black; white lettering "Queen Anne Rare Scotch Whisky"	Square/146 clipped corners	15.00	20.00	8.00
L-337	Ashtray	Black; grey/gold crest; white lettering "Queen Anne Rare Scotch Whisky"	Square/153	15.00	20.00	8.00
L-338	Water Jug	Mottled stone; black lettering "Queen Anne Scotch Whisky"	Round/177	25.00	30.00	12.00
L-339	Water Jug	Black; multi-coloured print, white lettering "Queen Anne Scotch Whisky"	Round/127	25.00	30.00	12.00

RAWLINGS

DRINK POURERS, c.1970–c.1980

These pourers are shape number 5455/1 and came with plastic tubes.

Photograph not available
at press time

Backstamp: Unmarked

No.	Description	Colourways	Shape/Size	U.S.$	Can.$	U.K.£
L-340a	Drink Pourer	Yellow/black; gold lettering "Rawlings"	Octagonal/40	30.00	35.00	15.00
L-340b	Drink Pourer	White/yellow; black lettering "Rawlings Mixing Waters"	Octagonal/40	30.00	35.00	15.00

REBEL YELL

DRINK POURER, 1995

This pourer has a rounded top and base and straight sides; it is shape number C57. It was produced with a metal tube.

Photograph not available at press time

Backstamp: Unmarked

No.	Description	Colourways	Size	U.S.$	Can.$	U.K.£
L-341	Round	White; grey lettering "Rebel Yell"	41	30.00	35.00	15.00

THE REVEREND JAMES ALE

TANKARD

This bulbous pint tankard is rimmed in gold lustre and decorated with a portrait of the Reverend James. It has a large round handle.

Photograph not available at press time

No.	Description	Colourways	Size	U.S.$	Can.$	U.K.£
L-342	Tankard	White; gold rim; black/red print	112	25.00	30.00	12.00

ROBYN HOODE DISTILLERIES

HORN DECANTER, 1993

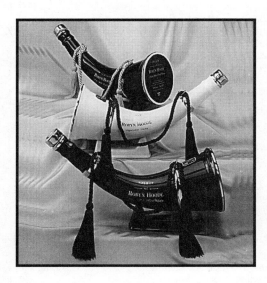

Backstamp: "Wade - England"

No.	Description	Colourways	Size	U.S.$	Can.$	U.K.£
L-343a	Decanter	White decanter, stand; gold decoration; black cord	360	80.00	100.00	40.00
L-343b	Decanter	Black decanter, stand; gold decoration, cord	360	80.00	100.00	40.00

ROMANOFF VODKA

ASHTRAY AND WATER JUG, 1969–1990

The ashtray was issued between 1984 and 1990. The jug, which has an open spout and is decorated with a print of two eagles, was issued between 1969 and 1984.

Photograph not available
at press time

Backstamp: A. "Wade pdm England"
B. "Wade p d m England"

No.	Description	Colourways	Shape/Size	U.S.$	Can.$	U.K.£
L-344	Ashtray	Black; white/red lettering "Romanoff Vodka"	Square/140	10.00	15.00	5.00
L-345	Water Jug	Black; gold print; red/white/black lettering "Romanoff Vodka"	Round/205	0.00	35.00	15.00

SACCONE & SPEED

ASHTRAY, 1962-1968

Photograph not available at press time

Backstamp: A. "Wade Regicor, London England," laurel leaves, large size
B. "Wade Regicor, London England," laurel leaves, small size

No.	Description	Colourways	Shape/Size	U.S.$	Can.$	U.K.£
L-346	Ashtray	Black; white lettering "Saccone & Speed"	Round/140	15.00	20.00	8.00

SAMUEL WEBSTER

Ash Bowl, 1984-1990

Backstamp: "Wade p d m England"

No.	Description	Colourways	Shape/Size	U.S.$	Can.$	U.K.£
L-347	Ash Bowl	Green; cream print, lettering "Samuel Webster 1838 Yorkshire"	Circular/250	30.00	35.00	15.00

SEAGRAM'S SCOTCH WHISKY

WATER JUG, 1984-1990

This water jug has an ice-check spout.

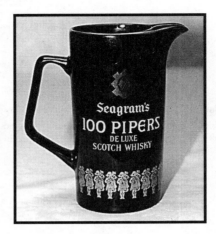

Backstamp: "Wade p d m England"

No.	Description	Colourways	Shape/Size	U.S.$	Can.$	U.K.£
L-348	Water Jug	Black; gold print; white lettering "Seagram's 100 Piper's De Luxe Scotch Whisky"	Round/175	25.00	30.00	12.00

SMIRNOFF VODKA

DRINK POURERS AND TANKARD, c.1970-1992

These pourers, shape C53, have a straight base and are found with a metal tube and spout. The issue date of the tankard is unknown. The print on the tankard is of the Smirnoff Vodka label.

Backstamp: "Wade Regicor Made in UK"

No.	Description	Colourways	Shape/Size	U.S.$	Can.$	U.K.£
L-349a	Drink Pourer	White; yellow crown; red lettering "Smirnoff Vodka"	Circular/41	30.00	35.00	15.00
L-349b	Drink Pourer	White; multi-coloured lettering "Smirnoff"	Circular/41	30.00	35.00	15.00
L-350	Tankard	Black; red/gold label	Pint/115	10.00	15.00	5.00

SPRINGBANK WHISKY

WATER JUG, 1969-1984

This water jug has an open spout.

Photograph not available at press time

Backstamp: "Wade pdm England"

No.	Description	Colourways	Shape/Size	U.S.$	Can.$	U.K.£
L-351	Water Jug	Black; gold/white lettering "Springbank Whisky"	Round/153	30.00	35.00	15.00

STAR BEERS

WATER JUG, 1960-1962

This jug has a recessed handle and open spout. It is decorated with a print of a town crier.

Photograph not available at press time

Backstamp: "Wade Regicor, London England," laurel leaves, large size

No.	Description	Colourways	Shape/Size	U.S.$	Can.$	U.K.£
L-352	Water Jug	White; black/red print; black lettering "Star Beers Brightest and Best since 1777"	Round/102	30.00	35.00	15.00

STONES BITTER

COUNTER DISPLAY AND WATER JUG, 1968-1995

The counter display was issued between 1968 and 1984, the water jug between 1990 and 1995.

Backstamp: **A.** "Wade pdm England"
B. "Wade P D M Made in England"

No.	Description	Colourways	Shape/Size	U.S.$	Can.$	U.K.£
L-353	Counter display	Dull yellow; gold/black print; red/black lettering "Stones Best Bitter"	Rectangular/210	25.00	30.00	12.00
L-354	Water Jug/ open spout	Yellow; white/red lettering "Stones Best Bitter"	Rectangular/133	15.00	20.00	8.00

STOWELLS OF CHELSEA

DRINK POURER

This drink pourer, shape C53, has a straight base.

Photograph not available
at press time

Backstamp: Unmarked

No.	Description	Colourways	Shape/Size	U.S.$	Can.$	U.K.£
L-355	Drink Pourer	White; plastic tube; blue lettering "Stowells of Chelsea"	Circular/41	38.00	50.00	15.00

STRONGBOW CIDER

ASHTRAY, 1969-1984

Backstamp: "Wade pdm England"

No.	Description	Colourways	Size	U.S.$	Can.$	U.K.£
L-356	Ashtray	Black; white print; yellow lettering "Strongbow"	175	30.00	35.00	15.00

TANQUERAY ENGLISH GIN

ASHTRAY, DRINK POURERS AND WATER JUG, 1969-1990

The ashtray was produced between 1984 and 1990 and the drink pourers and water jug between 1969 and 1984. The pourers, shape number C52A, have a notched base and shoulders. They were produced with plastic tubes. The water jug has an ice-check spout.

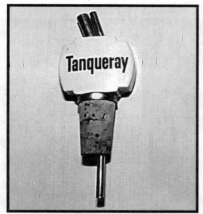

Drink Pourer (L-358a)

Water Jug

Backstamp: A. "Wade p d m England"
   B. "Wade pdm England," "Imported by the Buckingham Corporation New York. NY. Distilled Blended and Bottled in Scotland 86 Proof"

No.	Description	Colourways	Shape/Size	U.S.$	Can.$	U.K.£
L-357	Ashtray	Green; black lettering "Tanqueray English Gin"	Oval/177	10.00	15.00	5.00
L-358a	Drink Pourer	White; dark green lettering "Tanqueray"	Square/38	30.00	35.00	15.00
L-358b	Drink Pourer	Yellow; black lettering "Tanqueray"	Square/38	30.00	35.00	15.00
L-359	Water Jug	Dark green; white label; red/black lettering "Tanqueray Special Dry"	Round/177	25.00	30.00	12.00

TAUNTON CIDER PLC

CIDER JUGS, c.1985

These jugs, with a flat outer edge on the handle, were used on pub bars as advertising pieces and contained no cider. They were produced with various labels on the fronts which advertised Taunton products. Style L-359c has a circular plastic label on the front and stands on a base bearing the words "Made by Taunton Cider Co Ltd."

Small Jugs

Small and Large Jug (L-360a, L-362a)

Small Jug (L-361)

Backstamp: Unmarked

No.	Description	Colourways	Size	U.S.$	Can.$	U.K.£
L-360a	Cider Jug	Dark brown/red; black/yellow/white label "Autumn Gold Premium Cider"	Small/159	40.00	45.00	20.00
L-360b	Cider Jug	Dark brown/off white; black/white/gold label "Dry Blackthorn Cooled on Draught"	Small/159	40.00	45.00	20.00
L-360c	Cider Jug	Dark brown/off white; black/gold label "Cider Darts Champion Number One in Britain"	Small/159	50.00	70.00	25.00
L-361	Cider Jug	Dark brown/off white; black/white/yellow plastic label "Dry Blackthorn Cider"; brown plastic stand	Small/159	50.00	70.00	25.00
L-362a	Cider Jug	Dark brown/red; black/yellow/white label "Autumn Gold Premium Cider"	Large/210	70.00	90.00	35.00
L-362b	Cider Jug	Dark brown/off white; black/white/gold label "Dry Blackthorn Cooled on Draught"	Large/210	70.00	90.00	35.00
L-362c	Cider Jug	Dark brown/off white; black/yellow/gold label "Dry Blackthorn Cooled on Draught"	Large/210	70.00	90.00	35.00

LAMP

On the front of this "Cider Jug Lamp" is a black transfer print of two men and two horses turning a cider press. The lamp shade is white with a brown band around the rim, bearing the words "Taunton Cider" in large white letters.

Photograph not available
at press time

No.	Description	Colourways	Size	U.S.$	Can.$	U.K.£
L-363	Lamp	Dark brown/off-white jug; black print, lettering	210	60.00	80.00	30.00

LOVING CUPS

The Taunton Cider Company has a large collection of early 19th-century cider mugs and loving cups. Starting in 1973, Wade was given the task of reproducing some of the original designs onto loving cups and mugs. All the miniature loving cups were issued in pairs.

Apples and Blossom, 1986

"Apples and Blossom"

Backstamp: "A limited number of these traditional Cider Mugs were produced by Wade Potteries for the Taunton Cider Company"

No.	Description	Colourways	Size	U.S.$	Can.$	U.K.£
L-364	1986 Loving Cup	White; green leaves; red apples; white blossoms	1/2 pint/83	51.00	70.00	25.00

Apples and Leaves, 1985

This loving cup has bands of apple leaves printed around the inside rim and a garland of leaves around the centre design of apples.

Photograph not available
at press time

Backstamp: "500 of these Traditional Cider Mugs were reproduced by Wade Potteries For the Taunton Cider Company 1985"

No.	Description	Colourways	Size	U.S.$	Can.$	U.K.£
L-365	1985 Loving Cup	White; red/green print	1/2 pint/83	40.00	45.00	20.00

Apples and Leaves (Five), 1981

On the front and back of this loving cup are the words "Taunton Cider" with a print of five apples and leaves. A print of bunches of green leaves decorate the handles and inside the cup.

"Apples and Leaves"

Backstamp: "A Limited number of these traditional Cider Mugs were produced by Wade Potteries for the Taunton Cider Company 1981"

No.	Description	Colourways	Size	U.S.$	Can.$	U.K.£
L-366	1981 Loving Cup	White; green leaves; red apples; white blossom	1/2 pint/83	50.00	70.00	25.00

Arthur Moore–Blackthorn Cider Label

The half-pint loving cup has the story of Arthur Moore, the founder of the Taunton Cider Company, printed on the back.

Arthur Moore–Blackthorn Cider Label

Backstamp: "Wade pdm England"

No.	Description	Colourways	Size	U.S.$	Can.$	U.K.£
L-367	Loving Cup	White; black/white label, lettering "Taunton Dry Blackthorn Cider"	1/2 pint/85	50.00	70.00	25.00
L-368	Loving Cup	White; black/white label, lettering "Taunton Dry Blackthorn Cider"	Pint/120	50.00	70.00	25.00

Autumn Gold Cider Press, 1980, 1987

This loving cup has a transfer print on both sides showing men working on 19th-century Taunton Mill cider presses with the words, "Presented by The Taunton Cider Company." On version L-369a the print runs onto the handles; on version L-369b there is no print on the handles. They were produced in 1980. In 1987 a miniature limited-edition loving cup was issued.

No print on handles, left; print on handles, right

Backstamp: A. "Wade pdm England"
B. "Pair of 500 of these Traditional Cider Mugs were produced in miniature by Wade Potteries For the Taunton Cider Company 1987"

No.	Description	Colourways	Size	U.S.$	Can.$	U.K.£
L-369a	1980 Loving Cup	White; black print, print on handles	1/2 pint/83	50.00	70.00	25.00
L-369b	1980 Loving Cup	White; black print, no print on handles	1/2 pint/83	40.00	45.00	20.00
L-370	1987 Loving Cup	White; black print	Miniature/65	40.00	45.00	20.00

British Darts and Euchre Champions, 1981

These loving cups were produced for the British Dart Championships and the British Euchre Championships in 1981. The print is of a large *T* surrounded by apples.

Photograph not available
at press time

Backstamp: "A limited number of these traditional Cider Mugs were produced by Wade Potteries for the Taunton Cider Company"

No.	Description	Colourways	Size	U.S.$	Can.$	U.K.£
L-371a	1981 Loving Cup	Beige; black print, lettering "Taunton Cider British Darts Championship 1981"	Pint/120	50.00	70.00	25.00
L-371b	1981 Loving Cup	Beige; black print	Pint/120	50.00	70.00	25.00

Girl with Goat, 1976-1977

The quart loving cup was produced in 1976, and the miniature was issued in 1977.

"Girl with a Goat"

Backstamp: **A.** "500 of these Traditional Cider Mugs were reproduced by Wade Potteries for the Taunton Cider Company 1976"
B. "500 of these Traditional Cider Mugs were Produced in Miniature by Wade Potteries for the Taunton Cider Company 1977"

No.	Description	Colourways	Size	U.S.$	Can.$	U.K.£
L-372	1976 Loving Cup	White; black/yellow/red print	Quart/135	95.00	130.00	50.00
L-373	1977 Loving Cup	White; black/yellow/red print	Miniature/65	30.00	35.00	15.00

God Speed The Plough Loving Cups, 1973-1975, 1981

1973 God Speed the Plough

1974 God Speed the Plough

1981 God Speed the Plough

Backstamp: **A.** "500 of these Traditional Cider Mugs were reproduced by Wade Potteries for the Taunton Cider Company 1973"
B. "500 of these Traditional Cider Mugs were reproduced by Wade Potteries for the Taunton Cider Company 1974"
C. "Royal Victoria Pottery Staffordshire, Wade England"
D. "500 pairs of these Traditional Cider Mugs were produced in miniature by Wade Potteries for the Taunton Cider Company 1981"

No.	Description	Colourways	Size	U.S.$	Can.$	U.K.£
L-374	1973 Loving Cup	White; black/brown print	Quart/120	95.00	135.00	50.00
L-375	1974 Loving Cup	White; multi-coloured print	1/2 pint/83	95.00	135.00	50.00
L-376	1975 Loving Cup	White; multi-coloured print	Miniature/65	30.00	35.00	15.00
L-377	1981 Loving Cup	White; black/brown print	Miniature/65	30.00	35.00	15.00

Holly Leaves, 1994

Holly leaves and berries decorate this loving cup.

Photograph not available
at press time

Backstamp: "This Mug is one of five hundred specially commissioned by Taunton Cider. It is reproduced from a 19th century presentation original. 1994 Wade"

No.	Description	Colourways	Size	U.S.$	Can.$	U.K.£
L-378	1994 Loving Cup	White; green/red/gold leaves	Pint/120	60.00	80.00	30.00

Home Place, 1987

1987 The Home Place

Backstamp: "A limited edition of this Traditional Cider Mug was reproduced for Taunton Cider by Wade Potteries, Staffordshire"

No.	Description	Colourways	Size	U.S.$	Can.$	U.K.£
L-379	1987 Loving Cup	White; multi-coloured print	1/2 pint/83	50.00	70.00	25.00

19th-Century Floral Design, 1983-1984

The print on these cups is of flowers and leaves.

Photograph not available
at press time

Backstamp: **A.** "This Mug is one of a limited edition of five hundred specially commissioned by Taunton Cider. It is produced from a 19th Century original in the Taunton Cider collection 1983 Wade"
B. "500 of these Traditional Cider Mugs were reproduced by Wade Potteries for the Taunton Cider Company 1984"

No.	Description	Colourways	Size	U.S.$	Can.$	U.K.£
L-380	1983 Loving Cup	White; deep red/white flowers; green/yellow/ grey leaves; gold/blue rim	Quart/130	95.00	135.00	50.00
L-381	1984 Loving Cup	White; pale pink/blue flowers; green leaves	Quart/130	95.00	135.00	50.00

19th Century Floral Design, 1988

This cup is decorated with a 19th-century floral design.

Photograph not available
at press time

Backstamp: "A Limited edition of this Traditional Cider Mug was reproduced for Taunton Cider by Wade Potteries Staffordshire"

No.	Description	Colourways	Size	U.S.$	Can.$	U.K.£
L-382	1988 Loving Cup	White; black rim, base, handles; multi-coloured flowers	Pint/120	80.00	100.00	40.00

Peonies and Swallow, 1991

The Chinese-style print on this cup is of large peonies and a bird on a tree branch. "Taunton Cider May 1991" is printed around the base.

Photograph not available
at press time

Backstamp: "This mug is one of a limited eiditon of five hundred specially commissioned by Taunton Cider. It is produced from a 19th Century original in the Taunton Cider collection, 1991 Wade"

No.	Description	Colourways	Size	U.S.$	Can.$	U.K.£
L383	1991 Loving Cup	White; gold rim; blue/red/yellow/pink flowers, bird	120	100.00	145.00	55.00

Pastel Garden, 1992

"Pastel Garden"

Backstamp: "This Mug is one of a limited edition of five hundred specially commissioned by Taunton Cider. It is produced from a 19th Century original in the Taunton Cider collection, 1992 Wade"

No.	Description	Colourways	Size	U.S.$	Can.$	U.K.£
L-384	1992 Loving Cup	Pastel green; pink blossom; light brown leaves	Pint/120	95.00	135.00	50.00
L-385	1992 Loving Cup	Pastel green; pink blossom; light brown leaves	1/2 pint/90	80.00	110.00	40.00

Somerset Hunt Master of Hounds,1975

1975 "Somerset Hunt Master of Hounds," front   1975 "Somerset Hunt Master of Hounds," back

Backstamp: "500 of these Traditional Cider Mugs were reproduced by Wade Potteries For the Taunton Cider Company 1975"

No.	Description	Colourways	Size	U.S.$	Can.$	U.K.£
L-386	1975 Loving Cup	White; multi-coloured print	Pint/125	95.00	135.00	50.00

Note: See Commemorative Ware for the 1977 "Silver Jubilee Loving Cup."

Spitting Frog, 1995

This loving cup has a model of a spitting frog inside the cup. A blackberry print decorates the outside.

Photograph not available
at press time

Backstamp: "This Frog mug is one of a limited edition of five hundred specially commissioned by Taunton Cider. It is copied from a 19th century original in the Taunton Cider Collection. 1995 Wade PDM. Made in England"

No.	Description	Colourways	Size	U.S.$	Can.$	U.K.£
L-387	1995 Loving Cup	White; blue berries; light brown frog	Quart/120	100.00	145.00	55.00

Spring Flowers, 1990

A single transfer print of spring flowers, illustrated in the 19th-century style, is on this cup.

"Spring Flowers"

Backstamp: "500 of these traditional cider mugs were reproduced by Wade Potteries for the Taunton Cider Company 1990"

No.	Description	Colourways	Size	U.S.$	Can.$	U.K.£
L-388	1990 Loving Cup	White; black print	Pint/120	80.00	110.00	40.00

"T" Logo

"Taunton Cider" Loving Cup

"Taunton Tradition Draught" Loving Cup

Backstamp: "Wade pdm England"

No.	Description	Colourways	Size	U.S.$	Can.$	U.K.£
L-389	Loving Cup	White cup; orange apples; black lettering "Taunton Cider"	1/2 pint/83	50.00	70.00	25.00
L-390	Loving Cup	White; orange apples, red/black lettering "Taunton Traditional Draught"	Quart/140	50.00	70.00	25.00

Taunton Cider Story, 1978-1979

This loving cup has a large *T* on the front, with a cascade of apples on each side, and the words "The Taunton Cider Company." A print of a thatched-roof cottage is on the back with the story of Taunton Cider.

"Taunton Cider Story"

Backstamp: A. "A limited edition of 4,000 produced for the Taunton Cider Company by Wade Heath Potteries Staffordshire in the year of 1978"
B. "A limited edition of 4,000 produced for the Taunton Cider Company by Wade Heath Potteries Staffordshire in the year of 1979"

No.	Description	Colourways	Size	U.S.$	Can.$	U.K.£
L-391	1978 Loving Cup	White; red *T*; orange/red apples; yellow print	1/2 pint/85	80.00	100.00	40.00
L-392	1979 Loving Cup	White; red *T*; orange/red apples; yellow print	1/2 pint/85	80.00	100.00	40.00

Three-Handled Loving Cup, 1978

The three handles of this unusual loving cup are edged with gold. There is a spray of flowers between each handle.

"Three-Handled Loving Cup"

Backstamp: "500 of these Traditional Cider Mugs were reproduced by Wade Potteries For the Taunton Cider Company 1978"

No.	Description	Colourways	Size	U.S.$	Can.$	U.K.£
L-393	1978 Loving Cup	White; gold rim, base, handles; multi-coloured flowers	Pint/120	95.00	135.00	50.00

Views of Taunton, 1974, 1982

1974, 1982 Views of Taunton Miniature Loving Cups

Backstamp: **A.** "500 of these Traditional Cider Mugs were reproduced by Wade Potteries For the Taunton Cider Company 1974"
B. "This Mug is one of a limited edition of five hundred specially commissioned by Taunton Cider. It is produced from a 19th Century original in the Taunton Cider collection 1974 Wade"
C. "500 pairs of these Traditional Cider Mugs were produced in miniature by Wade Potteries For the Taunton Cider Company 1982"

No.	Description	Colourways	Size	U.S.$	Can.$	U.K.£
L-394	1974 Loving Cup	White; blue print	Quart/130	70.00	90.00	35.00
L-395	1974 Loving Cup	White; blue print	Pint/120	70.00	90.00	35.00
L-396	1982 Loving Cup	White; blue print	Miniature/65	40.00	45.00	20.00

The Wassailing Story, 1987

A transfer print of men firing guns into an orchard is on the front of this loving cup and the history of wassailing on the reverse with the words, "Taunton Cider keeps alive the tradition of 'Wassailing' the apple trees." Each year Taunton sponsors this event, in which the trees are annointed with honey and bread to assure a good harvest.

"The Wassailing Story"

Backstamp: "Produced exclusively for the Taunton Cider Company by Wade Potteries of Staffordshire"

No.	Description	Colourways	Size	U.S.$	Can.$	U.K.£
L-397	1987 Loving Cup	Cream; brown print	1/2 pint/83	80.00	100.00	40.00

MUGS

Chain of Flowers, 1977

"Chain of Flowers"

Backstamp: "500 of these traditional Cider Mugs were reproduced by Wade Potteries for the Taunton Cider Company 1977"

No.	Description	Colourways	Size	U.S.$	Can.$	U.K.£
L-398	1977 Mug	White; multi-coloured flowers	Pint/105	80.00	100.00	40.00

Floral Trees, 1980

An ornate design of flowers and trees was printed on this mug.

Photograph not available
at press time

Backstamp: "This Mug is one of a limited edition of five hundred specially commissioned by Taunton Cider. It is produced
from a 19th Century original in the Taunton Cider collection 1980 Wade"

No.	Description	Colourways	Size	U.S.$	Can.$	U.K.£
L-399	1980 Mug	White; red-brown/black print	Pint/120	80.00	100.00	40.00

Ladies With Parasols in Garden, 1989

An 19th-century scene of ladies with parasols walking under a bower of trees decorates this mug.

Photograph not available
at press time

Backstamp: 500 of these traditional cider mugs were reproduced by Wade Potteres for the Taunton Cider Company 1980

No.	Description	Colourways	Size	U.S.$	Can.$	U.K.£
L-400	1989 Mug	White; blue print	Pint/120	80.00	100.00	40.00

The Miller, 1977

1977 "The Miller" Mug

Backstamp: "500 of these tradition Cider Mugs were reproduced by Wade Potteries for the Taunton Cider Company 1977"

No.	Description	Colourways	Size	U.S.$	Can.$	U.K.£
L-401	1977 Mug	White; black print	Pint/105	80.00	100.00	40.00

Stock Exchange Floral, 1992

This mug is decorated with a gold-leaf design. It was produced to commemorate the listing of Taunton Cider on the stock exchange on July 23, 1992, and was presented to Taunton employees.

Photograph not available
at press time

Backstamp: "A limited edition drinking Mug copied from an original, dating from 1820, which is held in the Taunton Cider Collection. This mug was produced to Commemorate Taunton Cider's Listing on the Stock Exchange, 23rd July 1992, Wade No. 20"

No.	Description	Colourways	Size	U.S.$	Can.$	U.K.£
L-402	1992 Mug	Navy blue; gold decoration	Pint/120	200.00	275.00	100.00

"T", 1973-1974

"T" Mug

Backstamp: "Wade pdm England"

No.	Description	Colourways	Size	U.S.$	Can.$	U.K.£
L-403	Mug	Pink; black apples	Miniature /63	50.00	70.00	25.00
L-404	Mug	Yellow; red/orange apples	1/2 pint/83	50.00	70.00	25.00

Victorian Sporting Scenes, 1993

Victorian scenes of cricket and soccer players are printed on this mug.

Photograph not available
at press time

Backstamp: "This mug is one of a limited edition of five hundred specially commissioned by Taunton Cider. It is produced from a 19th century original in the Taunton Cider Collection. 1993 Wade"

No.	Description	Colourways	Size	U.S.$	Can.$	U.K.£
L-405	1993 Mug	White; pink print	Quart/120	60.00	80.00	30.00

PUMP HANDLES, 1970S

Beer-pump handles were produced by Wade PDM for Taunton, which installed them in the public houses that served their draught ciders.

Pump handle (L-406), Pump handle (L-407)

Backstamp: Unmarked

No.	Description	Colourways	Size	U.S.$	Can.$	U.K.£
L-406	Pump Handles	Brown; multi-coloured lettering "Taunton Traditional Draught Cider"	170	38.00	50.00	15.00
L-407	Pump Handles	White; red/multi-coloured lettering "Taunton T"	225	30.00	35.00	15.00

TEACHER'S SCOTCH WHISKY

ASHTRAY AND WATER JUGS, 1984-1990

The round jugs have ice-check spouts; the square jug has an open spout.

Jug (L-409)

Jug (L-410)

Backstamp: A. "Wade pdm England"
B. "Wade p d m England"

No.	Description	Colourways	Shape/Size	U.S.$	Can.$	U.K.£
L-408	Ashtray	Yellow; black print, lettering "Teacher's Highland Cream"	Round/153	10.00	15.00	5.00
L-409	Water Jug	Black; gold lettering "Teacher's Scotch Whisky in a class of its own"	Round/127	25.00	30.00	12.00
L-410	Water Jug	Cream; gold logo; black lettering "Teacher's Highland Cream Scotch Whisky"	Round/133	25.00	30.00	12.00
L-411	Water Jug	Black; gold lettering "Teacher's Scotch Whisky"	Square/125	25.00	30.00	12.00

TENNANTS

ASHTRAYS, 1955-1990

Ashtray (L-412a)

Ashtray (L-414)

Backstamp: **A.** "Wade Regicor, London England," laurel leaves, large size
B. "Wade pdm England"
C. "Wade p d m England"

No.	Description	Colourways	Shape/Size	U.S.$	Can.$	U.K.£
L-412a	Ashtray	White/dark green band; multi-coloured label, lettering "Tennants Gold Label Sparkling Barley Wine"	Round/140	15.00	20.00	8.00
L-412b	Ashtray	Green/white; multi-coloured label, lettering "Tennants Gold Label Sparkling Barley Wine"	Round/140	15.00	20.00	8.00
L-413a	Ashtray	White; multi-coloured label, lettering "Tennants Gold Label Sparkling Barley Wine"	Square/140	15.00	20.00	8.00
L-413b	Ashtray	Red; white lettering "Tennants Best Bitter"	Square/140	15.00	20.00	8.00
L-413c	Ashtray	Black; red lettering "Tennants Extra"	Square/140	15.00	20.00	8.00
L-414	Ashtray	White; red/black lettering "Tennants Glucose Stout for Vitality Plus"	Square/146	15.00	20.00	8.00

TENNENT'S LAGER

ASHTRAYS AND WATER JUGS, 1969-1995

All these jugs have open spouts.

Ashtray (L-415)

Ashtray (L-416)

Water Jug (L-417)

Water Jug (L-419)

Water Jug (L-420)

Backstamp: **A.** "Wade pdm England"
B. "Wade p d m England"
C. "Wade P D M Made in England"

No.	Description	Colourways	Shape/Size	U.S.$	Can.$	U.K.£
L-415	Ashtray	Black; white/yellow lettering "Tennent's Extra Export Lager"	Square/177	10.00	15.00	5.00
L-416	Ashtray	Black; white lettering "Tennent's Lager"	Square/177	10.00	15.00	5.00
L-417	Water Jug	White; blue/red lettering "Tennent's Lager"	Rectangular/114	25.00	30.00	12.00
L-418	Water Jug	White; red/blue lettering "Lots of Tennent's Lager"	Rectangular/140	25.00	30.00	12.00
L-419	Water Jug	White; red/black lettering "T Tennent's Lager"	Round/165	25.00	30.00	12.00
L-420	Water Jug	Royal blue; white lettering "Tennent's Lager"	Square/114	25.00	30.00	12.00

TETLEY ALES

ASHTRAY, 1984-1990

Photograph not available
at press time

Backstamp: "Wade p d m England"

No.	Description	Colourways	Shape/Size	U.S.$	Can.$	U.K.£
L-421	Ashtray	Yellow; red lettering "Tetley Ales"	Round/195	10.00	15.00	5.00

THEAKSTON ALE

ASHTRAY, 1990-1995

Photograph not available
at press time

Backstamp: "Wade P D M Made in England"

No.	Description	Colourways	Shape/Size	U.S.$	Can.$	U.K.£
L-422	Ashtray	White; black lettering "Theakston Traditional Ale"	Round/140	15.00	20.00	8.00

THORNE'S SCOTCH WHISKY

WATER JUG

This jug has an ice-check spout.

Photograph not available at press time

Backstamp: "Reginald Corfield Limited Redhill Surrey," "Wade Regicor England"

No.	Description	Colourways	Size	U.S.$	Can.$	U.K.£
L-423	Oval	White; black lettering "Thorne's 10 yr old Scotch"	165	30.00	35.00	15.00

THORNTON AND FRANCE SHERRY

SHERRY BARREL, 1980

This sherry barrel has a wooden tap and sits on a stand. The lettering is on the front of the barrel.

Photograph not available at press time

Backstamp: "Royal Victoria Pottery Staffordshire Wade England"

No.	Description	Colourways	Size	U.S.$	Can.$	U.K.£
L-424	Sherry Barrel	Brown; gold bands, lettering "Thornton & France produce of Spain Sherry"	224	115.00	130.00	85.00

TIA MARIA JAMAICAN LIQUEUR

WATER JUGS, 1969-1984

The style L-425 jug has an ice-check spout; style L-426 has a recessed handle and an open spout.

Water Jug (L-425)   **Water Jug (L-426)**

Backstamp: "Wade pdm England"

No.	Description	Colourways	Shape/Size	U.S.$	Can.$	U.K.£
L-425	Water Jug	Black; gold lettering "Tia Maria Liqueur"	Rectangular/165	25.00	30.00	12.00
L-426	Water Jug	Dark brown; yellow lettering "Tia Maria The Jamaican Liqueur"	Round/114	25.00	30.00	12.00

TOBERMORY WHISKY

DECANTER, 1991

Photograph not available
at press time

No.	Description	Colourways	Size	U.S.$	Can.$	U.K.£
L-427	Decanter	White; black/gold lettering "Tobermory Whisky"	305	60.00	80.00	30.00

TREBLE GOLD

ASHTRAY, 1955-1962

This ashtray has a print on it of a horseshoe.

Photograph not available at press time

Backstamp: "Wade Regicor, London England," laurel leaves, large size

No.	Description	Colourways	Shape/Size	U.S.$	Can.$	U.K.£
L-428	Ashtray	Pale green; red/white print; red lettering "Treble Gold"	Rectangular/225	10.00	15.00	5.00

TULLAMORE DEW SCOTCH WHISKY

WATER JUG, 1994-1996

This water jug has an open spout.

Photograph not available at press time

Backstamp: "Wade p d m Made in England"

No.	Description	Colourways	Size	U.S.$	Can.$	U.K.£
L-429	Rectangular	Black; white lettering "Tullamore Dew Finest Old Irish Whisky"	133	25.00	30.00	12.00

USHER'S SCOTCH WHISKY

WATER JUG, 1955-1962

This jug has an extra long spout.

Photograph not available at press time

Backstamp: "Wade Regicor, London England," laurel leaves, large size

No.	Description	Colourways	Size	U.S.$	Can.$	U.K.£
L-430	Round	Cream; black lettering "Usher's Scotch Whisky"	127	25.00	30.00	12.00

VAT 69 SCOTCH WHISKY

ASHTRAYS, DRINK POURERS AND WATER JUGS, 1955-1980

The drink pourers, shape C53, have a straight base. The jugs have an open spout and recessed handles.

Ashtray (L-431)

Ashtray (L-432b)

Water Jug (L-436a)

Backstamp: **A.** "Wade Regicor, London England," laurel leaves, large size
B. "Reginald Corfield Limited Redhill Surrey," "Wade Regicor England"
C. "Wade pdm England"
D. "Wade Regicor Make in UK"

No.	Description	Colourways	Shape/Size	U.S.$	Can.$	U.K.£
L-431	Ashtray	Black; white/gold lettering "Vat 69 Finest Scotch Whisky"	Round/101	15.00	20.00	8.00
L-432a	Ashtray	White/light blue; black/gold lettering "Vat 69 Scotch Whisky"	Round/101	15.00	20.00	8.00
L-432b	Ashtray	White/dark blue; black/gold lettering "Vat 69 Scotch Whisky"	Round/101	15.00	20.00	8.00
L-433	Ashtray	Blue; white lettering "Vat 69"	Square/140	15.00	20.00	8.00
L-434	Ashtray	Dark blue; white lettering "Vat 69"	Square/140 clipped corners	15.00	20.00	8.00
L-435a	Drink Pourer	Black; porcelain tube; gold line; white lettering "Vat 69"	Circular/41	30.00	35.00	15.00
L-435b	Drink Pourer	Cream; porcelain tube; gold lettering "Vat 69"	Circular/41	30.00	35.00	15.00
L-436a	Water Jug	Black; white lettering "Finest Scotch Whisky Vat 69 "	Round/108	30.00	35.00	15.00
L-436b	Water Jug	Black; white/gold lettering "Vat 69"	Round/108	30.00	35.00	15.00

VAUX BREWERIES

ASHTRAY, 1969-1984

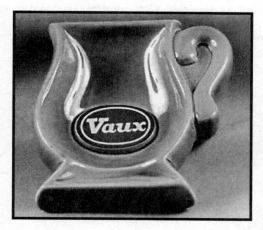

Backstamp: "Wade pdm England"

No.	Description	Colourways	Shape/Size	U.S.$	Can.$	U.K.£
L-437	Ashtray	Amber; red label; white lettering "Vaux"	Tankard/177	25.00	30.00	12.00

BEER STEIN, 1983

The one-pint "School of Sport Stein" was issued in 1983. It has purple lustre bands around the rim and several transfer prints of various sports with the words, "21st Anniversary—Vaux Sportsman and Sportswoman of the Year Vaux School of Sport—Lorimer & Clark Edinburgh, Liefmans Oudenaarde, Fred Koch New York State, Vaux Sunderland, Wards Sheffield, Darleys Doncaster—1983 Limited Edition."

See page 362 for illustration

Backstamp: "Wade pdm England"

No.	Name	Colourways	Size	U.S.$	Can.$	U.K.£
L-438	1983 School of Sport Tankard	White; purple lustre bands; grey/green/red prints	155	40.00	45.00	20.00

LOVING CUPS, MUGS, AND TANKARDS, 1977-1995

Since 1977 Wade PDM at the Wade Heath Pottery (now known as the "Hilltop Site" of Wade Ceramics) has produced seasonal loving cups, mugs and tankards for Vaux Breweries. They were presented as Christmas gifts to valued clients of the brewery. Most of these tankards differ from those usually associated with Wade in that they are shaped more like a tall mug with a wide mouth.

LOVING CUP, 1982

In 1982 Wade produced a two-handled, half-pint loving cup for Vaux, called the "Soldiers of the Maxim Gun Detachment Loving Cup." It has a purple lustre decoration on the rim and handles and a transfer print on the front of the Maxim Gun Detachment (Ernest Vaux was a colonel in this detachment, which fought in the Boer War).

See page 362 for illustration

Backstamp: "Wade p d m England"

No.	Name	Colourways	Size	U.S.$	Can.$	U.K.£
L-439	1982 Soldiers of the Maxim Gun Detachment	White; purple lustre; grey-green print	1/2 pint/83	50.00	70.00	25.00

MUGS, 1978-1995

In 1984 the pint-size "Vaux Delivery Lorries Mug" was produced. It has purple lustre bands and transfer prints of brewery delivery lorries of the early 1900s along with sheaves of barley and hops. The Vaux company names are printed around the base.

The "Eagles Head Crest Mug," is a pint-size mug produced in 1985. On one side is a print of an eagle's head inside a gold medallion with the words "Vaux Group founded 1806." On the other is listed the history of the Vaux Group.

There is a purple-lustre decoration on the 1986 " Vaux Brewery 1910 Mug." It also includes a photographic print showing workers in the courtyard of the Vaux Brewery, dated 1910.

In 1987 the "Vaux Fine Ales and Lagers Mug" was issued. It has a brewery label on the front and information on the ales and lagers on the back.

The "Double Maxim Premium Quality Ale Mug," issued in 1988, has a round Double Maxim Ale label on the front. The text on the back recounts the history of Maxim Ale, first produced to mark the homecoming of Colonel Vaux from the Boer War.

The 1989 "Maxim Light Mug" has a Maxim Light label on the front and Vaux Brewery information on the back.

In 1991 the pint-size "More Choice More Vaux Mug" was issued with a gold leaf decoration and a print of glasses of Vaux Ale.

Two pint-size mugs were issued in 1992. The "City of Sunderland Mug" was produced to mark the change in the designation of Sunderland, where Vaux is situated, from a town to a city on March 23, 1992. The mug has the coat of arms of the city on the front and a Vaux Fine Ales and Lagers label on the back with Vaux's toast to Sunderland. On the front of the base of the "Vaux Breweries Pub Signs Mug" are the words "Vaux Breweries A-Z Good Pub Guide 1992." There is also an all-over design of popular English pub signs and gold decorations.

The mug for 1993 was the "Samson Special Premium Bitter Mug." It has a Samson Special Premium Bitter label on the front with a text on the history and virtues of the ale.

The pint-size "Taste of Tradition Mug" for 1994 has the words "The Taste of Tradition" in black letters around the body. The mug is decorated with transfer prints of pump handles with pump clips for Double Maxim, Vaux Bitter, Lorimer Best Scotch, Vaux Samson, Wards Best Bitter, Vaux Mild, Vaux Extra Special and Thorne Best Bitter.

A new "Double Maxim Mug" was produced for Christmas 1995. Printed on this pint-size mug is a bottle label, which is a circle with a scroll across the middle. The text on the back recounts the history of the brew.

1992 City of Sunderland, 1994 Taste of Tradition   **1995 Double Maxim, 1993 Samson Special Premium**

Backstamp: **A.** "Wade pdm England"
             B. "Wade P D M Made in England"

No.	Name	Colourways	Size	U.S.$	Can.$	U.K.£
L-440a	1978 Sunderland Draught	White; purple lustre; red/black "Sunderland Draught Bitter Vaux"	Pint/108	70.00	90.00	35.00
L-440b	1981 Vaux Logos	White; purple lustre; grey-green logos, lettering	Pint/108	50.00	70.00	25.00
L-440c	1984 Vaux Delivery Lorries	White; purple lustre; grey-green/yellow-brown prints, red lettering	Pint/108	70.00	90.00	35.00
L-440d	1985 Eagle Head	White; gold lustre eagle; black lettering	Pint/108	70.00	90.00	35.00
L-440e	1986 Vaux Brewery 1910	White; purple lustre; black print, lettering "Vaux Brewery 1910"	Pint/108	70.00	90.00	35.00
L-440f	1987 Vaux Fine Ales and Lagers	White; gold bands; black/red/gold label, lettering "Fine Ales & Lagers Vaux Breweries Ltd"	Pint/108	70.00	90.00	35.00
L-440g	1988 Double Maxim	White; gold bands; red/brown/white label "Double Maxim"	Pint/108	70.00	90.00	35.00
L-440h	1989 Maxim Light	White; gold bands/stripes; gold/red/white "Maxim Light"	Pint/108	70.00	90.00	35.00
L-440i	1991 More Choice	White; gold decoration; multi-coloured print "More Choice More Vaux"	Pint/108	70.00	90.00	35.00
L-440j	1992 City of Sunderland	White; multi-coloured print, black lettering	Pint/108	70.00	90.00	35.00
L-440k	1992 Vaux Breweries Pub Signs	White; gold lustre; multi-coloured prints "Vaux Breweries A-Z Good Pub Guide 1992"	Pint/108	70.00	90.00	35.00
L-440l	1993 Samson Special	White; gold bands; yellow/red/black label, lettering "Samson Special Premium Bitter"	Pint/108	70.00	90.00	35.00
L-440m	1994 Taste of Tradition	White; gold bands; multi-coloured prints "Taste of Tradition"	Pint/108	70.00	90.00	35.00
L-440n	1995 Double Maxim	White; gold bands; gold/black/brown/red label "Double Maxim"	Pint/108	70.00	90.00	35.00

TANKARDS

The "Tavern Tankard," produced in 1977, resembles an early 18th-century pewter tankard. The "Lorimers Beers Tankard" produced in 1979, is a pint-size traditional tankard with a leaf thumb rest on the handle. It is decorated with a print of a Lorimers Beers label with sheaves of barley and corn. The Vaux tankard for 1980 was produced by another pottery. In 1981 Wade was back again, issuing the "Vaux Logos Mug," which is decorated with shields, inside which are the Vaux Company names and logos.

The "Horse-Drawn Dray Tankard," produced in 1990 is a traditional pint tankard with a leaf-shaped thumb rest. It is decorated with a print of a horse-drawn delivery dray leaving the brewery.

See page 362 for illustration

Backstamp: **A.** "Wade pdm England"
B. "Wade P D M Made in England"

No.	Name	Colourways	Size	U.S.$	Can.$	U.K.£
L-441	1977 Gold Tavern	Gold lustre	127	50.00	70.00	25.00
L-442	1979 Lorimer's	White; black/green label, print "Lorimer's Beer"	Pint/120	50.00	70.00	25.00
L-443	1990 Horse Drawn Dray	White; gold bands; green/black/yellow print	Pint/115	50.00	70.00	25.00

V - J GIN

WATER JUG, 1969-1984

This jug has an open spout.

Backstamp: "Wade pdm England"

No.	Description	Colourways	Shape/Size	U.S.$	Can.$	U.K.£
L-444	Water Jug	White; black print; red/black lettering "V - J Distilled London Dry Gin"	Square/114	30.00	35.00	15.00

WATNEYS BREWERIES

ASHTRAYS, 1955-1984

Ashtray (L-449)

Backstamp: "Wade pdm England"

No.	Description	Colourways	Shape/Size	U.S.$	Can.$	U.K.£
L-445	Ashtray	Green; cream lettering "Watneys Special"	D-Shaped/190	30.00	35.00	15.00
L-446	Ashtray	Purple; white/yellow lettering "Watneys Special Bitter"	Round/127	15.00	20.00	8.00
L-447	Ashtray	Cream; red lettering "Watneys Straight Eight"	Round/140	15.00	20.00	8.00
L-448	Ashtray	Green; white/red lettering "Straight Eight"	Round/153	15.00	20.00	8.00
L-449	Ashtray	Black; red lettering "Watneys"	Square/146	15.00	20.00	8.00
L-450	Ashtray	Dark red; red/white lettering "Watneys Red"	Square/153	15.00	20.00	8.00

WATNEYS SPECIAL BITTER LAMP, c.1979

This unusual dome-shaped lamp was produced to decorate public houses while advertising Watney's Breweries.

Backstamp: "Wade pdm England"

No.	Description	Colourways	Size	U.S.$	Can.$	U.K.£
L-451	Lamp	Green; yellow/brown lettering "Watneys Special Bitter"	250	160.00	240.00	80.00

WHITBREAD ALES

ASHTRAY, 1955-1962

Photograph not available
at press time

Backstamp: "Wade Regicor, London England," laurel leaves, large size

No.	Description	Colourways	Shape/Size	U.S.$	Can.$	U.K.£
L-452	Ashtray	White; black lettering "Whitbread"	Oval/171	15.00	20.00	8.00

FROG BADGE, 1987

Wade produced a limited edition of 3,000 of these reclining frogs, then they were sent to Enterprise Products, where they were mounted on a tin badge over a picture of a water-lily pad. The words "Whitbread Hopper" are also on the badge. The frog often came unglued from the badge and can be found unmounted. It can be identified by its flat back and a 5-millimetre diameter hole in the centre.

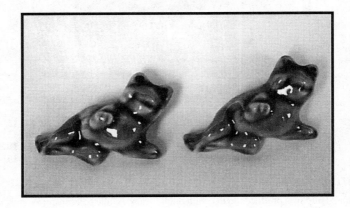

No.	Description	Colourways	Size	U.S.$	Can.$	U.K.£
L-453a	Frog Badge	White badge; green lily pad, frog; black eyes	14 x 55	40.00	45.00	20.00
L-453b	Frog (loose)	Green; black eyes	9 x 39	20.00	30.00	10.00

TRAIN DECANTER, 1979

In December 1978 Whitbread International, Belgium, commissioned Wade Heath to produce a limited quantity of "Train Decanters" to promote its pale ale. They resemble an American-style steam train with a cattle scoop on the front and the cork in the nose. The production run lasted from only February to March 1979, and 140 trains and 70 tenders were issued. After production ceased George Wade and Son Ltd. destroyed the moulds in agreement with the contract with Whitbread Breweries.

Backstamp: "Wade pdm England"

No.	Description	Colourways	Size	U.S.$	Can.$	U.K.£
L-454	Train	Dark brown; pale cream/orange Whitbread label	205 x 115			
L-455	Tender	Dark brown; pale cream/orange Whitbread label	130 x 105			
	Train and Tender				Rare	

WHITEHALL GIN

WATER JUG, 1969-1984

This jug has an open spout.

Backstamp: "Wade pdm England"

No.	Description	Colourways	Shape/Size	U.S.$	Can.$	U.K.£
L-456	Water Jug	Pale blue; black print, black/red lettering "Whitehall London Dry Gin"	Square/114	25.00	30.00	12.00

WHITE HORSE SCOTCH WHISKY

ASHTRAYS AND DRINK POURERS, 1955-1980

The ashtrays were produced between 1955 and 1980. There is no date known for the circular pourer with a straight base, shape C53. The "White Horse's Head Drink Pourer," produced in 1955, is the earliest known drink pourer produced by Wade. It is all porcelain. The date for the octagonal drink pourer, shape 5455/1, is unknown.

Ashtray (L-458)

Ashtray (L-459a)

Ashtray (L-459b)

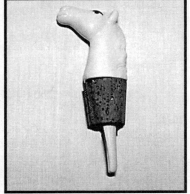

Drink Pourer (L-461)

Backstamp: A. "Wade Regicor, London England," laurel leaves, large size
B. "Wade pdm England"
C. "Wade Regicor Made in UK"

No.	Description	Colourways	Shape/Size	U.S.$	Can.$	U.K.£
L-457	Ashtray	Blue; white print; white lettering "White Horse"	Horseshoe/146	30.00	35.00	15.00
L-458	Ashtray	Cream; black/white print; red lettering "White Horse"	Horseshoe/205	30.00	35.00	15.00
L-459a	Ashtray	Dark blue; white print, lettering "White Horse Scotch Whisky"	Square/140	10.00	15.00	5.00
L-459b	Ashtray	Black; white lettering "White Horse Scotch Whisky"	Square/140	10.00	15.00	5.00
L-460	Drink Pourer	White; metal tube, spout; red/black lettering "White Horse"	Circular/41	30.00	35.00	15.00
L-461	Drink Pourer	White horse's head, black eyes	Horse's head/125	50.00	70.00	25.00
L-462	Drink Pourer	White/black; plastic tube; red lettering "White Horse Scotch Whisky"	Octagonal/40	30.00	35.00	15.00

WATER JUGS, 1984-1990

These jugs have prints of a horse on them, except for style L-464, which has a print of the bottle label on it and style L-465, which has a framed print of a horse's head. Styles L-463 and L-464 have ice-check spouts; style L-465 has no handle and an open spout; style L-466 has an open spout.

Water Jug (L-463)

Water Jug (L-465)

Backstamp: A. "Reginald Corfield Limited Redhill Surrey," "Wade Regicor England"
B. "Wade p d m England"

No.	Description	Colourways	Shape/Size	U.S.$	Can.$	U.K.£
L-463	Water Jug	Blue; white print, lettering "White Horse Whisky"	Round/133	30.00	35.00	15.00
L-464	Water Jug	White; yellow/red/black print, lettering "White Horse Whisky"	Round/140	30.00	35.00	15.00
L-465	Water Jug	Black; white/gold print; white lettering "White Horse Scotch"	Round/179	30.00	35.00	15.00
L-466	Water Jug	Black; white print, label, lettering "White Horse Whisky"	Round/140	30.00	35.00	15.00

WHYTE & MACKAY SCOTCH WHISKY

DECANTERS, 1983, 1991

The "Oast House Decanter" was produced in 1983, and the "Whyte & MacKay Decanter" was produced in 1991.

Oast House Decanter **Whyte & MacKay Decanter**

Backstamp: A. "Wade p d m England"
B. "Whyte & MacKay Scotland"

No.	Name	Colourways	Size	U.S.$	Can.$	U.K.£
L-467	Oast House	Gold; embossed "Whyte & MacKay"	250	40.00	45.00	20.00
L-468	Whyte & MacKay	Royal blue; gold print	235	40.00	45.00	20.00

WATER JUG, 1969-1984

This water jug has an ice-check spout and no handle.

Backstamp: "Wade pdm England"

No.	Description	Colourways	Shape/Size	U.S.$	Can.$	U.K.£
L-469	Water Jug	Cream; red print; brown lettering "Whyte & MacKay Scotch Whisky"	Round/177	25.00	30.00	12.00

WORTHINGTON

ASHTRAY AND WATER JUGS, 1955-1984

The water jugs were issued between 1969 and 1984. The triangular jug has an ice-check spout. The E-shaped jug, which has an open spout, looks like the letter *E* when facing right. On the back "Worthington" is spelled backwards, so that when the jug is standing in front of a bar mirror, the name can be read.

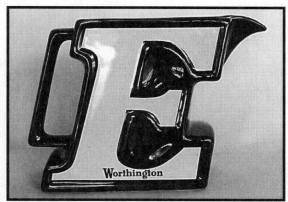

Water Jug (L-471)

Backstamp: **A.** "Wade Regicor, London England," laurel leaves, large size
B. "Wade pdm England"

No.	Description	Colourways	Shape/Size	U.S.$	Can.$	U.K.£
L-470	Ashtray	White/blue; blue lettering "You're Twice the Man on Worthington"	Round/140	15.00	20.00	8.00
L-471	Water Jug	Blue/white; blue lettering "Worthington"	E-shaped/140	50.00	70.00	25.00
L-472	Water Jug	Dark green; gold rim; blue/white lettering "Worthington"	Triangular/165	25.00	30.00	12.00

MISCELLANEOUS LIQUOR MAKERS

Between 1954 and 1995 Wade Regicor and Wade PDM produced hundreds of different products advertising brands of liquor. The companies that commissioned the following liquor products are unknown.

DECANTERS

Leaping Salmon Decanter, 1985-1986

It is believed that this decanter was produced for a Scottish distillery and was in production for a very short period of time. It has been found at antique shows minus its contents and labels.

Photograph not available
at press time

Backstamp: "Wade"

No.	Description	Colourways	Size	U.S.$	Can.$	U.K.£
L-473	Leaping Salmon	Pearlized grey/lilac; blue base	270	200.00	275.00	100.00

BOTTLE DECANTERS, 1993

These ribbed bottle-shaped decanters with porcelain stoppers were produced in a limited edition of 1,500 (500 of each version). Twenty-four of them (eight of each version) were presented to Queen Elizabeth. The transfer print on the front is of two cherubs on a wreath with the name of the drink in gold letters in the centre.

Backstamp: "Royal Victoria Pottery Wade England"

No.	Description	Colourways	Size	U.S.$	Can.$	U.K.£
L-474a	Sauternes	Creamy white; green wreath; gold lettering "Sauternes"	305	50.00	70.00	25.00
L-474b	Sherry	Yellow; gold wreath, lettering "Sherry"	305	50.00	70.00	25.00
L-474c	Vin Rose	Creamy white; pink wreath; gold lettering "Vin Rose"	305	50.00	70.00	25.00

DRINK POURERS

The print on version L-475a is of the King of Diamonds from a deck of cards; version L-475b shows the Queen of Clubs.

Photograph not available
at press time

Backstamp: Unmarked

No.	Description	Colourways	Shape/Size	U.S.$	Can.$	U.K.£
L-475a	Drink Pourer	White; plastic tube; multi-coloured print	Rectangular/48	30.00	35.00	15.00
L-475b	Drink Pourer	White; plastic tube; multi-coloured print	Rectangular/48	30.00	35.00	15.00

NOVELTY DRINK POURERS

Blue Horse's Head Drink Pourer, 1955

This drink pourer is from a different mould than the "White Horse's Head Drink Pourer" produced for White Horse Scotch Whisky. The horse depicted in this all-porcelain drink pourer is wearing a bridle, the head is further forward and the neck is shorter than that of the "White Horse's Head" model. This pourer may have been produced as a giftware item and not as a promotional product for liquor.

Photograph not available
at press time

Backstamp: Unmarked

No.	Description	Colourways	Shape/Size	U.S.$	Can.$	U.K.£
L-476	Drink Pourer	Pale blue; black eyes	Horse's head/110	40.00	45.00	20.00

Animal, Bird and Fish Drink Pourers, 1975-1982

These novelty shaped, all-porcelain drink pourers were produced by Wade Ireland. Those with more than two colours were produced first; later versions have only two colours shaded together.

Bush Baby

Eagle, with pointed spout

Eagle, rounded spout

Owl

Salmon

Songbird, pointed spout

Backstamp: Unmarked

No.	Description	Colourways	Size	U.S.$	Can.$	U.K.£
L-477a	Bush Baby	Beige/black; yellow eyes; green branch	120	70.00	95.00	35.00
L-477b	Bush Baby	Beige/grey	120	70.00	95.00	35.00
L-478	Golden Eagle	Honey; light green breast, pointed spout	138	70.00	95.00	35.00
L-479	Golden Eagle	Beige/grey, rounded spout	110	70.00	95.00	35.00
L-480a	Owl	Honey; green head, wings	110	70.00	95.00	35.00
L-480b	Owl	Beige; grey head, wings	110	70.00	95.00	35.00
L-481	Puppy	Beige/grey; green base	110	70.00	95.00	35.00
L-482a	Salmon	Honey; mottled green tail, base	120	70.00	95.00	35.00
L-482b	Salmon	Beige/grey	120	70.00	95.00	35.00
L-483	Songbird	Honey; dark brown tail; green branch; flat spout	170	70.00	95.00	35.00
L-483	Songbird	Honey/grey-brown; pointed spout	98	70.00	95.00	35.00

PUMP HANDLES c.1970-c.1980

These beer pump handles were produced by Wade PDM for various breweries.

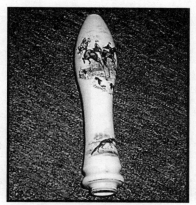

"Huntsmen and Fox"

Backstamp: Unmarked

No.	Description	Colourways	Size	U.S.$	Can.$	U.K.£
L-484a	Huntsmen	White; multi-coloured print	225	40.00	45.00	20.00
L-484b	Huntsmen and Fox	White; multi-coloured print	225	40.00	45.00	20.00
L-485	Grapes and Vine Leaves	White; green/yellow print	125	40.00	45.00	20.00

VETERAN CAR SERIES

Water Jugs, 1962

Round Jug, 1 1/2 Pint

Square Jug, 1/2-Pint

Square Jug, 1 Pint

Triangular Jug, 1 1/2 Pint

Backstamp: "Wade England"

No.	Description	Colourways	Shape/Size	U.S.$	Can.$	U.K.£
L-486	Bentley, 1 1/2 pint	Pale yellow; multi-coloured print	Round/115	30.00	35.00	15.00
L-487	Bentley, 1/2 pint	Pale yellow; multi-coloured print	Square/95	30.00	35.00	15.00
L-488	Bentley, pint	Pale yellow; multi-coloured print	Square/105	30.00	35.00	15.00
L-489	Bentley, 1 1/2 Pint	Pale yellow; multi-coloured print	Triangular/150	30.00	35.00	15.00

WINE DECANTER LABEL

Shape No.: Impressed shape number S52/3

No.	Description	Colourways	Shape/Size	U.S.$	Can.$	U.K.£
L-490	Wine Decanter label	White; gold rim; green/brown print, green lettering "Chilled Dry White Wine"	Oval/76	10.00	15.00	5.00

MONEY BOXES

Wade did not produce many money boxes. Those listed in this section were produced as giftware items. Others, such as the "National Westminster Bank Piggies," "Monster Muncher" and "Fried Green Tomatoes" money boxes, can be found in Advertising and Commissioned Products.

BACKSTAMPS

Transfer Prints

Most of these money boxes are backstamped "Wade England" with either a blue, red or black transfer print.

Impressed Backstamps

Some are marked with an impressed "Wade England."

Transfer print, c.1955-c.1960

Impressed, 1994

COMIC ANIMAL MONEY BOXES, 1994

In mid summer 1994, Wade introduced a set of four smiling-animal money boxes, produced in all-over, one-colour glazes. The original price direct from the Wade Pottery was £4.

Backstamp: Impressed "Wade England"

No.	Description	Colourways	Size	U.S.$	Can.$	U.K.£
MB-1	Bob the Frog	Green	120	25.00	30.00	12.00
MB-2	Gertie the Jersey	Orange brown	150	25.00	30.00	12.00
MB-3	Lucky the Rabbit	Grey	173	25.00	30.00	12.00
MB-4	Priscilla the Pig	Pink	112	25.00	30.00	12.00

ELEPHANT MONEY BOX, c.1960

Photograph not available
at press time

Backstamp: Black transfer print "Wade England"

No.	Description	Colourways	Size	U.S.$	Can.$	U.K.£
MB-5	Elephant	Dark grey; blue blanket	115	90.00	130.00	45.00

PAWS AT THE KERB PIG MONEY BOX, c.1955

The "Paws at the Kerb Pig Money Box" has on it a transfer print of a puppy sitting at a curb and the words "Paws at the Kerb" on one side and a schoolboy, a Belisha Beacon and the words "Look Right—Look Left—Look Right Again" on the other. The print was taken from the winning poster designed by an 11-year-old schoolgirl in a mid-1950s competition to promote British road safety.

Photograph not available
at press time

Backstamp: Blue transfer print "Wade England"

No.	Description	Colourways	Size	U.S.$	Can.$	U.K.£
MB-6	Pig	White; black transfers	115 x 160	60.00	80.00	30.00

SMILING PIG MONEY BOXES, 1955–c.1960

This novelty line of money boxes is found with various multi-coloured transfer prints of flowers, parasols and stars. The roses and violets designs were originally used on the Flair Tablewares of the mid 1950s and early 1960s, which were produced by the Wade Heath Royal Victoria Pottery. The parasols and shooting-stars designs were used on a series of vases and bowls, called Harmony Wares, made in the late 1950s to early 1960s . These money boxes are sometimes found with no backstamp.

Spring Flowers

Backstamp: A. Blue transfer print "Wade England"
          B. Unmarked

No.	Description	Colourways	Size	U.S.$	Can.$	U.K.£
MB-7a	Galaxy	White; gold inside ears; blue eyes; black stars	115	60.00	80.00	30.00
MB-7b	Galaxy	Yellow; black eyes, stars	115	60.00	80.00	30.00
MB-7c	Parasols	White; gold inside ears; blue eyes; red/yellow/blue parasols	115	60.00	80.00	30.00
MB-7d	Shooting Stars	White; blue eyes, nostrils; pink/green/black stars	115	60.00	80.00	30.00
MB-7e	Spring Flowers	White; gold inside ears; blue eyes, nostrils, flowers	115	60.00	80.00	30.00
MB-7f	Summer Rose	White; gold inside ears; blue eyes; pink roses	115	60.00	80.00	30.00
MB-7g	Summer Rose	White; gold inside ears; blue eyes; yellow roses	115	60.00	80.00	30.00
MB-7h	Summer Rose	Yellow; blue eyes; orange roses	115	60.00	80.00	30.00
MB-7i	Violets	White; gold inside ears; blue eyes; violet flowers	115	60.00	80.00	30.00

SHAVING MUGS, 1985

This small series of shaving mugs was produced at the Royal Victoria Pottery in 1985. There is one hole in the top of the mugs. These models are more dainty and more rounded than the Addis and Culmak mugs, which are listed in Advertising and Commissioned Products.

The following backstamp is found on the *Royal Victoria Shavings Mugs*.

Red transfer print, 1985

ROYAL VICTORIA SHAVING MUGS, 1985

Cricketer

Galleon and Dinghy

Galleon and Sailboat

Backstamp: Red transfer print "Royal Victoria Pottery Wade England"

No.	Description	Colourways	Size	U.S.$	Can.$	U.K.£
SM-1a	Cricketer	White mug; brown batsman and background	85	25.00	30.00	12.00
SM-1b	Fisherman	White mug; multi-coloured print	85	25.00	30.00	12.00
SM-1c	Galleon and Dinghy	White mug; brown sails, hull, dingy	85	25.00	30.00	12.00
SM-1d	Galleon and Sailboat	White mug; yellow sails; brown hull	85	25.00	30.00	12.00
SM-1e	Golfer	White mug; yellow/brown golfer; blue sky	85	25.00	30.00	12.00

INDEX

The Charlton Press

Dear Collector:

The Charlton Press has an ongoing commitment to excellence and completeness in the production of all its Wade reference works.

Our 1996 schedule will include:

The Charlton Standard Catalogue of Wade, Volume 1, General Issues, 2nd Ed.
The Charlton Standard Catalogue of Wade, Volume 2, Decorative Ware, 2nd Ed.
The Charlton Standard Catalogue of Wade Whimsical Collectables, 3rd Ed.

Our 1997 schedule will include:

The Charlton Standard Catalogue of Wade, Volume 3, Tableware, 2nd Ed.
The Charlton Standard Catalogue of Wade Whimsical Collectables, 4th Ed.

We ask that collectors having information not included in any of our pricing references to please send it along to our editorial offices in Toronto.

We will consider editorial additions or corrections regarding colourways, varieties, series, issue dates, designs and styles, as well as well as other information that would be of interest to collectors. Photos of models that were unavailable in previous issues are particularly welcome. Black and white, unscreened photos are best, but colour is also suitable.

Your help in providing new or previously unobtainable data on any aspect of Wade models or collecting will be considered for inclusion in subsequent editions. Those providing information will be acknowledged in the contributor's section in the front of every catalogue.

Please send your contributions together with your name, address and phone number to:

The Charlton Press
Editorial Office
2010 Yonge Street
Toronto, Ontario M4S 1Z9 Fax (416) 488-4656